Where Islam and Judaism Join Together

Where Islam and Judaism Join Together

A Perspective on Reconciliation

Shai Har-El

palgrave
macmillan

WHERE ISLAM AND JUDAISM JOIN TOGETHER

Softcover reprint of the hardcover 1st edition 2014 978-1-137-39100-1

First published in 2014 by
PALGRAVE MACMILLAN®
in the United States—a division of St. Martin's Press LLC,
175 Fifth Avenue, New York, NY 10010.

Where this book is distributed in the UK, Europe and the rest of the world, this is by Palgrave Macmillan, a division of Macmillan Publishers Limited, registered in England, company number 785998, of Houndmills, Basingstoke, Hampshire RG21 6XS.

Palgrave Macmillan is the global academic imprint of the above companies and has companies and representatives throughout the world.

ISBN 978-1-349-48283-2 ISBN 978-1-137-38812-4 (eBook)
DOI 10.1057/9781137388124

Library of Congress Cataloging-in-Publication Data

Har-El, Shai, author.
Where Islam and Judaism join together : a perspective on reconciliation / Shai Har-El.
pages cm
Includes index.

1. Islam—Relations—Judaism. 2. Judaism—Relations—Islam. I. Title.

BP173.J8H36 2014
297.2′82—dc23 2013050455

A catalogue record of the book is available from the British Library.

Design by Newgen Knowledge Works (P) Ltd., Chennai, India.

First edition: July 2014

10 9 8 7 6 5 4 3 2 1

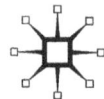

I dedicate this book to all those who work diligently across the religious divide to promote understanding and fellowship among the children of Abraham and who see Jerusalem, the City of Peace, as a place of their reconciliation and a beacon for the prophetic vision of peace: "*For mine house shall be called a house of prayer for all people*" (Isaiah 56:7).

Contents

Illustrations

Figures

Tables

Prefatory Notes

On Transliteration

For the cross-language transliteration of Hebrew and Arabic words, the system set forth below will be followed. The same diacritical marks will be used in both languages. In the case of long vowels (in Hebrew: *tenu'ōt*, with focus on accentuating *mil'ēl* for prefix and *milrā'* for suffix; in Arabic: *ḥarakāt*), a special column is set forth to the right of the consonants to help the reader in proper pronunciation. The following are the transliteration alphabet:

Hebrew	Arabic	English	Long Vowels
א	ء ,ى,آ,ا	a,'	ā
ב		v	
בּ	ب	b	
ג		g	
	ج	j	
ד	د	d	
[vowel]		e	ē
ה	ه	h	
ו		v,u,o	ū,ō
	و	w,u	ū
ז	ز	z	
	ذ	dh	
ח	ح	ḥ	
ט	ط	ṭ	
	ظ	ẓ	
י	ى	y, i	ī
כ	خ	kh	
כּ	ك	k	
ל	ل	l	
מ	م	m	
נ	ن	n	

Hebrew	Arabic	English	Long Vowels
ס	س	s	
ע	ع	ʿ	
	غ	gh	
פ	ف	f	
פּ		p	
צ		tz	
	ص	ṣ	
	ض	ḍ	
ק	ق	q	
ר	ر	r	
שׁ	ش	sh	
שׂ	س	s	
ת	ت	t	
	ث	th	

A simplified system of Romanization omitting diacritical marks has been used in transliterating geographical names (e.g., Canaan, Beersheba, Hebron, and Mecca); proper names (e.g., Muhammad, Abraham, Hagar, and Ishmael); and commonly used names of classical Jewish texts (e.g., Torah, Talmud, Mishnah, and Midrash).

On Translation

For the most part, translations of scriptural verses are from the following sources:

For the *Hebrew Bible*: *The Holy Scriptures: According to the Masoretic Text.* Philadelphia: The Jewish Publication Society of America, 1955, and the online program *Navigating the Bible II* in http://www.bible.ort.org.

For the *Qur'ān*: *The Holy Qur'ān: Text, Translation and Commentary, New Revised Edition*, trans. and ed. 'Abdullah Yusuf 'Ali. Brentwood, Maryland: Amana Corporation, 1989, and online collection of Qur'ān translations offered by http://www.altafsir.com (published by the *Royal Aāl al-Bayt Institute for Islamic Thought*, Jordan).

For the *Jewish Prayer Book*: *Siddūr Tehillāt Hashēm* [A Praise of the Lord]: With English Translation, trans. Rabbi Nissen Mangel. Brooklyn, NY: Merkos L'Inyonei Chinuch, 2002.

To simplify the translation of scriptural texts, I took the liberty to replace the archaic dative forms (e.g., thou, ye) with their modern equivalents (i.e., you).

On Terminology

Since the book focuses on the relations between Islam and Judaism, the terms "BC" and "AD," which are conventionally used in the West, are not appropriate. The alternative terms "BCE" (Before the Common Era) and "CE" (Common Era) are used instead.

When quoting verses from the Bible and the Qur'ān, the word "God" was generally used in translating the Names "Adonai" and "Allah" respectively. When quoting verses from the Talmud and Midrash, the conventionally used "the Holy One, blessed be He" for God's Name is not used in this book. The alternative, simplified Name, "the Blessed Holy One," is used instead.

Acknowledgments

Although it would be impossible to acknowledge all the people who have influenced me in this book, I still want to express my deepest appreciation to a few of them.

It is a pleasure to first acknowledge my gratitude to Dr. Abidullah Ghazi, founder and executive director of the IQRA' International Education Foundation, who was the catalyst that inspired me through many years of interfaith dialogues. This book grew out of a series of interactions with him and his colleagues. I also want to acknowledge the late Hajj Anwar Zainal, a friend and a peace-loving individual who enthusiastically introduced me to his devotional life and "his" Islam. I am proud to express my indebtedness to both of them and thankful to everyone who allowed me to enter into their spiritual life.

There is no limit to my debt and gratitude to my teachers, who taught me how to read text and how to approach it with critical judgment. Many years have passed since I was an undergraduate and graduate student at Tel Aviv University, but what I learned from all of my teachers has never departed from me. It is not possible here to note every one of them. However, I want in particular to recall Professor Shimon Shamir, a rare scholar of Middle Eastern Studies, from whom I have learned immensely, particularly during our fruitful exchanges when he served as my MA advisor.

In the course of my doctoral studies in Middle Eastern History at the University of Chicago, in the late 1970s, I was privileged to study under a scholarly giant and an internationally renowned master, Professor Halil Inalcik, who taught me about late medieval Islam and Ottoman history. I have never forgotten nor ceased to be astounded by his immense learning and his willingness as my PhD advisor to share his knowledge and private Ottoman archives in the course of writing my dissertation.[1] I also owe a special debt to the late Professor Fazlur Rahman, who patiently guided me through some of the intricacies of Islamic religion and encouraged me to research and write about complex subjects, the benefits of which I reaped while writing this book.

Many friends and scholars have read the manuscript of the book and have given me the benefit of their counsel. I particularly want to thank my friend Fadel Abdallah, lecturer of Arabic in John Hopkins University, whose suggestions have contributed immeasurably to my final formulations.

I like to express my great appreciation to Professor Douglas Giles, my editor, whose careful editing of the manuscript and invaluable comments on the text have meant much to me.

Words are incapable of expressing my special gratitude to my wife, Rosalie. She has been my *'ēshet ḥāyil* (woman of valor), a treasured life companion, a never-ending source of encouragement, and a friendly and honest critic of style and clarity. Indeed, in the immortal words of the famed sage Rabbi Akiva, "Shelī ve-shelakhēm shelāh hū'"[2]—everything that I have learned and written, are truly hers. She is the most precious gift that the Blessed Holy One has granted me.

I am deeply indebted to you, my readers. After all, it is your interest in world peace and interreligious reconciliation that has inspired me to write this book.

Finally, as I complete the preparation of this manuscript, I thank God for allowing me to finish this book. And may He grant us the fulfillment of the following prayer for the peace of Jerusalem in our times:

Our feet are standing within your gates, O Jerusalem;
Jerusalem that is built as a city that is united together.
[...] Pray for the peace of Jerusalem;
May those who love you be serene.
May there be peace within your walls,
serenity within your palaces.
For the sake of my brethren and friends,
I ask that there be peace within you.
(Psalms 122:2–8)

Introduction: Jerusalem's Gate of Mercy as a Context

As an epigraph to my book, I chose verses from Psalm 122, because they send a message that is close to my heart—peace within the City of Peace, Jerusalem. Whenever I visit my homeland, Israel, I make sure to *be* in Jerusalem. One cannot comprehend what this holy city is all about without *being* there spiritually, experiencing the intense presence of the Divine, and having the inner understanding of the mystical Ladder Dream of the Patriarch Jacob, when he said, "How full of awe is this place! This is none other than the house of God and this is the Gate of Heaven."[1]

When I am in Jerusalem, I sense what Jewish sages wrote, inferring from the above citation: "When a man prays in Jerusalem, it is as though he prays before the throne of glory, for the Gate of Heaven is in Jerusalem and a door is always open for the hearing of prayer."[2] When I am in Jerusalem, I try to listen to its ancient stones telling primeval stories about how the faith of Abraham—venerated as the common forefather, patriarch, and spiritual ancestor of the three monotheistic religions—had begun four millennia ago. I try to understand why it is that the City of Peace—where peace should have reigned and conflicts been kept out—has been, for so long, a focus of powerful and intertwined passions of religion and politics that caused Islam and Judaism to be in a fierce contention over this place. I wonder why this place is called the Golden City, "Jerusalem of Gold, and of bronze, and of light" in the famous Hebrew song, when its long history down to our days is stained and darkened with intolerance and bloodshed. After many spiritual pilgrimages to this magnetic city, I realized that perhaps the answer to these questions may be found right there. Perhaps only in this city of contrasts, where Islam and Judaism are so much apart, can they truly join together in peace. For this reason, and because of the symbolism that the Holy City of Jerusalem offers, I chose this place as the context for my book.

The Holy City, also known as the Old City—considered by many nations to be the metropolis and sanctuary of the world, where heaven and earth meet—is surrounded by ancient walls with eight gates that are open and one that is closed. Seven of the open gates were built by the Ottoman Sultan Suleiman the Magnificent, between 1535 and 1538 and one by the Ottoman Sultan Abd al-Hamid in 1889. Every gate carries several names from different centuries-old traditions. Each gate has its own special timeless look with its unique geometric design and floral ornamentation. There is one gate, however, that is more beautiful than all of them and that is totally sealed by stone slabs. Seemingly standing blind to its surroundings, this earthly gate gives the impression of a heavenly sense of sight that transcends human comprehension. It is known in both Jewish and Muslim traditions as the Gate of Mercy (*Shā'ar ha-Raḥamīm* in Hebrew; *Bāb ar-Raḥmah* in Arabic). What does this "gate of all gates" possibly see that we may be blind to?

Figure 0.1 Image of the Gate of Mercy, Jerusalem.

The Gate of Mercy, through which Jews believe the Messiah (Hebrew: *Mashīyaḥ*) would enter Jerusalem when he comes, is part of the eastern wall that surrounds not only the Old City but specifically the Temple Mount (Hebrew: *Har ha-Bāyyit*), which is considered highly sacred to both Jews and Muslims and is one of the most contested religious sites in the world. Jewish traditions identify this as the summit of Mount Moriah, where Abraham passed the trial of faith by his willingness to sacrifice his son, Isaac, to the will of God. It is the site where the Jewish Holy Temple has stood, until Titus and the Roman legions destroyed it in 70 CE, and where the magnificent *Qubbat aṣ-Ṣakhrah*, or Dome of the Rock, was built by the Muslims 60 years after the conquest of Jerusalem by the Caliph 'Omar ibn al-Khaṭṭāb. "The Rock" refers to the Foundation Stone (Hebrew: *'Ēven ha-Shetiyyāh*) located at the heart of the Dome and considered in Jewish traditions to be part of what was the Temple's Holy of the Holies, the place that served Abraham as the altar for the binding of Isaac, and the foundation of planet Earth. The building of the Dome on the site of the Jewish Temple and over the Foundation Stone has been interpreted as a symbolic act placing Islam in the lineage of Abraham and dissociating it from the precursory monotheistic religions Judaism and Christianity.[3] That site was considered by Jewish sages as the Gate of Heaven, and by the Muslims as the point where Prophet Muhammad ascended to heaven to commune with God face-to-face, a journey known in Islamic tradition as the *mi'rāj*.[4] Here, over the Temple Mount, on the plaza of *Al-Ḥaram ash-Sharīf*, or the Noble Sanctuary, we find *Al-Masjid al-Aqṣa'*, the third holiest mosque in Islam. After the Arab conquest of Jerusalem, *Madīnat Bayt al-Maqdis*, or the City of the House of the Holy (referring to the Hebrew name for the Holy Temple, *Beit Ha-Miqddāsh*), became synonymous with Jerusalem and eventually shortened to simply *Al-Quds* meaning "The Holy."

The Gate of Mercy is also special because of its double-entry structure and because it is more significant in size and ornamentation than the open gates. The earliest mention of the Gate can be found in the writings of Arab historians and Muslim travelers, who referred to it by its two names, one for each of its entries: the northern entry, the Gate of Repentance, and the southern gate, the Gate of Mercy. They say that when a Muslim prays to God, he stands in front of the Gate of Mercy, and then turns in front of the Gate of Repentance to receive God's answer. Although the Jews referred to the Gate by a single name, the Gate of Mercy, there are several medieval accounts by Jewish pilgrims mentioning the two entries to possibly allow the traffic in and out of the Temple compound. The Christians, believing that it is the "beautiful gate" mentioned in the New Testament, named it the Golden Gate, an appellation picked up by all the languages of Europe.[5]

When visiting the place, one can see a distinct difference between the inside and the outside of the Gate. It appears from outside to be composed of two adjoining facades and crowned by twin arches of equal height and weight, but its interior is actually a unified structure built into the wall. Perhaps this monumental gate sees what it represents—the special bond between Islam and Judaism. Like the Gate of Mercy, they are one faith from the inside made of two religions from outside. Although they represent two ways of worship, one by the descendents of Isaac and the other by the descendents of Ishmael, and they pray separately through the Gate of Mercy's double entry, their prayers eventually reach God through a single entry, "the Gate of Heaven." The two together form a unity of faith—a shared belief in One God. Because of what it symbolizes, the Gate of Mercy in this book is dedicated to the shared heritage of these sister religions and selected as the context for this book.

One of the verses in the Qur'ān speaks of a gate in a certain wall and makes a clear distinction between the inside and outside sections of that wall: "So a wall will be put up between them, with a gate therein; inside there will be mercy throughout, while outside facing it there will be punishment."[6] It has a symbolic meaning for us: just like in the case of the Gate of Mercy, the interior that is dominated by unity of faith represents mercy, whereas the exterior that is dominated by division between the two contending religions represents punishment.

Making this message even more powerful is the addition of another symbol. A certain Islamic decorative motif appearing in the ornamentation of the Gate of Mercy is a knotted rope.[7] This reminds us of the beautiful words of the Qur'ān: "Hold firmly, all together by the rope of God and be not divided among yourselves; and remember with gratitude God's favor upon you, for you were enemies and He joined your hearts in love, so that by His grace, you become brothers."[8] To be the knotted rope of God that joins people in brotherhood, Islam and Judaism can no longer relate as separate ropes dangling next to each other. In order for them to tie their ropes together, to bind them into a knot that is much tighter, each rope must give up little, surrender a bit of its original length, to achieve a stronger unity.

So we all have a choice: either we become the knotted rope of God that binds us together, or we continue to exist as separate ropes apart from each other. Either we live in unity as brothers and enjoy God's mercy, or we live apart as enemies and suffer punishment. Like one of Martin Luther King's pearls of wisdom, "We must learn to live together as brothers or perish together as fools."[9]

It is in this spirit of harmony and brotherhood that I wrote this book—as a place where I attempt to bridge between Islam and Judaism, and as a tool to promote a greater understanding and appreciation of the two Abrahamic traditions. It is my hope that both Jews and Muslims, in their search for common ground, will adopt the symbol of sharing and bonding represented by the unique structure of the closed Gate of Mercy and the knotted rope. It is my prayer that they will carry out their search *from the inside out* by allowing the oneness and compassion that dominate the interior of the Gate of Mercy to influence the exterior of interreligious relationship.

* * *

This book presents the Abrahamic concept as an alternative to "Judeo-Christian," a term used to describe the moral traditions thought to be held in common by Judaism and Christianity and considered a fundamental basis for the body of concepts and values in the modern Western world. It has been argued, however, that Judaism and Christianity are entirely autonomous of one another, that there is no shared and ongoing "Judeo-Christian Tradition," and that there is not now, and there never has been, a dialogue between them.[10] This term has been used only by Western scholars and was never adopted by Jews or by Muslims, whereas the term "Abrahamic" has been accepted by all three monotheistic religions—Judaism, Christianity, and Islam—as a term of both historical relevance and future significance. Labeling them "Abrahamic" acknowledges that all three religions come from one source, Abraham, whose biblical name means "the father of a multitude of nations," and whose primordial creed can be used as a unifying force to bring all of them together.

In this book I chose to concentrate only on Islam and Judaism, sister religions that are closely related to one another, with roots intertwined in the land, in the language, and in the memories of shared history. Of all religions, they are by far the closest to each other in their fundamental religious tenets, practices and systems of law, and their social, cultural and ethical traditions. (On the similarities between the two systems of law, see Appendix 1). Since Abraham (*Avrahām* in Hebrew; *'Ibrāhīm* in Arabic) is claimed by Jewish tradition as the ancestor of the Jews through his son Isaac (Hebrew: *Yitzḥāq*), and by Muslim tradition as ancestor of the Arabs through his son Ishmael (Arabic: *'Ismā'īl*), the need to build bridges of understanding between these historical antagonists and to seek better understanding and peaceful coexistence between their religions is, in my opinion, much stronger.

It is important to mention one historical fact right away. There are many examples of relative well-being enjoyed by Jews in the Arab and Muslim lands. The classical example is that of Andalus, Muslim Spain, in the ninth to the eleventh centuries. While Jews fared there better, overall, than those in the Christian lands in Europe, Jews were no strangers to persecution and humiliation by Muslims. Nevertheless, Professor Bernard Lewis, one of the world's greatest historians of the Middle East, observed that—although "there were unambiguously negative attitudes towards Jews in the Muslim lands as part of the 'normal' feelings of a dominant group towards subject groups"—"There is little sign of any deep-rooted emotional hostility directed against Jews...such as the anti-Semitism of the Christian world."[11]

Given the spirit and message of peace in this book, I used the following guidelines in writing it:

1. I based my work, almost entirely, on the scriptural sources: the Bible (primarily the first book, Genesis) for the Jewish tradition and the Qur'ān for the Islamic tradition.
2. I let the Torah (both the Written, i.e., the Five Books of Moses, and the Oral, i.e., the Talmud) and the Qur'ān (as well its classical commentary, i.e., *Tafsīr*) speak for themselves and did my best to avoid the type of modern suggestive commentaries that use the text to subserve one's own ideological passions or particular political affiliation.
3. I accepted the integrity of both scriptures and treated them as "these and those are the words of the Living God" (Hebrew: *'ēilu ve-'ēilu divrēi 'Elohīm ḥayyīm*), to use the classical Talmudic model of dialogue and tolerance within Jewish Law.[12] The belief in the divine origin of both the Torah and the Qur'ān is supported by the Qur'ān's own words: "This Qur'ān could not have been produced by other than God; on the contrary, it is a confirmation (*taṣdīq*) of what was before it and elaboration (*tafṣīl*) of the Book [of Torah], wherein is no doubt [revealed] from the Sovereign of the Universe."[13]
4. I concentrated on those scriptural verses that support mutual acceptance and tolerance and avoided those that may indicate or infer a negative treatment of others. As the Qur'ān states: "Goodness and evil are not alike; repel [evil] with something that is far better, and notice how someone, who is separated from you because of enmity, will become your intimate friend."[14]

Given the spirit and purpose of this book, I made a decision that neither the exhaustive research by Jewish and Christian scholars on the influence of the Bible, the Midrash (a collection of exegetical or homiletical commentaries on the biblical narrative) and other classic Jewish sources on the Qur'ān,[15] nor the traditional polemical claim by Muslims that the Jews have corrupted or altered some portions of the Bible,[16] should become the subject of this work. While they definitely help in understanding the tumultuous history of Jewish-Muslim relations, they do not forward the intent of this book—reducing the gulf between Jews and Muslims. They only cause the debasement and dilution of the authentic revelation of their scriptures, which is at the core of their religions. I also made a decision to limit the discussion of the Qur'ānic verses that speak of intolerance and violence against non-Muslims to an appendix and let a Muslim scholar reflect on this subject (see Appendix 5). My purpose is not to blur the differences between the two religions, but to accentuate the similarities so that a common denominator is established for serious dialogue. The emphasis of unity over separation creates a context of love, compassion, mutual respect, and understanding, one in which peace and reconciliation are possible.

Because the relationship between Islam and Judaism is an extremely loaded subject, I must state at the very onset of this book that nowhere in its pages did I allow my Jewish faith to interfere with the integrity of my research and writing. On the contrary, the task of carefully navigating between the texts of the Bible and the Qur'ān and producing this sensitive bridgework was undertaken in the spirit of service to the noble cause of amity and peace among Jews and Muslims.

Abraham is the central figure in my book. From my perspective, as one who believes the Bible, there was such a person. For me, and for all Jews and Muslims, he represents one common religious tradition and the foundation on which all three monotheistic religions have built their faith over the course of history, and from which each has developed a set of beliefs and practices that sets them apart from others. Whether Abraham is historically a real person or a mythological figure, as some scholars question, is irrelevant for our purpose.[17] History, any history, especially the one that is based heavily on scriptural narratives, is a record of imperfections. The narratives are scarce and fragmentary, and we don't know if they are true. What we care about here, however, is that they are held as true. So although this record is inherently imperfect, it is one of great potential. It tells us about the old world, but also about our world. Although it is rooted in the historical past, it sets the context for understanding our present. It actually opens for us a window through which we can look at the present, a gate through which we can enter in order to take action. It can teach a moral lesson; Abraham's willingness to sacrifice his son may serve as one example. It can help us understand current situations; thus, the conflict between Abraham and his Philistine neighbor in the south over water continued into Isaac's time, setting the stage for the bitter conflict between Israel and the Palestinians over water four millennia later. It can influence diverse groups of people to come together around a shared belief; thus, Abraham's code of ethics may serve as a source of inspiration for both Jews and Muslims about the possibility of reconciliation.

* * *

Because the Gate of Mercy, the *closed* "master gate," represents the overall context for the book, I divided it into eight chapters corresponding to the eight *opened* gates to the Holy City of Jerusalem. In the Jewish tradition, the number eight has a spiritual meaning. It refers to a higher, more sublime level than that which is represented by the seven days of Creation. It represents the first day, the opening, of the new creation. It symbolizes the human power to rise beyond one's natural limitations. We would need such power if we, you and I, were to succeed in our noble efforts to reconcile between Islam and Judaism. Each chapter, or "gate" (*shā'ar* in Hebrew; *bāb* in Arabic), is designed to serve as a gateway to the Abrahamic faith shared by Jews and Muslims and to the understanding of the complex relationship between them:

1. In Gate 1, we will reflect on the ethical dimension of God's Oneness and focus, primarily from an Islamic perspective, on five elements that bond Jews and Muslims together: the creedal, human, ethical, historical, and cooperative.
2. In Gate 2, we will explore the linguistic commonality between the two "holy tongues," Hebrew and Arabic, and find out what we can learn from the Names of God, commonly used in the two sister languages, in order to bridge between those who speak them.
3. In Gate 3, we will look at several customs and rites shared by both Jews and Muslims and suggest that they are much closer than apart.
4. In Gate 4, we will review the characteristics of the creed of Abraham and find out whether his primal religion, particularly his code of ethics, can serve as a model for us to follow in our pursuit of peace.
5. In Gate 5, we will discuss the gap in the biblical narrative about the relationship between Abraham and Ishmael and attempt to reconstruct the story by filling in the gap with information from extracanonical sources.
6. In Gate 6, we will review the Jewish and Islamic traditions about Abraham's attempted sacrifice of his son and outline the moral lessons Jews and Muslims can learn and apply to their contemporary relations.
7. In Gate 7, we will reexamine, from Jewish and Islamic theological perspectives, the historical rights to the disputed Holy Land and offer a vision that may resolve the Israeli-Palestinian conflict.
8. In Gate 8, we will argue that the problem of Truth is the truth of the problem in Jewish-Muslim relations and present two ethical arguments that can serve the cause of harmony and understanding between them.

I subdivided the book into three thematic parts. I have preceded the eight chapters with a prologue in which I share my own personal experiences and reflections as a peacemaker. I follow them with an epilogue that seals the book with a few poems I wrote on the oneness of humanity as the foundation of Jewish-Muslim reconciliation.

I hope that by the time you "enter" all eight "gates" and finish reading this book, the *Gate of Mercy* will metaphorically break open for you and allow you to see the possibility of peace through it. Especially nowadays, when the Muslim world and the West have been poised on the edge of an apocalyptic battle to defend their sacred "isms," the world ought to realize that Islam and Judaism can and must reconcile their terribly bitter and unholy differences. This reconciliation is not just possible, it is critical; it would forward the cause of world peace, in general, and help defuse the Arab-Israeli conflict, an age-old hostility trigger in the Middle East, in particular.

The virtue of *mercy* is a colorful thread interwoven throughout the chapters of this book. This is for a good reason. The Merciful, says a Jewish prayer, "directs His world with kindness and His [human] creatures with mercy,"[18] and He, according to the Qur'ān, offers "mercy to all [His] creatures."[19] The world as we know it today, though, is inflicted by so many merciless onslaughts contrary to God's teaching. It is my prayer that as He, "Who each day opens the doors of the eastern gates and unlocks the apertures of heaven [. . . to] illuminate the whole world and its inhabitants, which He created with the attribute of mercy,"[20] this book you are about to read will also do the same—create an opening in the minds of the Jewish and Muslim readers to see the light at the end of the dark hostility tunnel and encourage them to embrace each other as brothers and sisters. The ultimate course requires, however, far more than a shift in thinking. The key is action—the actual translation of this mind shift into concrete implementation in the form of peacebuilding and peacemaking.

Consider *Where Islam and Judaism Join Together* an unfinished book, one that unceasingly evolves and hopefully develops into a force strong enough to affect public opinion about the possibility of reconciliation between Islam and Judaism. Let this book be a sacred gateway, where readers of all nations can embark on a journey of exploration of other people's culture. Let it be not a monologue but a start of an open dialogue, a conversation that nurtures mutual respect and understanding. You are invited to participate by sharing your ideas and communicating your thoughts to shai@MEPNetwork.org.

RABBI DR. SHAI HAR-EL
Highland Park, IL USA
Winter 2013

Prologue: Our Father Avrahām/'Ibrāhīm

This book is the result of many years of thinking, speaking and writing about peace. It was planted during the 1993 convention of the Parliament of the World's Religions in Chicago, during which I moderated a panel of scholars and clergyman on "Building a Common Ground: Jews, Christians and Muslims Working Together." The event was sponsored by the Middle East Peace Network (MEPN), a Chicago-based not-for-profit organization I founded and led during the early 1990s and reactivated in the spring of 2011.[1] Made up originally of Arab and Jewish Americans, this organization spread the message that people-to-people relationship building, citizen diplomacy, and unofficial human interaction could enhance the prospects of the long-sought Arab-Israeli peace.

My peace advocacy led me naturally to interfaith dialogue as an alternative peacemaking framework. I have always regarded religion as a critical, yet ignored, track for the resolution of the Arab-Israeli conflict. While some use religion as a political instrument to spread division and hatred, I believe religion is all about unity and tolerance. This premise has always been at the core of my interfaith encounters.

As a result of my interaction with many Muslims, I was introduced to the heart of Islam, or rather to the "Islam of the heart," and to many precious people. I had numerous soulful conversations with Hajj Anwar Zainal, a devout Muslim of Iraqi origin, who spoke highly about Muslims' descent from the Patriarch Abraham, whom he called *'Abūna 'Ibrāhīm* (our father Abraham). Being a proud and observant Jew, I saw Abraham mostly as our own father, *Avrahām Avīnu*, the first Hebrew and the founder of the Jewish people. I also had the privilege of engaging with Dr. Abidullah Ghazi, a Muslim educator of Indian descent, who had opened his heart and the doors of his educational institute to me. There, I shared many intimate spiritual moments with Fadel Abdallah, an excellent Arabic teacher, and other Muslim devotees, who welcomed me as their brother in the spirit of God's calling in the Qur'ān: "[I] made you as [diverse] nations and tribes so that you may be acquainted with each other,"[2] and be enhanced by the presence of the other.

During my journey into Muslims' devotional life, I was invited in 1993 to a mosque in northern Indiana, where I gave a sermon to a crowded congregation about the commonality between Islam and Judaism (see Appendix 2 for a news report). The sermon in its entirety appears in the following chapter. As a Jew of Israeli descent, making a public presentation in a mosque was an unforgettable experience. For the Muslim congregants, it was a refreshing surprise to see a Jew flipping through the pages of their Holy Qur'ān and quoting Arabic verses in support of religious pluralism and word peace.

My human interactions with Muslims continued on different levels, finding common grounds for sharing our joys and our distresses. We visited each other at weddings and other personal events and never stopped communicating with one another. I will not forget how one night in the fall of 1994, a group of Arab Muslim friends, led by my long-time friend Suheil Nammari, a civil engineer of a Palestinian descent, came to my house to offer me their condolences, when I was "sitting" for my father's *shiv'āh,* the Jewish seven-day mourning after death. I invited Muslim friends to celebrate a Passover *sēder* with my family, and during Ramaḍān, they invited me to "break bread" with them as they assembled for the evening *ifṭār.*

I believe that it is essential to build bridges of understanding between Jewish and Muslim community leaders, and enhance opportunities to do so especially when tragedy strikes. When Muslim Bosnians were brutalized in their homeland, I was privileged to join on August 11, 1995, Chicago community leaders for an emergency interfaith gathering and sign a public statement expressing concern with the plight of the Bosnian people, condemning the ethnic cleansing, and calling for intervention by the international community. When the Chicagoland Muslim community seemed to be under siege and suffered from an unfair backlash after the events of September 11, 2001, I felt it was vitally important to join the Muslim community's gathering and prayer in Villa Park, Illinois, to show my moral support. I also invited Muslim friends and community leaders to visit my *sukkāh,* during the Feast of Tabernacles, a joyous Jewish holiday known for its universality.

* * *

Where Islam and Judaism Join Together appears at a time when world attention is focused on the seemingly unfolding clash between Islam and the West as civilizations. There is a growing use of the term "clash of civilizations," coined by Professor Samuel Huntington of Harvard University,[3] as a password to the understanding of the antagonistic relations between the two worlds. In this book, I wish to introduce an alternative context for the future: one that can be called "interaction of civilizations" instead; one that can generate new conversations about an interreligious dialogue and new ways to create a community of religions; one that can help the children of 'Avrahām of the Torah and the children of 'Ibrāhīm of the Qur'ān radically transform their underlying assumptions about and behavior toward each other. How can we create this kind of a community of religions?

One way is to learn a lesson of history. The experience of community relations and cultural interaction among Jews, Muslims and Christians during the Spanish Golden Age of the fifteenth to seventeenth centuries provides us a living example of inter-religious, intellectual, cultural and social interaction. The words "Golden Age" (*Siglo de Oro* in Spanish) connoted religious communities living in harmony with each other and developing their creative potential in a wide variety of fields of science, arts and literature. Spanish historians called this phenomenon of interaction *convivencia*, which is loosely defined as "coexistence." For Jews and Muslims, in particular, this phenomenon should be encouraging, offering them a model for future Jewish-Muslim cooperation and amity.[4]

The current world community of religions, as we know it, is influenced by two vectors, two moving forces that run in opposite directions: unity and separation. To understand these forces, one needs to view this community or family of religions as a wheel with a hub and a rim connected by spokes in one structure. The hub represents the One God, the ultimate core shared by all religions. The outer rim represents humanity, to which the spokes—the different religions each with its own set of beliefs and practices—are connected. As the spokes come closer to each other at the hub, the spiritual paths come closer to each other seeking the One God and each other. As the spokes approach the outer rim, the paths distance themselves from each other. The vector of separation is the force of particularism and exclusivism that drives people away from the center, whereas the vector of unity is the force of universalism and inclusivism that drives them toward the center. The vector of separation is natural within each religion—it sets boundaries and wants to expand by emphasizing differences. We, humanity as a whole, are the catalyst for the vector of unity that generates reconciling actions that emphasize similarities. Though the two forces seem to be diametrically opposed to each other, they are not in conflict, but are rather self-neutralizing. The ultimate goal is to mitigate the tendency of the vector of separation to go to the extreme by finding a happy medium. There, religions can join together and collaborate for peace, reconciliation, preservation of the planet, and establishment of a global ethic that responds to critical issues around the world. The vector of unity is expected to curb the pressures by the vector of separation to be distant and different by instilling ethical virtues, such as mercy, compassion, empathy, brotherhood, and love. *Where Islam and Judaism Join Together* is just one tool designed to support those who are in the service of unity and to counter those who foster separation.

Scholars, analysts, and policymakers have continuously reexamined the resurgence of religion on the world stage and its growing role in human affairs. One of them is the Dalai Lama, the spiritual leader of the Tibetan people. In his recently published book, he explores ways to transcend the differences between religions so that they are genuinely appreciated and not turned into sources of conflict.[5] Another is Professor Philip Jenkins of Penn State University, one of America's best scholars of religion. He holds an opposite view claiming that "the twenty-first century will almost certainly be regarded by future historians as a century in which religion replaced ideology as the prime animating and destructive force in human affairs, guiding attitudes to political liberty and obligation, concepts of nationhood, and, of course, conflicts and wars."[6] If this alarming apocalyptic observation is accurate, then it is time for soul searching and genuine reassessment of the role of religion in global conflicts and violence. But more importantly, it is time to challenge Professor Jenkins's thought-provoking prediction by harnessing our power to create a different future, by coming together and allowing the true expression of the generosity of our cultures creating a force of peace and harmony.

It is our obligation to reject the argument that religion is a source of conflicts and emphasize the role of religion as a resource for resolving them. Religion can, best of all, serve peace and speak the language of conflict resolution and reconciliation, as studied by numerous scholars.[7] We have all seen how religious leaders exhibited remarkable capacities to serve others. It is therefore essential to treat religion as relevant to foreign policy and include religious actors in the diplomatic efforts in conflict regions.[8] Religious leaders may be especially more effective in offering faith-driven solutions to religious conflicts. This supposition is qualified by a special report of the United States Institute of Peace, which stated that "faith-based non-governmental organizations (NGOs) are increasingly active and increasingly effective in international peacebuilding," and that they "have a special role to play in zones of religious conflict."[9] One example is the historic First Alexandria Declaration of the Religious Leaders of the Holy Land issued on January 21, 2002 (see Appendix 4), where 14 religious leaders in Israel and Palestine used their influence to support the peace process.

I recognize the centrality of the Israeli-Palestinian conflict within the overall context of Jewish-Muslim relations. Most Muslim leaders still argue that as long as this conflict is not resolved, resolution for the Jewish-Muslim rift is impossible. I disagree. If anything, an historical rapprochement between the two religions can only help Israelis and Palestinians find peace together. The passions of religious antagonism between Islam and Judaism only aggravate the Middle East conflict. Nothing is more dangerous than turning this conflict into a war of beliefs and exporting it outside the boundaries of that region. True, in the Middle East, politics and religion are quite intertwined, and it is difficult sometimes to distinguish between the two. But the frequent misuse of religion by Middle East governments and leaders, in their conflict with each other, has only distorted the attitudes of Muslims and Jews toward one another.

It is time Jewish and Muslim leaders move beyond this polarization and publicly acknowledge that we are brothers in faith and blood. We both believe in One God (*'Elōha* in Hebrew; *Allah* in Arabic). We have the same faith (*'emunāh* in Hebrew; *'īmān* in Arabic). We keep similar acts of worship (*'avodāh* in Hebrew; *'ibādah* in Arabic). We share the same genealogical ancestor, "Our Father," Avrahām/'Ibrāhīm. It is time to market these reconciling common denominators and "unmarket," not necessarily ignore, the differences that separate us. While law and practice vary, faith is the same for all, and our relationship with God, regardless of our religion, is judged by our relationship to fellow men.

Inconsistent with this fundamental injunction of Islam (see chapter 1: The Gate of Unity, for details) is the culture of denial that has plagued some intellectual and religious centers in the Muslim world with respect to my Jewish narrative. The deniers blatantly dismiss the most fundamental truths of the Jewish story. They frequently claim that there was no Jewish People, no Land of Israel, no Holy Temple in Jerusalem, and no Holocaust. What should I tell my children and grandchildren about their ancestors? What should I tell them about my Eastern European grandparents (from my father's side), who perished in the concentration camp of Auschwitz? What should I tell them about my Yemenite great-grandparents (from my mother's side), who in the late nineteenth century left south Arabia for what they believed to be their sacred Land of Israel and settled in Jerusalem so that they could pray at the Western ("Wailing") Wall (Hebrew: *Ha-Kōtel ha-Ma'ravī*) of the Temple Mount? What does it say about all those Muslims, who need to assault my remarkable history and my core identity and redefine me out of my glorious heritage and national existence? What kind of a world would we be living in, if everyone denies another's history and identity? I admit there is a vocal but fringe radical right in Israel that insists that there are no Palestinian people. But most Israelis, as well as Jews all over the world, understand the Palestinian narrative and believe in a two-state solution to the Israeli-Palestinian conflict. The collective stories of nations and the integrity of their identity must be honored.

We need to fight the fanatics among us—those who manipulate religion and turn it into an instrument of hatred and violence—while supporting the voices of peace among us. We need to reject all cultures of denial and allow infrastructures of mutual trust and reconciliation to be erected instead. We need to cast aside exclusivist religious visions and violent passions and replace them with relationships marked by mutual human care and compassion. We need to combat the forces of chaos and darkness that divide people and create for them instead peaceful ecology, where they can rejoice in the human diversity of experience, the colorful tapestry of expression, and the noble acceptance of each other. We need to condemn all senseless wanton acts of violence and engage in peace education in our schools, places of worship, and media networks so that our children and grandchildren live in a safe world and enjoy a brighter future. A personal perspective on intolerance and violence in Islam is offered by Imam Jamal Rahman, a Seattle-based Muslim Sufi interfaith minister (see Appendix 5).

Professor Khaled Abou El Fadl of UCLA, a distinguished scholar of Islamic Law, admits in his article "The Place of Tolerance in Islam: On Reading the Qur'ān and Misreading it," that the Qur'ān and other Islamic sources offer possibilities of intolerant interpretation that are exploited by contemporary supremacists. He made the following explanation with which I agree: "Ultimately, the Qur'ān, or any text, speaks to its reader. This ability of human beings to interpret texts is both a blessing and a burden. It is a blessing because it provides us with the flexibility to adapt texts to changing circumstances. It is a burden because the reader must take responsibility for the normative values he or she brings to the text. Any text, including those that are Islamic, provides possibilities for meaning, not inevitabilities. And those possibilities are exploited, developed and ultimately determined by the reader's efforts—good faith efforts, we hope—at making sense of the text's complexities. Consequently, the meaning of the text is often only as moral as its reader. If the reader is intolerant, hateful, or oppressive, so will be the interpretation of the text."[10]

The book you have just started to read is a sincere effort to go back to our sacred texts and reinterpret their teachings so that an open space is created to embrace religious pluralism and respect of other people's truths.[11] Jewish sages observed that "Torah scholars increase peace in the world, for it is said (in Isaiah 54:13): 'And all your children shall be taught [the Torah] of the Lord, and great shall be the peace of your children.'"[12] But, expounding on words of the Psalmist (Psalms 119:165), they suggest a twist to the Hebrew word for "children": "Do not read *banāyikh* (your children), but *bonāyikh* (your builders)."[13] Conclusion: Those who engage in the study of their Sacred Law, whether they are Jews or Muslims, have a role to play as peace builders. Thus, the Psalmist urges us to "seek peace and pursue it."[14]

Avōt d'Rabbi Nathan, one of the minor tractates of the Talmud, expounds on this verse and says: "If a man sits in his place and keeps silent, how can he pursue peace in Israel between man and man? But let him leave his place and roam about in the world, and pursue peace in Israel, as it is written 'seek peace and pursue it'. How: Seek peace in your own dwelling place, and pursue it in another place."[15] This commendable course of action applies to Jews and Muslims alike. Peace building is a ceaseless effort, a day-to-day action, an everlasting undertaking. Teachings on peace by Jewish sages are compiled in a noncanonical section of the Babylonian Talmud called The Chapter on Peace (see Appendix 3).

I hope this book will contribute to this noble mission and continuously remind us of the words of the Psalmist cited earlier: "Pray for the peace of Jerusalem," and keep her "as a city that is united together" (*ke-'īr she-ḥubrāh lah yaḥdāv*).[16] Not only united horizontally, that is, between its physical entities—Arab and Jewish sections and various quarters and communities—but more so vertically as a holy city where heaven and earth kiss, that is, between its spiritual entities—Heavenly Jerusalem (*Yerushalāyim shel Mā'lah*) and Earthly Jerusalem (*Yerushalāyim shel Māṭah*). Not only united, but unifying as well; a mosaic city with a holistic unity-within-diversity and with a unique quality that brings us "together" (*yaḥdāv*) and makes all of us "friends" (*ḥaverīm*).[17]

I am confident that the presence of God will help us transcend the seemingly unbridgeable chasm that separates Islam and Judaism and transform the historical confrontation into harmony and cooperation. I respectfully ask all Jewish and Muslim spiritual leaders, scholars, educators, opinion makers, and community leaders to join hands, in the spirit of the Torah and the Qur'ān, and open a constructive interfaith dialogue to which this book is a modest contribution. I also invite you to read my Open Letter to My Muslim Friends, a public appeal published online in both English and Arabic.[18] I always believed that, with our shared vision of peace and prayer of hope, we together could succeed where politicians have failed miserably.

May you all embrace the following inspirational message of the Arab poet and philosopher Khalil Gibran (1883–1931):

> I love you, my brother, whoever you are
> whether you worship in your church,
> kneel in your temple,
> or pray in your mosque.
> You and I are all children of one faith,
> for the diverse paths of religion
> are fingers of the loving hand of one Supreme Being,
> a hand extended to all,
> offering completeness of spirit to all,
> and eager to receive all.[19]

Part I

Two Religions, One Faith

Chapter 1

The Gate of Unity

We Are Bound Together—an Appeal to Muslims

As the president of the Middle East Peace Network (MEPN), I was invited on December 12, 1993, to address the congregants of The Islamic Center of Michigan City, Indiana (see a new report in Appendix 2). The following edited version of this sermon is dedicated to the inviter, the late Hajj Anwar Zainal, a good friend, a wise man, and a spiritual devotee, who served in the leadership team of MEPN in its early days and contributed immensely to the understanding between Islam and Judaism.

* * *

Bismillāh al-Raḥmān al-Raḥīm, al-Ḥamdulillāh Rabbi-l-'Ālamīn (In the Name of God, the Merciful, the Compassionate, Praise be to God, Sovereign of the Universe).

Brothers and sisters, distinguished friends:

As a Jew, I am deeply honored by the gracious invitation extended to me to address such a gathering of devout Muslims. As a longtime student of Islamic studies and an ardent devotee of peace in the Middle East, I deem your place of worship to be the most appropriate forum to talk about the Islamic central doctrine of *tawḥīd*—the Oneness of God—and its relationship to the ideal of peace. I use the words of Moses cited in the Qur'ān as a prayer: "O my Lord! Expand me my heart, ease my task for me, and loose a knot from my tongue, so they [you] may understand whatever I say."[1]

In its broad definition, the doctrine of *tawḥīd*, in my opinion, is composed of three concentric circles: first, the inner most core of our being, the source of all things, is the Unity of God; second comes the Unity of Faith (Arabic: *waḥdat al-'īmān*); third is the outer circle, the Unity of Mankind (Arabic: *waḥdat an-nās*). These three circles are not separate, but are part of the whole with God as the Ultimate Source. In the case of Jews and Muslims, we may add another circle, the Unity of Kinship (Arabic: *waḥdat an-nasab*) that can explain the ancestral relationship between them.

Indeed mankind is divided into different religions; some are monotheistic and some are not. What concerns us here are the three monotheistic religions—Judaism, Christianity, and Islam—whose doctrine is based on divine revelation (Arabic: *waḥy*), the starting point for each of the three religions. One word about the Islamic term "People of the Book" (Arabic: *ahl al-kitāb*), commonly used of the Jews and Christians, who, like the Muslims, each received their own book of revelation, the Torah and the Gospels respectively. This term is not originally Islamic. Because of the giving of the Torah to the People of Israel, they have always been called worldwide the "People of the Book" (Hebrew: *'am ha-sēfer*), a nation I am proud to belong to.

In spite of the theological differences between all three monotheistic religions, the Qur'ān repeatedly reminds Muslims of five common elements that bond them with members of their sister religions:

1. The creedal element—the common belief in One God.
2. The human element—the common bond with Adam, the primordial man.
3. The ethical element—the common principle that piety, righteousness, and morality are the only criteria for a fair judgment of people.
4. The historical element—the common link to one ancestor, Abraham, and to a chain of the same holy prophets.
5. The cooperative element—the common ground for a dialogue.

I am not here to elaborate on *the creedal element*. As we all know, the first and foremost tenet and guiding principle of Islam—and of all the three Great Religions—is the Oneness of God. Our declarations of faith: both my *Shemā'* ("*Adonāi 'Elohēinu Adonāi 'Eḥād*—the Lord is our God, the Lord is One") and your *Shahādah* ("*lā ilāha illā Allāh*—there is no God but Allah") proclaim the infinite Unity of God. As a practicing Jew, I pray three times a day, "He is our God, there is none else; truly He is our King, there is nothing besides Him."[2] So my God is your God. The Qur'ān says: "God is our Lord and your Lord" ("*Allāhu rabbunā wa-rabbukum*").[3] The Arabic word for "Lord," *rabb*, used in the *Bismillāh* blessing, is etymologically related to the Hebrew word *ribbōn*, meaning "Sovereign." In *Shmonēh 'Esrēh* ("Eighteen Benedictions"), the silent standing prayer I say throughout the week, I thankfully acknowledge that "You [God] are the Lord our God and God of our fathers, the God of *all flesh*."[4] The word "flesh," meaning humankind, is etymologically related in both sister languages—it is *basār* in Hebrew and *bashar* in Arabic. Here is another similarity: The common Arabic phrase *Allāhu Akbar*, usually translated as "God is Great" or "God is [the] Greatest" and recited by Muslims as a call for prayer, reminds us of the Psalms-based opening prayer recited by Jews at the Welcoming of Sabbath (*Qabbalāt Shabbāt*): "Let us come before His presence with thanksgiving, let us shout for joy to Him with psalms. For the Lord is a great God, and a great King above all gods."[5]

What I want to concentrate on today, however, is the unity of mankind—the human aspect of the Unity of God, the ethical dimension of monotheism—a cardinal yet sometimes forgotten principle, introduced by Prophet Muhammad to all human beings.

The Human Element

Although Jews and Muslims trace their genealogy to the Patriarch Abraham, the Bible begins with the story of the creation of Man. This shows that a long genealogical chain connects us all to the deepest roots of humanity, even before the history of civilization had begun.

In his farewell sermon on Mount Arafat, near Mecca, just before he died, Prophet Muhammad spoke on the equality of mankind: "O Mankind! Your Lord is One and you have but One Father. You all descended from Adam, and Adam was made of clay. Surely, the noblest among you in the eyes of God is the one with the most righteous conduct. None is superior to another [...] except with God-fearing (*taqwā*)."[6]

Sometimes, we hear the offensive remark "the enemies of God," when referring to another religious community. I ask you: if God, as we know Him, is the All-Father, can He have enemies? "Have we not all one father? Has not one God created us? Why do we deal treacherously every man against his brother?" asked Prophet Malachi.[7] And if God is indeed Almighty and All-Powerful, why should He be afraid of enemies among the humans?

As you all know, the Qur'ān calls upon mankind as a whole, saying: "O Mankind! Your Lord Who created you from one soul (*min nafsi waḥidati*)."[8] The Arabic word for "mankind," *nās*, is etymologically related to the Hebrew word *'enōsh*. The Qur'ān also says: "He who has made everything which He has created so fine: He began man from clay; then He made His progeny by creating from an extract of discarded water; next He fashioned him and breathed some of His own spirit into him."[9]

With these words, the Qur'ān reinforces two interrelated ideas: one, that we all come from one single source, Adam, whom God fashioned to His liking and breathed into him His own spirit; and two, that God recognizes the sanctity of each individual human being and each individual life, because we all carry His spirit.

This reminds me of an Islamic legend about Adam's creation told by *Qiṣaṣ al-Anbiyā'* ("Stories of the Prophets"), an Islamic text compiled by the thirteenth-century Turkish judge Al-Rabghūzī. The legend has it that God commanded Angel Izrael (*'Izra'īl*), after Angels Gabriel and Michael failed in their missions, to go down to Earth and bring back a handful of soil. He also ordered him to gather soil from all parts of the Earth, from its east and west, from its valleys and mountains, in order to create a new creature to rule, as His deputy, over His creation. As for the soil, the legend continues, some of it was pure and some of it salty, some sweet, some bitter, some of it black and white, some was yellow and green, red and blue, hard and soft, clean and unclean. So are the children of Adam, who inherited all these properties. This is why, the legend explains, they do not resemble one another.[10] Similarly, an ancient Jewish legend tells that God gathered soil (in Hebrew, "soil," *adamāh,* has the same root as "man" *adām*) from the four corners of the world and mixed it with water of all the seas to create *one* human being, so that no one could claim superiority over another.[11] We, the family of mankind, are all descended from one Adam. Unsurprisingly, the word "Adam" in both Hebrew and Arabic does not come in plural; human beings are called "sons of Adam" (*bnai Adām* in Hebrew; *banū Ādam* in Arabic). Like God, Adam is one—the true foundation of the unity of mankind.

In His wisdom, God spread mankind into different countries and climates and developed different languages, as told by the Qur'ān: "Among His signs is the creation of heaven and earth, as well as the diversity in your languages and colors; surely in that are signs for those who have knowledge."[12]

God did not create human beings as coins, clones, or look-alike robots. He made us different, so we can enjoy the diversity, be enriched by our particular gifts and qualities, and be able to grow. He made each and everyone of us individually unique, entirely different from any other human being that ever existed. A Jewish tradition offers us an illuminating parable. It tries to find the reason why Adam was created alone and gives the following answer: "In order to show the greatness of the King of Kings, the Blessed Holy One; whenever a man casts one-hundred coins with a single stamp, all the coins look alike. But, the King of Kings, the Blessed Holy One, casts all humans with the stamp of the first Man, and no one is similar to his fellow man."[13]

God must have had some special purpose in creating individualistic humans in a pluralistic humanity. Mankind is the product of His creative hand, "God's own handiwork" (Arabic: *fitrat Allāh*), and human diversity is "the true religion" (Arabic: *ad-dīn al-qayyim*), as the Qur'ān puts it: "So set your face truly towards the [true] religion, God's handiwork along which lines He patterned mankind. There is no way to alter God's creation. That is the true religion, though most men do not realize it."[14]

Since all humankind was created equal, a Muslim is encouraged to accept and respect diversity within human society. The Qur'ān relates this following important declaration made by Prophet Muhammad in his last sermon: "O Mankind! We created you all out of a single [pair of] a male and a female, and made you as [diverse] nations and tribes so that you may be acquainted with each other."[15]

The concept of human diversity, as part of God's intent, purpose, and predesign of Creation, is emphasized throughout the Qur'ān. The following verses are considered by many scholars to be expressions of Islamic tolerance toward the other religions and the recognition that we may have a single Truth with many tracks leading to it:[16]

> Mankind was once just one single community, but differed; [later] had it not been for a Word [of God] that went forth from your Lord, their differences would have been settled between them.[17]
>
> If your Lord had wished, He would have made all mankind one single community, but [He wished it otherwise and so] they continue to have differences, except those who may have God's grace [in dealing with their differences]. And for that end [of testing human beings in how they handle their differences and deal fairly with one another] has He created them.[18]
>
> We have prescribed each of you a [different] law and custom (*shir'ah wa-minhaj*). If God had wished, He would have made you all one single community; but [His plan] is to test you through what He sends to you, so you may compete with one another in doing what is good.[19]

The last phrase, "So you may compete with one another in doing what is good," leads me to the next principle.

The Ethical Element

The Qur'ān goes further and explains that living a righteous life is an essential element of a true religion. Religion is not merely praying to the east or to the west but engaging in *'ibādah*, a devotional service of God. God does not care where people direct their prayer. He cares whether the worshipers compete with each other in doing "good deeds." Says the Qur'ān:

> Righteousness is not that you turn your faces [in prayer] towards the east or the west; but righteousness means that one believes in God, in the Last Day, in the Angels, in the [scriptural] Books and in the Prophets; that, for the love of God, one gives of his wealth to his kindred and to the orphans and to the needy and to the way-farer and to those who ask, and to effect the freedom of the slave; that one observes prayer and pays the poor; that is of those who are faithful to their engagements, when they have engaged in them, and endured with fortitude poverty, distress and moments of peril—such are the people of Truth, the God-fearing.[20]
>
> Everyone is given a direction to which he turns. So strive to be the first [to do] good deeds (*faistabiqū' al-khyrāti*). Wherever you are, God will bring you together. For God has power over all things.[21]

The competition between people to do good deeds is not limited here to the Islamic community, but to humanity as a whole. The true test in the relations between religious groups is not who is the "winner" in a theological debate or in the struggle over Truth; it is the ethical principle that God prefers to see what is guiding the relations between religions.[22]

The Qur'ān states clearly that God does not distinguish between the righteous, whether they are Muslims, Jews, or Christians. It is speaking to all the children of Abraham when it says:

> Surely, the most honored of you in the eyes of God is one who is the most righteous.[23]
>
> Those who believe [i.e., Muslims] and those who profess Judaism, and the Christians and the Sabians[24]—any of those who believe in [One] God and the Last Day and act righteously—shall have their reward with their Lord.[25]

Like in the last citation, whenever the Qur'ān refers to "those who believe" or "the believers" (Arabic: *al-mu'minīn*), it means Muslims. But now pay attention to the Qur'ān's definition of who is a true believer: "Believers are only those who feel a tremor in their hearts when God is mentioned, and whose faith is strengthened whenever His messages are conveyed to them, and who put [all] their trust in their Lord; [and] who establish regular prayers and spend on others out of what We have given them for sustenance. It is they who are truly believers."[26]

This is a broad definition that any believer of the three monotheistic religions can identify with. There is nothing in this definition that confines it to believers of the Islamic faith only. If we apply this definition to all believers, then the following verse has a powerful implication: "[All] the believers are but brothers, therefore seek reconciliation (*aṣliḥū'*) between your two [contending] brothers, and fear God, so that you may be blessed with His mercy."[27]

Also, the *Book of Psalms* (known in Islamic tradition as the *Zabūr*), revealed to King David (who is recognized in the Qur'ān as a prophet), says, "Open for me the gates of righteousness, that I will enter them to thank God. This is the gateway to the Lord, the righteous shall enter through it."[28] It does not say Jews shall enter into it; it does not say Christians, nor does it say Muslims. It says the righteous shall enter into it. In praying, "Open for me the *gates* of righteousness," David uses the plural, as if to say there are many gates of righteousness, many ways to reach God. Similarly, the Jewish Midrash (commentaries on the Bible) says: "The Blessed Holy One disqualifies no human creature, but receives them all. The gates are always opened, and all who wish to enter can enter."[29] In the same spirit, the Qur'ān quotes the Psalms, reminding us of God's words: "My righteous servants shall inherit the earth."[30]

Our God, whom we all pray to, is not an exclusive God. He is the Sovereign of the Universe (*rabbi-l-'ālamīn*) and the Lord of Mankind (*ilāhi-n-nās*), as the Qur'ān states: "Say: 'I believe in whatever [scriptural] Book God has sent down; and I am commanded to deal justly between you. God is our Lord and your Lord. We have our deeds, while you have your deeds. There is no contention between you and us. God will bring us together, and towards Him is the final goal.'"[31]

This perfectly leads me to the next principle.

The Historical Element

The Qur'ān neither cancels out the messages of previous prophets, nor does it make any distinction between them. It mentions 28 prophets, of which 18 are Hebrew Bible figures. They all, according to the Qur'ān, represent an unbroken chain of divine revelations; they all symbolize the continuity and variety of the religious experience of mankind; they all represent but one faith, One God:

> Say: "We believe in God and in that which has been revealed to us [i.e. the Qur'ān] and revealed to Abraham, Ishmael, Isaac, Jacob and the Tribes, and that which was given to Moses, Jesus, and the Prophets by their Lord. We make no distinction between any one of them."[32]

> For you has He established the [same] religion, which He enjoined on Noah and which We have revealed to you, and which We enjoined on Abraham, Moses, and Jesus, saying: "Observe this religion, and create no divisions within it."[33]

The key statement here is that God has established for mankind one universal religion—*ad-dīn*—using various holy prophets as transmitters of His revelation. All revealed books, according to the Qur'ān, had one heavenly source, the Preserved Tablet (*al-lawḥ al-maḥfūẓ*), also called Mother Book (*'umm al-kitāb*).[34] The Qur'ān gives us a beautiful parable that illustrates God's universality: "God is the Light of the heavens and the earth. The parable of His Light is as if there were a niche and within it a lamp. The lamp is enclosed in glass. The glass is [shining] like a radiant star, lit from a blessed tree—an olive tree that is neither of the east nor of the west, whose oil would well nigh glow [of itself] even though fire had not touched it. Light upon Light! God does compose parables for mankind; God does know everything."[35]

It is clear that the Light cannot be identified wholly with one of its carriers, but is common to them all. The Light is "for mankind" (*li-n-nās*); it shines in the heart of every individual, who walks "in the path of God" (*fī sabīl Allāh*) in piety and righteousness, regardless whether he is Muslim, Jewish, or Christian. The example of the olive tree alludes to the continuity of divine revelation, which springs from one source and branches into a variety of religious experiences. It is not confined by any one particular tradition or locality; it is "neither of the east nor the west."

I learned from my dear friend Reverend Bassam Abdallah of the United Evangelical Lutheran Church in Hammond, Indiana, the following analogy: The three Great Religions offer mankind a whole structure: Moses built the foundation, Jesus erected the walls, Prophet Muhammad placed the roof above. Thus, each prophet made his contribution to humanity by building part of the House of God.[36]

Indeed, the Qur'ān, in order to mark its disapproval of the tendency to regard one prophet as superior to another, or of accepting one and rejecting another, declares: "Those who believe in God and His messengers and make no distinction between any of them, We shall soon give [them] their [due] rewards."[37] The Qur'ān calls upon us to accept without discrimination all the Prophets and all the Books revealed to them, and God's Truth, which they all contain, regardless of the language in which it is expressed. "[God's] Truth stands out clear from error,"[38] says the Qur'ān. The rest is all human interpretation, and there is a lot of it all over the world. Unfortunately, the vocal among many of the contemporary religious leaders are spiteful extremists, who in their over-zealous interpretation of the scripture and law, use and abuse their religious authority to create separation rather than cooperation. Jewish and Muslim leaders have a responsibility toward their faith and a duty to their respective constituencies to counteract this destructive exploitation of their religious communities and to draw their attention to the worthy principle of cooperation and interaction among the children of Abraham sanctioned in their revealed scriptures.

This leads me to the last principle.

The Cooperative Principle

Islam's principle of freedom of worship and religious pluralism is clearly expressed in an early *sūrah*. "Say: 'O non-believers! I do not worship what you worship, nor do you worship what I worship; and I will not worship what you have worshiped, nor will you worship what I worship. You have your religion, and I have mine.'"[39]

But, the Qur'ān does not mean an exclusive, noncooperative relationship. To the contrary, its call is very clear for us: "Cooperate with each other in righteousness and piety, and do not cooperate with each other in sin and transgression."[40] Coercion is incompatible with God's religion, as the Qur'ān clearly states that "there must be no compulsion in matters of religion (*lā ikrāha fi-d-dīn*)."[41]

Finding common ground, based on the Unity of God, and establishing a dialogue are urged instead:

> Say: "O People of the Book! Let us come to common terms between you and us as we worship none but God; and associate no partners with Him, nor shall any of us take on others as lords other than God."[42]
>
> Invite [all] to the Way of the Lord with wisdom and beautiful preaching; and dispute with them *in the politest manner*. For your Lord knows best who has strayed from His path and who has consented to guidance (emphasis added).[43]
>
> Do not dispute with the People of the Book except *in the politest manner*, unless those of them it be with who do wrong. And say [as you enter in dialogue with them]: "We believe in the revelation which has come down to us and in that which came down to you; our God and your God is [the same] One and it is to Him we submit" (emphasis added).[44]

Where is the influence of the Qur'ān that teaches us to dispute "in the politest manner"? Disputing "in the politest manner" means more than rendering lip service to benevolent ideals, which our sacred scriptures teach us.

It does not mean to be quiet. It means to speak openly on behalf of peace and reconciliation and to communicate it across the boundaries of peoples and nations. It means to talk clearly and unmistakably about our intentions and concerns. It means to freely exchange ideas and information and openly share feelings and hopes. It also means to condemn anyone, particularly our own leaders, when they engage in a hostile rhetoric and equate the use of force to resolve conflicts with the doing of God's will.

The Qur'ān teaches you to be kind and compassionate to others as He is to you. It says to "be kind as God has been kind to you,"[45] and also "the All-Merciful is kind to those who are kind to others."[46] By the way, the most popular pair of God's Names, "The Merciful, the Compassionate," appears in both Arabic and Hebrew: in Arabic *Ar-Raḥmān ar-Raḥīm*, in Hebrew *Ha-Raḥamān* and *ha-Raḥūm* respectively. The Qur'ān even calls Muslims to be compassionate with those whom they perceive as enemies: "May God still grant love between you and those whom you hold as enemies, for God is Powerful and God is Oft-Forgiving, Merciful."[47] Where is our compassion? I am afraid most of us forgot the first element of this virtue—becoming aware of others' needs and responding to their cries of distress and suffering. We are stuck in our own belief systems, unable to transcend beyond our partisan loyalties, whether they are religious or political, and unwilling to challenge some of our leaders who feed us with polarizing rhetoric.

There is a two-word *ḥadīth* (one of Prophet Muhammad's sayings and actions) that equals a whole book of thought: "*Ad-dīn al-mu'āmalatu*,"[48] which means your faith is judged by your treatment of others. You cannot claim to be a person of piety by simply going to a place of worship. You are what you do. Your true faith would be evident in the way you treat, or deal with, others. It is not by coincidence that human beings are called humankind or mankind. But, we forgot to be *kind* to each other.

The Muslim tradition of *sujūd*, the practice of kneeling down in praying, is a wonderful symbol of humility and submission to the will of God to which any human being can relate. However, let me share with you my own *tafsīr*, an interpretation, regarding *sujūd*. The way I see it, this is the symbolic act of placing your head below your heart, allowing the heart to take precedence in your relationship with God.

I believe the following poem of Hafiz (ca. 1320–1389), the most revered poet of Persia, is a beautiful representation of the spiritual meaning of *sujūd* I am referring to:

> There I bow my head.
>   at the feet of every creature.
> This constant submission and homage,
>   of kissing God all over.

Someday,
every lover will do.
Only there I prostrate myself,
against the beauty of each form
For when I bring my heart close to any object
I always hear the Friend say,
"Hafiz, I am
Here."[49]

The *sujūd* is about allowing the heart to take precedence in relationship not only with God, but with your fellow man as well. Love of God and love of man go hand in hand. One cannot truly love God without truly loving human beings. The oneness of man's heart is a manifestation of the Oneness of God. Doesn't the Qur'ān say: "God has not made for any man two hearts in his one body?"[50]

Once, the greatest Jewish master and leader of our generation, Rabbi Menachem Mendel Schneerson (1902–1991), who has come to be known worldwide as "The Lubavitcher Rebbe," was asked: "Which is greater, love of God or love of your fellow man?" He answered: "Love of your fellow man. For then you love that which your Beloved [i.e., God] loves."[51] Here is what one *ḥadīth* tells us: "Do you love your Creator? Love your fellow men first."[52] We see here one identical message from two totally different sources, one Jewish and the other Islamic.

I must say here some words about brotherhood. There is a Jewish folktale, based on a Midrash, about a wise father who asked each of his sons to take a stick and break it in half. They did so, very easily. Then he put the same number of sticks together and bound them with a string. Again the father asked his sons to break the sticks. They couldn't. "You see, my sons," he explained, "our strength is as one, by our bonding together, not as isolated individuals."[53] Doesn't the Qur'ān raise the question, "Have We not made the earth [as a place] to draw [us] together"?[54] Doesn't the Torah say: "You are all children of the Lord, your God"?[55] This reminds me of the beautiful lines of an ancient prayer for peace and brotherhood chanted by the Essenes, a Jewish religious group that flourished from the second century BCE to the first century CE:

And all shall work together in the garden of brotherhood
Yet each shall follow his own path
And each shall commune with his own heart.
Though the brothers be of a different complexion
Yet do they all toil in the vineyard of the Earthly Mother
And they all do lift their voice together in praise of the Heavenly Father.
There shall be no peace among peoples
Till there be one garden of brotherhood over the earth.[56]

We, Jews and Muslims, are brothers. We share the same genealogical ancestry of Abraham, our father (*Abūna 'Ibrāhīm* in Arabic; *Avrahām Avīnu* in Hebrew). "The closest people to Abraham," says the Qur'ān, "are those who follow him (*inna awla-n-nās bi-'Ibrāhīm la-ladhīna attaba'ūhu*)."[57] So let's all follow his way of life: when his herdsmen were fighting with the herdsmen of his nephew Lot, he called on Lot and told him, "I beseech you! Let there be no strife between me and you, and between my herdmen and your herdmen, for we are brothers."[58] So let us follow Abraham's tradition of fellowship, the way you, brothers and sisters, offered it to me today in extending your hospitality. Let us follow the Psalmist David who sang, "Behold, how good and pleasant it is for brothers to dwell together in unity."[59] Let us, as the ancient poem beautifully calls upon us, "work together in the garden of brotherhood."

Whether He is called Allah, 'Elōha, or the Lord, God wants us to turn the entire Earth into a place of worship for Him. And as long as we—Jews, Christians, and Muslims—ignorantly refer to Him as a Jewish God, or a Christian God, or a Muslim God, we are *not* one with God and, therefore, we violate the *tawḥīd*, the cardinal principle of the Oneness of God. Thus, the Jewish prayer *'Alēinu* (that calls upon Jewish worshipers "to praise to the Master of All") questions whether we truly have One God. It suggests instead that only at the End of the Days, on the Day of Judgment, "when God shall be acknowledged King of all the Earth, on that day, God shall be One and His Name One."

Similarly, the famed Rabbi Abraham Isaac Ha-Cohen Kook (1864–1935), the first Ashkenazi chief rabbi of the British Mandate for Palestine, offers, in his monumental work *Orōt* ("Lights"), the following universalistic approach: "The Blessed Holy One was generous with His world; he did not grant all the qualities to one place, to one person, to one people, to one country, to one generation or to one world. But the qualities are spread, and it is the need for wholeness (Hebrew: *shlemūt*), the most ideal driving force, that drives us toward the exalted unity that must come to the world; and 'on that day, God shall be One and His Name will be One.'"[60]

When, according to the Qur'ān, Abraham traveled as far as Arabia to rebuild, purify, and establish the *Ka'bah* as the "House of God,"[61] he also expected us to apply this act to man's sanctuary of love, the heart. So I call upon you, brothers and sisters: let's purify our hearts from the mischief of disputes and conflicts. Let's replace them with the loving care of God, with the empowering grace of God, with the liberating peace of God. Do not forget that one of God's names, both in Islamic and Jewish traditions, is Peace, *Salām*, *Shalōm*. God is the source of all peace. If we follow His way, we then pursue peace in our relationship with our fellow men. We should all integrate the spiritual message of *sujūd*—placing our head below our heart—to our everyday life and trust the Light of God, "*Allāhu-nūr*." We should all invite His light to our hearts and to the whole world, especially to its dark corners. The world would then look totally different, very enlightened, and human experience would inevitably go through a truly radical transformation, so would the relationship between Jews and Muslims. *Inshāllāh*, God willing!

Final Thoughts

The Jewish "Grace after Meals" contains a beautiful verse that has a universal appeal, a blessing for "food to all [human] creatures." The entire universe is invited to eat at the heavenly table, the earth, and enjoy God's blessing:

> Blessed are You, Lord our God, King of the universe, who, in His goodness, provides sustenance for *the entire world* with grace, kindness and mercy. He gives food *to all flesh* [*le-khōl basār*], for His mercy is everlasting. Through His abundant goodness to us, we have never lacked [food]; and may we never lack food, for the sake of His great Name. For He, benevolent God, provides sustenance and nourishment for *all* [*la-kōl*], does good *to all*, and prepares food for *all His creatures* [*le-khōl briyotāv*] whom He has created, as it is said: Blessed is the Lord, who provides food *for all* (emphasis added).

Both the Torah and the Qur'ān proclaim God's sovereignty as the Lord of Mankind. In this spirit, I wish to end my remarks first with a phrase from the Jewish silent standing prayer during the service of Rosh Ha-Shanāh, the Jewish New Year festival: "And so, Lord our God, let Your awe be manifest in all Your works, and instill a reverence for You upon all that You have created; so that all [Your] works shall be in awe of You, all the creatures [*bru'īm*] may bow down to You, *and all of them unite in one fellowship* [*ve-ye'asū khulām agudāh 'aḥāt*] to carry out Your will with a perfect heart (emphasis added)."

The last chapter of the Qur'ān, *Sūrat an-Nās*, is an ideal conclusion, as it declares God as the Master of Mankind, One who protects us from the mischief of all evil thinkers and doers among us:

> Bismillāhi ar-Raḥmān ar-Raḥīm,
>
> *Qul*: "a'ūdhu bi-Rabbi-n-nās, maliki-n-nās, llāhi-n-nās, min sharri-l-waswāsi-l-khannās alladhi yuwaswisu fī surdūri-n-nās min al-jinnati wa-n-nās."
>
> In the Name of God, the Merciful, the Compassionate,
>
> *Say*: "I seek refuge with the Master of Mankind, the King of Mankind, the God of Mankind, from the mischief of the whisperer who whispers into the hearts of mankind whether among evil spirits or mankind."[62]

The Torah praises "the righteous" people (*tzadiqīm*), who seek peace and spread goodness in the world, while criticizing "the wicked" (*resha'īm*), who rejoice at the destruction of the world.[63] He who desires good and rejoices at it, the Psalmist suggests, "his soul shall abide in good fortune,"[64] whereas "he who is glad at calamity shall not remain unpunished."[65]

Likewise, the Qur'ān makes a clear distinction between makers of peace and creators of antagonism. Those who mediate "reconciliation (*iṣlāḥ*) between people" are considered even better than those who devote themselves to prayer, fasting, and charity and are rewarded and supported by God in all His affairs.[66] On the other hand, those who sow hatred and enmity among people, the so-called *al-mufsidīn*, will not attain their purpose and God will not set right their work.[67]

Remember, our God is the God of Peace. His name is Peace, *Salām*, *Shalōm*. He is all about peace, as one of your prayers beautifully states:

> Allāhumma anta as-salām wa-minka as-salām wa-'ilaika yariji'u as-salām.
>
> Hayyina rabbanā bis-salām wa-'adkhilnā dāra as-salām.
>
> Tabārakta yā dha-l-jalāli wa-l-'ikrām.
>
> O God! You are peace, and from you come peace, and unto you peace returns.
>
> Salute us, our Master, with peace and let us enter the abode of peace.
>
> Blessed and exalted are you, O Lord of all glory and honor.

As-salāmu 'alaykum! Peace be upon you!

Chapter 2

The Gate of Discourse

Holy Tongue—a Cultural Commonality

As mentioned earlier, somewhere in Heaven, according to the Qur'ān, God keeps a common, eternal book called the Preserved Tablet or the Mother Book. This celestial scripture, to which Jewish mystical texts of Kabbalah refer as the Jewel of Wisdom,[1] serves as the shrine of God's unchanging Truth from which Divine Wisdom (*ḥokhmāh* in Hebrew; *ḥikmah* in Arabic) descended to the lower material world in revealed forms, such as the Torah, the New Testament, and the Qur'ān, through several messengers, starting with Abraham and Moses and ending, according to Islam, with Muhammad. Each holy book was delivered in a different language, in Hebrew to Abraham and Moses and in Arabic to Prophet Muhammad.

We are told in the Bible that initially, prior to the building of the Tower of Bavel (Babylon),"the whole earth was of one language and of uniform words."[2] It is suggested by Jewish sources that the "holy tongue," Hebrew, was the common language of the world. But, over time, mankind has spread to different regions, with each nation developing its own native tongue. During the building of the Tower, they already spoke 70 new languages, losing the unity provided to them by the single tongue.[3] This language split is supported by the Qur'ān.[4]

Also, according to one Jewish Midrash, when God revealed Himself on Mount Sinai, He spoke in 70 tongues so that all nations would vocally witness the giving of the Torah to the People of Israel.[5] Another Midrash limits the number of the tongues to four: Hebrew, Roman (Latin), Arabic, and Aramaic.[6] With the exception of Roman, three of the four are linguistically related; they belong to the linguistic family conventionally termed as Semitic. In this family, Hebrew and Aramaic commonly belong to the northwestern branch; Arabic and the extinct Ethiopian (Ge'ez) commonly belong to the southern branch, whereas the extinct Akkadian belongs to the western branch.[7]

The blood ties between Isaac, the ancestor of the Hebrews, and Ishmael, the ancestor of the Arabs, and the historical cross-cultural relationship between their societies, explain the linguistic kinship between Hebrew and Arabic. Ironically, this kinship has never prevented the historical antagonism between the two peoples. The fact that both of them regard their language as a "holy tongue" (*lashōn qōdesh* in Hebrew; *lisān muqaddas* in Arabic) has not prevented them from using those languages to wage a war of words against each other. Even the supposition supported by biblical evidence that Hebrew is the first language in the world and that Abraham, the ancestral forefather of both peoples, spoke Hebrew has not helped in bringing them together.[8]

Perhaps the following chapter that addresses the linguistic commonality between Hebrew and Arabic, particularly in reference to the Names of God in both traditions, will serve as a unifying element and a bridge-maker between Jews and Muslims, who believe in One God. This chapter is not a study in linguistics, but rather a study of peoples' normative system as it is reflected in their language. Since language represents the peculiar mindset of those who speak it, it would be useful to do a comparative study of Hebrew and Arabic, with a focus on the vocabulary of faith and worship, and find out whether Jews and Muslims are linguistically, and therefore culturally, compatible.

General Vocabulary of Faith and Worship

Linguistically, Jews and Muslims are more alike than different. Their words for faith (*'emunāh* in Hebrew; *'īmān* in Arabic) and believer (*ma'amīn* in Hebrew; *mu'min* in Arabic) use the same root *a.m.n.* They believe in the Unity of God, and their word for unity (*yiḥūd* in Hebrew; *tawḥīd* in Arabic) is based on the same root *a.ḥ.d.* Therefore, God is called *'eḥād* in Hebrew and *al-aḥad* in Arabic. Their belief systems include angels (*mal'akhīm* in Hebrew; *malā'ikah* in Arabic), Satan (*saṭān* in Hebrew; *shayṭān* in Arabic), prophets (singular *navī'* in Hebrew; *nabī* in Arabic), the Last Day or End of the Days (*aḥarīt ha-yamīm* in Hebrew; *yawm al-'ākhiri* in Arabic), and the fight against idol-worshipers or nonbelievers (singular: *kofēr* in Hebrew; *kāfir* in Arabic). All of these terms are based on the same roots. The Muslims' Holy Book, the Qur'ān, and the common Jewish name for the

Bible, Miqrā', etymologically derive from *q.r.a.*, meaning "to read." They keep similar acts of worship (*'avodāh* in Hebrew and *'ibādah* in Arabic are based on *'a.v/b.d.*). They wash before prayer to keep their body and soul in a state of purity (*ṭaharāh* in Hebrew and *ṭahārah* in Arabic are based on *ṭ.h.r.*) and make a blessing (*berakhāh* in Hebrew and *barakah* in Arabic are based on *b.r.kh/k.*).

The Muslims' main blessing, *Bismillāh ar-Raḥmān ar-Raḥīm* (in the Name of God, the Merciful, the Compassionate), considered in Islamic tradition the second in importance after *Allah*, uses the same Names of God in the Jewish tradition *Ha-Raḥamān* and *Ha-Raḥūm*. However, the most frequently used pair of Names in the Bible and other Jewish sources are *Ḥanūn ve-Raḥūm* (Gracious and Compassionate),[9] or vice versa *Raḥūm ve-Ḥanūn,*[10] such as the short prayer chanted during the Festivals: "The Lord, the Lord, God, *Compassionate and Gracious,* Slow to Anger, and Abundant in Loving-kindness and Truth."[11]

Etymologically, the common root for mercy *r.ḥ.m.* derives from "mother's womb" (*rēḥem* in Hebrew; *raḥīm* in Arabic)—the ultimate source of compassion, the organ that holds, nurtures, and protects the fetus. As the Jewish German leader and Bible commentator Rabbi Samson Raphael Hirsch (1808–1888) explains: "Just as a mother has compassion for the life of all the children of her womb, we should have compassion for all of God's creations."[12] But not only a mother, but father too, as the Psalmist writes: "As a father has compassion upon his children, so has the Lord compassion upon them that fear Him."[13] The two Names of God may represent two dimensions of compassion, one active and outpouring (*Ha-Raḥamān* in Hebrew; *Ar-Raḥmān* in Arabic); and one passive and accepting (*Ha-Raḥūm* in Hebrew; *Ar-Raḥīm* in Arabic). Similar is the Hebrew pair of God's Names, *Ṭov 'u-Meṭīv* (Good and Does Good) that appears in the Jewish standing prayer of *Shmonēh 'Esrēh*.

This has a moral implication. Both Jews and Muslims are expected to emulate God's attributes, the chief of which is mercy (*raḥamīm* in Hebrew; *raḥmah* in Arabic) toward fellow men. Being the most commonly used word in Jewish and Muslim prayers, mercy seems to be the only human response to a world that is becoming more and more dehumanizing and demonizing. We need to remember that just as a mother showers unconditional love onto her children, God does the same for His creatures, and it is our mission to follow suit.

Both Jews and Muslims interweave the Names of God into their daily conversations, and in many cases they use the same idiomatic forms and etymological sources. "God willing!" ("*'im yirtzēh ha-Shēm*" in Hebrew; "*'inshallāh*" in Arabic), "praise to God!" ("*ha-shēvaḥ la-'El*" in Hebrew; "*subḥānallāh*" in Arabic), "God will protect!" ("*'Elohīm yishmōr*" in

Hebrew; "*Allāh yistor*" in Arabic), and "God is with you!" ("*adonāi 'imkhā*" in Hebrew; "*Allāh ma'ak*" in Arabic) are just a few examples.

The similarity in the actual Names of God, the numerous designations or attributes ascribed by Jews and Muslims to the Almighty is even more astonishing, as one can see from the following sections. It is not only the shared belief in One God, but also the shared use of God's Names that brings the two religions together.

Names of God in Judaism

In Judaism, the Names of God represent the Jewish conception of the Divine and of the relation of God to the Jewish people.[14] One of the morning blessings on the Torah in the Jewish prayer book states, "Make the teachings of Your Torah, Lord our God, pleasant . . . so that we, and our children, and the children of Your entire people, the House of Israel, *may all know Your Name* and learn Your Torah for its own sake."

One may identify three categories of Names:

The primary Names, which are originated in the Torah, are sometimes called "the seven." The "Great Eagle" of Jewish learning and the greatest Jewish thinker since the close of the Talmud, Rabbi Moshe ben Maimon (1138–1204), best known in the Western world as Maimonides and in the Jewish world by his acronym Rambam, calls them in his *Mishnēh Torāh* "the sacred and pure Names."[15] They are:

1. *YHVH*—The not-to-be-pronounced four-letter Tetragrammaton (*yod, hay, vav, hay*), termed as "the Ineffable Name" (Hebrew: *Ha-Shēm ha-Meforāsh)*. In English translation, it often appears in the reconstructed forms of Yahweh or Jehovah. A derivative, composed of the first two letters, is pronounced and written as *Yah*.[16]
2. *Adonāi*—"Master of All." The way *YHVH* is pronounced in vocalized prayer texts; usually printed in prayer books as *YY*, read in English versions as "Lord," and customarily written and pronounced as *Ha-Shēm* ("The Name") to avoid the violation of the Third Commandment against taking the Name of God in vain.
3. *'El*—The most common singular noun for God, which has cognates in other Semitic languages and which denotes either the chief god or a general word for any god. It is commonly found in the Bible in connection with God's Names (e.g., *'El 'Elyōn*—"the Exalted God"), sacred places (e.g., *Beth 'El*—"the House of God"), and proper names (e.g., *Israel*—"one who wrestled with God").

4. *'Elohīm*—The frequently used Name of God in the Bible (also appears in its singular form *'Elōha*, mainly in the book of Job).
5. *'Ehyēh-Ashēr-'Ehyēh*—"I am that I am" (or just *'Ehyēh*). A Name revealed to Moshe,[17] who unlike the Patriarchs dared to ask God for His proper name.[18]
6. *Shaddāi*—"The Mighty" (appears frequently as *'El Shaddāi*).
7. *Tzeva'ōt*—"Hosts" (appears frequently with the hybrid name of *Adonāi YHVH Tzeva'ōt*).

The inclusion of God's Names in the *Shema'*, the Jewish affirmation of faith and the keynote of all Judaism, "*YHVH* (Lord),'*Elohēinu* (our God), *YHVA* (Lord) *'Eḥād* (is One)," signifies their unification in the One Name and confirms that the God of Israel is both the many and the One. This is confirmed in the Jewish standing prayer the *Shmonēh 'Esrēh,* made during the Sabbath afternoon prayer (*Minḥāh*), when Jews say "You are One and Your Name is One." The Kabbalist sage, Rabbi Joseph Gikatalia (1248–1323), in his important mystical treatise about Jewish meditation on God's Names *Sha'arēi 'Orāh* ("Gates of Light"), writes that "YHVH is like the trunk of a tree, while other Divine Names are like its branches." In his teaching of the Ten *Sefirōt*, the cosmic structure of divine emanations, he attached ten hybrid forms of the seven Names to that structure.[19]

The Patriarch Abraham was familiar with the Names of God. As soon as he reached the Land of Canaan, he built his first altar and addressed God as "*YHVH*."[20] In his conversation with the King of Sodom, he refers to God as "*YHVH 'El 'Elyōn Qonēh Shamāyim va-'Āretz*" (the Lord, God the Most-High, Maker of Heaven and Earth).[21] During the vision of the Covenant between the Parts ("*Brīt bein ha-Betarīm*"), he refers to Him as "*Adonāi YHVH*,"[22] and during the vision of the Covenant of the Circumcision, God introduces Himself as "*'El Shaddāi*" (God, the Mighty One)[23] and refers to Himself as "*'Elohīm*."[24] When he planted an *'ēshel* (tree) in Beersheba, he proclaimed the Name *Adonāi, 'El 'Olām* (Everlasting God or God of the Universe)."[25]

The secondary names originated in the rabbinic postbiblical period. The following are the most common:

1. *Adōn 'Olām*—"Master of the Universe"
2. *Avīnu Malkēinu*—"Our Father, our King"
3. *Ha-Borē'*—"The Creator" (also *Borē' 'Olām*—Creator of the World)
4. *Ha-Qadōsh Barūkh Hu*—"The Holy One, blessed be He," or for short, the "Blessed Holy One."
5. *'Elohēi Avrahām, 'Elohēi Yitzḥāq ve-'Elohēi Ya'aqōv*—"God of Abraham, God of Isaac, and God of Jacob."

6. *Ha-Maqōm*—literally "The Place", meaning "The Omnipresent."
7. *Ribbonō shel 'Olām*—"Sovereign of the Universe" (also *Ribbōn Ha-'Olamīm*—"Sovereign of the Universe[s]")

The appellations (Hebrew: *kinnnuyīm*), a long list of Names that are originated in the Bible and considered as divine traits (Hebrew: *middōt*).

Most of them appear throughout the Jewish prayerbook (Hebrew: *siddūr*). The Jewish standing prayer *Shmonēh 'Esrēh*, for example, contains many of them, such as the opening phrase, "the Great, Mighty, and Fearsome God, Exalted God, Who bestows bountiful kindness, Who creates all things, Who remembers the piety of the Patriarchs, and Who brings redemption to their children's children, for the sake of His Name, in love." Also the phrases: "[You are] a King, a Helper, a Savior and a Shield," "Who is like You, Mighty One! And who can be compared to You, King, Who brings death and restores life, and causes deliverance to spring forth," "Blessed are You Lord, Who revives the dead," and "You are Holy and Your Name is Holy." *Pirkēi Avōt* ("Sayings of the Fathers"), the first chapter of the Mishnah and the most well-known collection of rabbinic ethical perspectives in the Talmud, records the following Names: "And become aware that He is God, He is the Fashioner, He is the Creator, He is the Discerner, His the Judge, He is the Witness, He is the Plaintiff, He will hereafter sit in judgment."[26]

Names of God in Islam

Like in Judaism, God's Names and attributes are a central component of Islamic doctrine.[27] One may identify in Islam the same three categories of God's Names:

In the first category, *Allāh* (a combination of *Al*, the definite article of the Arabic language, and *Ilāh*, the High God of ancient pre-Islamic Arabia[28]) is used as the proper Name of God and the dominant one in the Qur'ān.

In the second category, we find a few Names, the most popular one being *Rabb*—"Sovereign" (the most common derivative is *Rabb al-'Ālmaīn*, or "Sovereign of the Universe"), which is identical to the Hebrew Name. Both are etymologically derived from the same root.

The third category is known as "The Ninety-Nine Beautiful Names of God" (Arabic: *Asmā' Allāh al-Ḥusnā*). All revealed in the Qur'ān and Sunnah (the way and deeds of Prophet Muhammad), these Names are attributes (mostly adjectives) of God. Even though the Names exceed 99, Muslims believe that there is an elite group of Names, or the best Names, which number 99. In a famous *ḥadīth*, Prophet Muhammad is reported to have said, "Verily, there are ninety-nine Names of God, one hundred minus one. He who enumerates them would get into Paradise."[29] The one hidden Name is Allah, known to Muslims as "The Greatest Name of God" (*'Ism Allāh al-A'zam*). The Qur'ān states that "God has the most beautiful Names, so call on Him by them,"[30] and suggests that we "call upon Allah, or call upon al-Raḥmān, by whatever Name you call upon Him [it is fine], for to Him belong the Most Beautiful Names."[31]

The Qur'ān, for example, in three consecutive verses, lists many of these designations: "He is God; there is no other god but He. He is the Knower of both the invisible and the visible; He is the Merciful, the Compassionate. He is God; there is no other god but He. He is the Sovereign, the Holy, the Peaceable, the Guardian of Faith, the Preserver, the Mighty, the Powerful, the Majestic: Glory be to God. [High is He] above all the partners they associate with Him. He is God, the Creator, the Maker, the Fashioner. To Him belong the Most Beautiful Names: whatever is in the heavens and on earth declares His praises and glory: and He is the Mighty, the Wise."[32]

God, says the *Qiṣaṣ al Anbiyā'*, gave a sermon for Adam and Eve's marriage. He opened the sermon with a litany of His Names: "*Al-Ḥamd* is My laudation, *Allāh* is my name, *ar-Raḥmān* is the key to My treasure houses and the key to My pardoning of rebels and sinners, *ar-Raḥīm* is the key to My indulgence towards rebels and sinners, *al-'Azamah* ("Majesty") is My loincloth and *al-Kibriyā'* ("Magnificence") is My outer garment, *al-'Izz* ("Might") and *al-Ghūd* ("Generosity") are My splendor, and *al-Jamāl* ("Beauty") and al-*Jalāl* ("Loftiness") are My praise."[33]

Table 2.1 is a selected listing taken from "The Ninety-Nine Names of God," according to the tradition of Islam, and the corresponding Names in the Jewish tradition. Pay attention to the etymological similarity between the Names in both traditions and the moral virtues they represent for human behavior.

Final Thoughts

At the basis of the theological concept of One God with many Names is ethical monotheism. The One God is the cornerstone of faith, whereas the multiple Names of God represent ethical attributes for the worshiper to integrate into his life. Thus, God becomes not only the ultimate address for worshiper's prayers, but more importantly His Names and attributes become a model for man to follow and a roadmap to fulfill the divine potential embodied in Him.

Table 2.1 Cross-Language Comparison of God's Names

	Arabic Name	Hebrew Name	Common Root	Meaning
	Ar-Raḥmān (الرحمن)	Ha-Raḥamān (הרחמן)	r.ḥ.m.	The Merciful
	Ar-Raḥīm (الرحيم)	Ha-Raḥūm (רחום)	r.ḥ.m.	The Compassionate
	Al-Malik (الملك)	Mēlekh (מלך)	m.l.k.	The King
	Al-Quddūs (القدوس)	Qadōsh (קדוש)	q.d.s[h].	The Holy
	As-Salām (السلام)	Shalōm (שלום)	s[h].l.m.	The Peaceable
	Al-Mu'min (المؤمن)	Ne'emān (נאמן)	'a.m.n.	The Faithful
	Al-'Azīz (العزيز)	'Ezūz (עזוז)	'a.z.z.	The Mighty
	Al-Jabbār (الجبار)	Gibbōr (גבור)	j[g].b.r.	The Powerful
0	Al-Mutakabbir (المتكبر)	Kabbīr (כביר)	k.b.r.	The Majestic
2	Al-Bāri' (البارئ)	Borē' (בורא)	b.r.i'.	The Creator, the Maker
3	Al-Muṣawwir (المصور)	Yotzēr (יוצר)	y.s.r. [H.] s.w.r. [A.]	The Fashioner
4	Al-Ghaffār (الغفار)	Salḥān (סלחן)		The Forgiver
7	Ar-Razzāq (الرزاق)	Mekhalkēl (מכלכל)		The Provider
6	As-Samī' (السميع)	Shomē'a [tefillōt] (שומע)	s[h].m.i'.	The All-Hearing
8	Al-Ḥakam (الحكم)	Shofēṭ or Dayyān (שופט) (דיין)		The Judge
3	Al-'Aẓīm (العظيم)	Adīr (אדיר)		The Magnificent
4	Al-Ghafūr (الغفور)	Sallāḥ (סלח)		The All-Forgiving
5	Ash-Shakūr (الشكور)	'El Ha-Hoda'ōt (אל ההודאות)		The Worthy of Thanksgiving
6	Al-'Aliyy (العلي)	'Elyōn (עליון)	'a.l.y.	The Exalted
7	Al-Kabīr (الكبير)	Kabbīr (כביר)	k.b.r.	The Great
9	Al-Muqīt (المقيت)	Zan (זן)		The All-Nourishing

continued

#	Arabic Name	Hebrew Name	Common Root	Meaning
42	Al-Karīm (الكريم)	Ḥanūn (חנון)		The Gracious
46	Al-Ḥakīm (الحكيم)	Ḥakhām (חכם)	ḥ.k[h].m.	The Wise
47	Al-Wadūd (الودود)	Yadīd (ידיד)	w[y].d.d.	The Loving
49	Al-Bā'ith (الباعث)	Meḥayēh Ha-Metīm (מחיה המתים)		The Reviver of The Dead
51	Al-Ḥaqq (الحق)	'Emēt (אמת)		The Truth
53	Al-Qawiy (القوى)	Ḥazāq (חזק)		The Strong
56	Al-Ḥamīd (الحميد)	Mehulāl (מהלל)		The Extolled
60	Al-Muḥyī (المحيى)	Meḥayēh (מחיה)	ḥ.y.h.	The Restorer of Life
61	Al-Mumīt (المميت)	Memīt (ממית)	m.w[v].t.	The Bringer of Death
62	Al-Ḥayy (الحي)	Ḥay (חי)	ḥ.y.y.	The Ever-Living
63	Al-Qayyūm (القيوم)	Qayyām (קיים)	q.y.m.	The Eternal
66	Al-Wāḥid (الواحد)	Meyuḥād or Yaḥīd (מיוחד) (יחיד)	w[y].ḥ.d.	The Unique
67	Al-'Aḥad (الاحد)	'Eḥād (אחד)	'a.ḥ.d.	The One
73	Al-Awwal (الأول)	Rishōn (ראשון)		The First
74	Al-'Akhir (الأخر)	Aḥarōn (אחרון)	'a.ḥ.r.	The Last
75	Aẓ-Ẓāhir (الظاهر)	Niglāh (נגלה)		The Manifest
76	Al-Bāṭin (الباطن)	Nistār (נסתר)		The Hidden
78	Al-Muta'āli (المتعالي)	Na'alēh (נעלה)	'a.l.i[h].	The Most High
81	Al-Muntaqim (المنتقم)	'El-Neqamōt (אל נקמות)	n.q.m.	The Avenger
82	Al-'Afuw (العفو)	Moḥēl (מוחל)		The Pardoner
84	Malik al-Mulk (مالك الملك)	Mēlekh Ha-'Olām (מלך העולם)	m.l.k.	King of [His] Sovereignty
97	Al-Wārith (الوارث)	Morīsh (מוריש)	w[y].r.th[sh].	The Bestower of Inheritance

In keeping with one of the 613 Jewish-prescribed commandments, "And you shall walk in His ways,"[34] and with the principle that man was created in God's image, after His liking,[35] Jewish sages turned the Names of God into one of the foundations of Judaism.[36] They suggested that "to walk in His ways" and to be like "His image" means to imitate God, to emulate His righteous ways and do the things He does, exactly as Abraham did. The reason that the prophets continuously mentioned God's ethical attributes and that the prayerbook contains many of them (Merciful, Compassionate, Forgiver, Holy, Good, etc.) was that man might strive after those attributes, rise to His lofty standards and stay on track with "the way of the Lord." Thus, Maimonides quotes the Talmud (Shabbāt 133b) and explains in his *Mishnēh Torāh* that the Hebrew prophets described God by all kinds of attributes "to inform us that these traits are good and right and man ought to conduct himself according to them and to imitate Him as much as he can."[37]

Here is what Jewish sages said:

> Just as the Blessed Holy One is called Compassionate (*raḥūm*), so you too must be compassionate; just as the Blessed Holy One is called Gracious (*ḥanūn*), so you too must be gracious; just as the Holy Blessed One is called Righteous (*tzadīq*) as it is said (in Psalms 145:17), "the Lord is righteous in all His ways and benevolent in all His works" you too must be righteous; just as the Blessed Holy One is called Benevolent (*ḥasīd*) as it is said "and benevolent in all His works," you too must be benevolent.[38]
>
> And Rabbi Hama ben Rabbi Hanina said, "What is the meaning of the verse: 'after the Lord your God shall you walk'? (Deuteronomy 13:5). Is it all possible for a man to walk after the Divine Presence [*shekhināh*]? Has it not been said: 'for the Lord your God is a consuming fire' (Deuteronomy 4:24). But [the meaning is that] one must walk after the traits of the Blessed Holy One. Just as He clothes the naked, as it is written, 'and the Lord God made for Adam and his wife coats of skin and clothed them' (Genesis 3:21), so should you clothe the naked. [Just as] the Blessed Holy One visited the sick, as it is written [about Abraham], 'And the Lord appeared to him by the oaks of Mamre' (Genesis 18:1), so should you visit the sick. [Just as] the Blessed Holy One comforted the mourners, as it is written, 'and it came to pass after the death of Abraham that God blessed Isaac his son' (Genesis 25:11), so should you comfort the mourners. [Just as] the Blessed Holy One buried the dead, as it is written, 'and He buried him in the valley' (Deuteronomy 34:6), so should you bury the dead."[39]
>
> Abba Saul says: "O try to be like Him: Just as He is Gracious and Compassionate, you too be gracious and compassionate," for it is said, "The Lord, the Lord, God, Compassionate and Gracious" (Exodus 34:6).[40]

Mercy is the most frequently used trait of God one must follow. The Talmud says, "Anyone who is merciful towards [human] creatures clearly belongs to the descendents of Abraham, our father. Anyone who is not merciful towards [human] creatures clearly belongs not to the descendents of Abraham, our father."[41] Maimonides picks up this principle and writes in his *Mishnēh Torāh* that "Cruelty is frequently to be found only among the heathen who worship idols; the descendants of Abraham, our father [...] are merciful towards anybody." In speaking of mercy as "one of the divine attributes of the Blessed Holy One, which He has commanded us to imitate," he quotes the Psalmist saying: "The Lord is good to all, and His mercy is over all His works (Psalms 145:9). He then writes, "Whoever is merciful will receive mercy, as it is written (in Deuteronomy 13:18, and Talmud Bavlī, Shabbāt 152:2): 'He will bestow mercy unto you and be merciful upon you and multiply you.'"[42]

Compassion, a derivative of mercy, is a central theme in the writings of Rabbi Shmuel David Luzzatto (1800–1865), one of the greatest sages of Italy. He writes, "Compassion, the first element [in the Torah], is the special means for the reparation of the traits (*tikkūn ha-middōt*). The trait of compassion is imprinted within man since the beginning of his creation, and it is the root of love, loving-kindness, and honesty." Luzzatto believes that compassion alone is enough to turn man to choose good and reject evil, and that this trait is applied to the entire world. "Like God's compassion, it is directed at all His creatures. No [human] race is outside of this [universal] law, because all human beings, according to the teaching of Judaism, are brothers, children of one father, all of whom were created in the image of God."[43]

Although the Judeo-Christian concept of imitating God, a concept known as *Imitatio Dei*, is alien to Islam, given that Islam strictly prohibits having partners or associates to God, we still can find references in the Qur'ān to the attributes of God as guidance to humanity. There, mercy is the chief attribute of God and the moral virtue that presides over everything. This is why it is part of the most frequently used invocation of *Bismillāh Ar-Raḥmān ar-Raḥīm* (In the Name of God, the Merciful, the Compassionate). God says in the Qur'ān, "We have merely sent you as a mercy (*raḥmah*) for [everybody in] the universe,"[44] and also "He then became one of those who believes, recommends patience, and encourages mercifulness (*marḥamah*)."[45] Therefore, Muslims regarded Muhammad as the Prophet of Mercy. The Qur'ān says that to forestall God's wrath after the Golden Calf ordeal, Moses appealed to God for forgiveness for himself and his brother Aaron, saying "admit us to Your mercy, for You are merciful of those who show mercy (*adkhilna fī raḥmatika wa-anta arḥamu ar-raḥimīn*).[46] This principle of God's mercifulness and of the expectation of man to show mercy to his fellow men is repeated throughout the Qur'ān.[47]

Likewise is God's attribute of goodness (Hebrew: *ṭovāh*) in Judaism. The Jewish prayerbook is filled with references to God's abounding goodness, which is the reason for His mercy. It contains expressions such as "the Lord is good to all, and His mercies extend over all His works," and "You are good and forgiving God," and "You are a good God, Who bestows goodness," and "in His goodness He renews each day, continuously, the work of Creation." This is why the Hebrew Prophet Amos advised, "Hate the evil, and love the good."[48] This is why among the virtues of the Word of God listed in the Jewish prayerbook is "good and beautiful" (*ṭov ve-yafēh*). In this respect, the Psalmist provides us with a fundamental teaching: "Who is the man who desires life, who loves long life that he may see goodness therein? Guard your tongue from evil, and your lips from speaking deceitfully. Turn away from evil and do good, seek peace and pursue it."[49]

The word used in Islam for good is *iḥsān*, meaning good or beautiful. It derives from *ḥusn*, which is the quality of being good and beautiful. In describing the creation of human beings, the Qur'ān writes that God has made human beings in a beautiful form and nature, and for this reason, they have an obligation to behave in a beautiful way in their lives and in their relationships with others. It says, "Do what is good, as God has been good to you."[50] And when you do good, you are rewarded with goodness: "Those who do good will receive goodness [even] in greater proportion,"[51] and "the one who believes and acts righteously shall be rewarded with goodness."[52] The Qur'ān is very clear that "God loves those who do good,"[53] and that "God's mercy is near to those who do good (*al-muḥsinīn*)."[54]

The Qur'ān also brings up God's teaching, "Say to My servants that they should only say those things that are the best,"[55] advises, "who is better in speech than one who prays to God, does right, and says: I am of those who surrender [to Him],"[56] and warns us that not practicing what we preach (*lam taqūlūna mā lā taf'alūna*) is "grievously odious in the sight of God."[57] In other words, a person who appeals to God in prayer and acts honorably is one whose word reaches the highest mark of human speech. For a true Muslim, according to these citations, there is no gap between his words and his deeds, no disparity between his prayer and his conduct. So it is for a true Jew, who is advised to follow the rabbinic teachings, "good is the one who practices what he preaches (*na'ēh dorēsh ve-na'ēh meqayēm*),"[58] and "preaching is not essential but the practice (*lo ha-midrāsh hu ha-'iqār elā ha-ma'asēh*)."[59]

What is the conclusion we can draw from the above teachings? Mercy and goodness are not only words or concepts; they are not just appellations of God. They must be real things, be realized in oneself and society. They must be part of our being, as much as it is part of God's being. To be true to our word, to be in integrity with our belief, every believer must say: God is Merciful, therefore I am. God is Compassionate, therefore I am. God is the Forgiver, therefore I am. And so on. What do we see instead? We see how hate-mongering extremists, operating on the fringes of Islam and abusing its teachings, "play God." They imitate one of His Names, "The Bringer of Death" (*Al-Mumīt* in Arabic) by indiscriminately killing innocent people in their fanatical and cruel belief that they are carrying out God's will. This is a clear desecration of God's Name and a sheer destruction of the image of God. Such a widespread violation of a basic universal commandment prescribed by all the three monotheistic religions is just one infectious ill of society that has to be eradicated from the earth.

In praying and chanting daily, "He Who makes peace in His heavens, may He make peace for us,"[60] Jews allude to the dynamic relationship between heaven and earth, between divinity and humanity. According to many mystical traditions, there must be correspondence between the terrestrial and celestial planes of existence—*as above so below*. Whatever humans do in the lower world affects the Divine in the upper world, and vice versa. Thus, Jewish sages tell us: "It is accounted to anyone who makes peace on earth, as if he makes it in heaven."[61] It is, therefore, our responsibility as human beings to reciprocate to God and say: "We, who make peace on earth, may we make peace for Him in His heavens." You may think heaven and earth are two separate worlds; they are not. They are essentially one and shall become one when we, the bridge-builders between the two worlds, will be Godlike in our behavior and integrate His attributes into our lives.

Making the world a better place will happen only when we ourselves become an embodiment of God, a realization of His positive traits on earth. Mahatma Gandhi said, "We must become the change we want to see in the world." Clear and simple! You don't have to go far. Just look at your prayers, watch God's Names as you recite them daily, and apply His traits to your life. Just resolve to "be the change you wish to see in the world." Just be kind, generous, loving, and compassionate, and you will see a new, enlightened, humanizing world emerging before your eyes.

Chapter 3

The Gate of Practice

Rituals and Rites—Closer than Apart

The Qur'ān established for the Muslims five acts of worship, known as "the Pillars of Islam" (*arkān al-Islām*). The first is the *Shahādah*, the profession of faith by bearing public witness to the Oneness of God. The second is the *Ṣalāh*, prayer performed five times a day. The third is the *Ṣawm*, fasting during the month of Ramaḍān. The fourth is the *Zakāt*, alms-giving, sharing one's savings with the poor and needy, and *Ṣadaqah*, the free-will offerings. The fifth is the *Ḥajj*, making pilgrimage to the Sacred Mosque in Mecca at least once in a lifetime. The five Pillars are obligatory (*farḍ*) for every Muslim man and woman.

Why did Prophet Muhammad establish only those five acts of worship? Seeing the elaborate ritual system of the Jews and their numerous commandments, he apparently wanted to simplify his new religion and make it easier for his followers. Prior to his listing of the Pillars, he has explained: "He has chosen you, and has imposed no difficulties on you in religion; it is the religion of your father Abraham."[1] At the end of the second *sūrah*, Prophet Muhammad placed the following words of prayer in the mouth of the Muslims: "Our Lord, do not lay on us a burden like that which You placed on those before us. Our Lord, do not lay on us a burden greater than we can bear."[2] In referring to "those before us," he meant the Jews. The Qur'ān says that prior to the introduction of the whole array of commandments by Moses, Abraham's system of rituals was simple and elementary, and this is why Islam adopted it.

Nevertheless, many elements of each Pillar appear in Judaism. Jews have their own confession of faith in the Oneness of God, the *Shemā'*. Their

Tefillāh, prayer, is composed essentially of three daily prayers and four during the service of the Sabbath and the three Festivals. They observe one major day of fasting, the *Tzom* of Yom Kippūr, the Day of Atonement, and five minor fasts. They observe the commandment of charitable giving, *Tzedaqāh*. But the pilgrimage, or *'aliyāh la-rēgel*, to the Holy Temple in Jerusalem, made during the festivals, has been replaced today by traditional visits to the Western Wall, also called the Wailing Wall. The act of worship, the service of God, is the same in both lexicons: *'ibādah* in Arabic and *'avodāh* in Hebrew. The root verb "to serve" is the same in both Hebrew and Arabic languages, *'a.v.d.* and *'a.b.d.* respectively. Thus, a worshiper is called a "servant of God": *'Abdallah* in Arabic and *'Ovayāh* in Hebrew.

Given the centrality of the Old Testament in both Judaism and Christianity, these monotheistic religions appear to be theologically closer to each other. But on a deeper level, there is a greater resemblance between Judaism and Islam. While all three religions concern themselves with fulfilling God's commandments and adhering to their divine laws, Christianity downplays correct action based on religious laws in favor of correct faith. Although the codes of laws in Judaism and Islam, known as *Halakhāh* and *Sharī'ah* respectively, differ in content, they do share much in context. In the course of history, they even developed similar legal systems (see Appendix 1), which led to many similarities in the devotional life of the traditional Jewish and Muslim communities. Below is a sampling of these similarities.

Islam in the Eyes of Maimonides and His Son

Maimonides is the first Jewish spiritual leader who viewed Islam as a flawless monotheistic faith. Although he did not find in Islam's teachings any theological novelty, and he denied the validity of Muhammad's prophecy, he believed in the purity of Islamic faith and the purposefulness of its mission. He truly believed that the religions that stemmed from Judaism have contributed to swaying people away from idolatry toward monotheism, a worldwide activity that only helps facilitate the coming of the true Messiah.[3] When discussing the idea of the coming of the Messiah in his monumental work, *Mishnēh Torāh*, he writes: "All the deeds of Jesus Christ and the Ishmaelite (Muhammad) who arose after him will only serve to pave the way for the King Messiah ['s coming] and repair the entire world, so that [everyone] serves God together, as it is said (in Zephaniah 3:9) 'I will make the peoples pure of speech that they will all call upon the Name of God and Serve Him with one consent.' "[4]

In his response to a query by Rabbi Shmuel Ibn Hisdai of Alexandria, Egypt, Maimonides wrote: "As to your question regarding the status of the [gentile] nations, you should be aware that the Merciful seeks the intention of the heart. Therefore, our sages stated (in Tosefta, Sanhedrīn 13) that the righteous among the world's nations have a portion in the World-to-Come, if they achieved what is achievable in knowing the Creator and have learned good virtues (*middōt ṭovōt*). Undoubtedly, anyone who educated himself about the good virtues and came to recognize their faith in the Creator is clearly among the inhabitants of the World-to-Come."[5]

Given the invaluable influence Maimonides exercised on the future development of Judaism, such an inclusive treatment of Islam is crucial in Jewish-Muslim relations. One who was personally influenced by the theological legitimacy he gave to Islam was his son, Rabbi Abraham (1186–1237), who succeeded his father as leader of the Egyptian Jewish community, so-called *Ra'īs al-Yahūd* (Chief of the Jews). He was mostly known for being deeply influenced by Sufism, a form of Islamic mysticism.[6] He wrote a great Sufi compendium named *Rif'at al-'Ābidīn* ("The Ultimate Book for the Worshipers"), in which he tried to win his generation over to the Sufi way of life. Rabbi Abraham argued that Islam, especially in its Sufi version, preserved many elements of the practices and teachings of the ancient Jewish sages. Among these elements were kneeling and prostration during prayer, ritual immersions, nightly prayers, and so on. Early Islam, in his view, adopted these ceremonies, and the attending feelings of awe for the Day of Judgment. In the world of Islam, all of these elements were developed in a special way in the Sufi movement, and that is why they are so closely related to the ancient Jewish sages. He believed that in following the Sufi-like practices, he was able to preserve the ancient Jewish acts of worship.

Rabbi Abraham did not content himself with theoretical study alone. His conviction induced him to demand the return to the ancestral customs by imitating the Muslim surroundings, for instance in the matter of prayer. In one section of his work, he suggests the removal of pillows from synagogues to be replaced by prayer mats and carpets on the floor, as in the mosques, and to prostrate as the Muslims did in prayer. He also praises the respectful silence in the mosques, which was in flagrant contrast to the noise and lack of devotion in the synagogues of his day. Rabbi Abraham's suggestions, however, were not adopted, as we learn from the documents found in the *Genizāh*, the depository of the Cairo synagogue. The members of his congregation filed a complaint against him with the ruler, al-Malik al-'Adil, the brother and heir of Saladin, alleging that he tried to force upon them innovations (Arabic singular: *bid'ah*) forbidden by their religion. This was in violation of Islamic laws, which in this respect were also applied to the non-Muslim communities under his jurisdiction. Rabbi Abraham was compelled to apologize to the Muslim ruler and to announce that he did not intend to abuse his authority as leader of the Jewish community by introducing such religious innovations.

Although Rabbi Abraham and his children represent the highest level of Sufi influence, we know of other Jewish sages who integrated Sufi traditions into their lives and recognized them as a source of inspiration for their writings. One of them is Rabbi Bahya ibn Paquda, a philosopher and the author of *Ḥovōt ha-Levavōt* ("Duties of the Heart"), which was translated from the original book in Arabic entitled *Al-Hidāyah ilā Farā'id al-Qulūb* ("Book of Direction to the Duties of the Heart").[7]

Genizāh documents tell of Jewish-Arab Muslim business contacts and partnerships, of Jews visiting Arab neighbors during their festivals, and of Arabs attending a festive reading of the Scroll of Esther during Purim. The *Genizāh* treasures also contain many Arab religious and secular works, some translated into Hebrew. These include books on medicine, philosophy, and theology. Copies of the Qur'ān in Hebrew translation and in Arabic, and Sufi literature translated into Hebrew, were also found there. Although life for Jews in the Islamic society in Cairo in the Middle Ages was far from idyllic because they were regarded as *Ahl adh-Dhimmah* (People of Protection), inferior subjects of the Islamic state,[8] these findings from the Cairo *Genizāh* are evidence of the dynamic social interaction between the Jewish and Muslim communities, in both practical and spiritual spheres, and the high degree of integration of Jewish culture into Muslim society.[9]

Sūrat al-Fātiḥah—The Heart of Muslims' Prayer

If prayer is the heart of religion, *Sūrat Al-Fātiḥah*, the "opening" chapter of the Qur'ān, is the heart of Islamic prayer. Revered as the essence of the Qur'ān and the summary of its whole teaching, this short *sūrah* was selected by Prophet Muhammad to be recited by Muslims as their public prayer.

> *In the name of God, the Merciful, the Compassionate.*
> Praise God, Sovereign of the Universe!
> the Merciful, the Gracious!
> Master of the Day of Judgment!
> It is You we worship and You we ask for help.
> Guide us in the straight path,
> the path of those whom You have bestowed Your Grace,
> not [the path] of those who earn Your anger,
> nor of those who go astray.
> [And let us say] Amen.

When reading this little prayer, which perhaps not by accident does not mention Prophet Muhammad's mission, one is stricken by its universality. It appeals to every human being, Jew, Christian, or Muslim, who believes in the centrality of mercy as an ethical value, in the Day of Judgment, and in walking "the straight path." There is nothing in this prayer that conflicts with the Jewish spirit or is contradictory to the Jewish faith. To a certain degree, it is idiomatically consistent with many expressions in the Bible and in Jewish liturgy.

The prayer is sometimes called *Sab'a al-Mathani* or "the Seven Oft-repeated Verses,"[10] perhaps to allude to its magical power to reach God quickly by piercing through "the seven planetary heavens." It looks like a short form of the Jews' most sacred prayer, the silent meditation *Shmonēh 'Esrēh*. It is structured in the form of a psalm (*mizmōr*) from King David's *Book of Tehilīm* (Praises), known as Psalms and, in the Islamic tradition, *Zabūr*. It begins with *Bismillāh* (in the Name of God), the opening that precedes every *sūrah* (with the exception of *sūrah* 9). This salutation reminds us of the prefatory verse that is taken from the Psalms[11] and said by observing Jews before they recite the *Shmonēh 'Esrēh*: "My Lord, open my lips, that my mouth may declare your praise." In both cases, these prefatory verses set the tone for and purpose of the prayer—an opportunity for the believer to stand in the presence of God and to recognize His greatness. After the invocation of *Bismillāh* there comes the beautiful form of praise, *Al-Ḥamdulilāh* or "Praise be to God," which is identical to the Hebrew *Haleluyāh* that begins and/or ends many of the Psalms.[12]

Interestingly, Maimonides opens each of the three parts of his philosophical work, *Guide to the Perplexed*, and almost all his treatises, with the epigraph, "*Be-Shēm Adonāi 'Ēl 'Olām*" (In the Name of the Lord, God of the Universe).[13] Although he uses the biblical citation referring to Patriarch Abraham's way of worshipping God, "He called upon the Name of the Lord, God of the Universe,"[14] one can only be amazed by Maimonides' choice of this two-part prefatory phrase, because it is very similar to the Islamic salutation. The first part, *Be-Shēm Adonāi*, is identical to *Bismillāh*, both meaning "In the Name of the Lord," whereas *'Ēl 'Olām* is almost identical to *Rabb al-'Ālamīn*, meaning "Sovereign of the Universe." The fact that Maimonides wrote his books in Arabic, that he exchanged communications with contemporary Muslim thinkers, and that he lived in an Islamic milieu, means his choice of this specific phrase is not surprising at all.

There is a natural sequence in the calling of God's Names that represent divine attributes. The first one, "Sovereign of the Universe," or "Sovereign of the Worlds," is the same in both traditions, *Rabb al-'Ālamīn* in Arabic and *Ribbōn Ha-'Olamīm* in Hebrew.[15] As previously explained, "The Merciful, the Compassionate," known as *Bismillāh*, appears in both Arabic as *Ar-Raḥmān ar-Raḥīm* and in Hebrew *Ha-Raḥamān* and *ha-Raḥūm*.

Although the exact formulation "Master of the Day of Judgment" cannot be found in Jewish sources, we do find in Proverbs, "A king that sits on the throne of judgment."[16] We know that the term King appears as one of God's Names (see above) and the Day of Judgment, *Yawm ad-Dīn* in Arabic, is exactly the same as the Hebrew term *Yom Ha-Dīn*, referring to the day when man, after his demise, faces the Creator to receive His last judgment.[17] This term is mentioned several times during the *Ve-Netanēh Tōqef* prayer on Rosh Ha-Shanāh.

The next section of the prayer is composed of two parts: the first part is the acknowledgment to God that man serves Him alone and seeks His help only, reminding us of the biblical citation "Direct your hearts unto the Lord, and serve Him only."[18] This manner of expression fulfils the central condition of faith, the Muslim *Tawḥīd* and the Jewish *Yiḥūd*, the Unity of God that everyone must observe. The second part focuses on the idea of "the straight path" (*Ṣirāṭ al-Mustaqīm* in Arabic; *Dērekh Ha-Yashār* in Hebrew), which will be discussed in detail later. Here the believer seeks God's guidance similar to the verses in Psalms, "And He guided them in a straight path" and "Teach me Your way, O Lord; and lead me on the straight path,"[19] and in the Proverbs, "In all your ways know Him, and He will make your paths straight,"[20] which remind us of the opening words of *Qiṣaṣ al-Anbiyā'* ("Stories of the Prophets"), "And [He] Who led us to the path of righteousness, honoring us with His guidance, [and Who] delivered us from the path of wickedness."[21] The prayer finally ends with "*Amīn*," or Amen, the customary conclusion of a prayer in most traditions.

Jewish Prayer in a Mosque

Judaism and Islam have chosen similar ways of sanctifying God's House and assembling their faithful for communal prayer. In the Jewish tradition, a space can be made a synagogue (Hebrew: *beit knēset*) by simply placing the Ark containing the Torah Scroll in the wall facing Jerusalem. The congregants pray in that direction. In the Muslim tradition, a space can be made a mosque (Arabic: *masjid*) by decorating the walls with quotations from the Holy Qur'ān and setting the *miḥrab* niche in the wall facing the Ka'bah in Mecca. This niche indicates the direction, or *qiblah*, of prayer.

It was, therefore, not surprising to see Rabbi Ovadiah Yosef, the former Sephardic Chief Rabbi of Israel and spiritual leader of the Shas Party in Israel, issued a ruling permitting a Jew to pray in a mosque, in the absence of a nearby synagogue.[22] Rabbi Yosef bases his ruling on a response by Maimonides to Rabbi Obadiah the Proselyte of Spain, in which Maimonides clarifies his position on Islam. He states that even though the original Muslims are considered to be idol worshipers, "the Ishmaelites (i.e., Muslims) of today do not believe whatsoever in idolatry; it was completely erased [from their creed]. They believe in the unification of God."[23]

There is a similar response written seven hundred years after Maimonides by Rabbi Yitzchak Elchanan Spektor (1817–1986), the rabbi of Kovno and a leading Talmudic sage of his generation. Rabbi Spektor cites a ruling by Tur, a fourteenth-century code of Jewish law,[24] and other sources, including Maimonides, to rule that "in the houses of prayer of the Ishmaelites, where idol worship is not brought in [...] it is permissible [for Jews] to pray and study there."[25]

Also, Rabbi Menachem Ha-Meiri (1249–c.1310), a preeminent fourteenth-century Talmudic scholar and author of the monumental work *Beit Ha-Beḥirāh* ("The Chosen House [i.e., the Temple]"), argued that his contemporary Christians and Muslims were in another category altogether from the ancient idolaters mentioned in the Torah and Talmud and had a moral code that fully complied with the divinely revealed Noahide Laws. In his opinion, both Islam and Christianity are legitimate ways to serve God.[26] Like Maimonides, Ha-Meiri believed that "Every Noahide whom we see, who accepts upon himself the Seven Commandments, is one of the pious of the [gentile] nations of the world and is in the category of the religious and he has a portion in the World-to-Come."[27]

Nothing can be found in Islamic law that disallows Jews from praying in any place that is regarded as holy by Muslims. There is nothing in Jewish prayer that can be offensive to Muslims. The holy city of Mecca, on the other hand, is off-limits to non-Muslims. Indeed, we find a reference by the Arab historian of early Islam and a biographer of Prophet Muhammad, Ibn Ishaq (c. 704–c. 773), to instructions by Muhammad to 'Ali to tell gathering pilgrims that "a non-believer shall not enter paradise and a polytheist shall not make pilgrimage after this year, and a naked person shall not circumvent the [Ka'bah] shrine."[28] But, Muhammad referred here to the Arab pagan tribes residing around Mecca, not to the People of the Book. Didn't the Qur'ān state clearly that "We made the House [of God] a place for mankind (*lil-nās*)"[29] and "God made the Ka'bah as the Sacred House for mankind"?[30] May the time come when King Abdullah bin Abdul Aziz Al Saud, Custodian of the Two Holy Cities, will open the doors for mankind, specifically for non-Muslim visitors under the broad definition of *mu'minīn* or believers mentioned earlier.

Prostration—an Islamic Practice and Jewish Too

The practice of prostration is an integral part of Muslim ritual prayer. The Qur'ān instructs Muslims: "'O you who believe! Bow down, prostrate yourselves, and adore your Lord; and do good, so that you may prosper."[31] But the origin of this practice can be traced back to biblical times. We are told that Abraham "fell on his face, and God talked with him."[32] When God spoke to Moses and Aaron, it is also written that "they fell upon their faces."[33] Job "fell down upon the ground and worshiped."[34] In the Temple times, it was a common practice for the priests, taking part in the Service, to prostrate themselves on completing their tasks. At the conclusion of the Service, all the priests and worshipers in the Temple court bowed down after each Shofār (ram's horn) blast.[35] The Talmud relates that the Service in the Temple included three forms of prayer: bowing (*qidāh*), kneeling (*kri'āh*), and falling prostration (*hishtaḥvayāh*).[36] In his *Mishnēh Torāh*, Maimonides defines these forms of prayer as follows: "How do we practice prostration? After one lifts his head from the fifth kneeling, he should sit on the ground and fall upon his face on the ground and supplicate all the supplications he desires. Kneeling that is mentioned in every place [is to be done] on the knees; bowing [is to turn down] the face; prostration means the stretching out of hands and feet until one is flat upon his face on the ground."[37]

We are told in *Pirkēi Avōt* about one of the miracles of the Temple: when Jewish worshipers congregated there to celebrate the Festivals, "they stood pressed closely together and yet found ample space to prostrate themselves."[38] The miracle, and the message to both Jews and Muslims, is that when we are completely humble before God, when we utterly submit to His will, we make room for everyone else around us. It is said that Rabbi Akiba, the most eminent of all rabbis, bowed and prostrated so much he was all over the room when he prayed.[39]

One section in the Jewish prayer on Sabbath morning beautifully illustrates the reason behind the prostration: "For every mouth shall offer thanks to You, every tongue shall swear by Your Name, every eye shall look to You, every knee shall bend to You, all who stand erect shall prostrate themselves before You, all hearts shall fear You, and every innermost part shall sing to Your Name, as it is written [in Psalms 35:10]: 'All my limbs shall declare: Lord, who is like You?' "

In the Jewish closing prayer, *'Alēinu*, worshipers say: "And we bend our knee, prostrate, and offer praise before the supreme King of kings, the Blessed Holy One." In the same way that we prostrate down to the feet of a human king, so Jews were required to do the same to the King of Kings, as the Sabbath morning prayer says, citing one of the Psalms: "Exalt the Lord our God, and prostrate at His footstool, holy is He."[40] The Prophet Isaiah explains, "Thus says the Lord: The heaven is My throne, and the earth is My footstool."[41]

After the destruction of the Temple and the rise in the practice of bowing and prostration among the Christian sects, the rabbis prohibited the daily practice of falling prostrate. Unable to wipe it out entirely, they severely curtailed it and limited its use to Rosh Ha-Shanāh and Yom Kippūr, when reading the *'Avodāh*—an account of the ancient sacrificial ritual in the Temple—and reciting the closing prayer of *'Alēinu*. On those occasions, the Jewish worshipers, as a reenactment of the Temple ritual in biblical times, fall down on their knees and spread their hands flat out on the floor, like the Muslims. They keep, however, a slight separation between their foreheads and the bare stone floor, as required by Jewish law.[42] In his textbook on the Jewish prayer book and prayer, Adin Steinsaltz, a noted rabbi, philosopher, and scholar, shows a drawing of prostration that has a striking similarity to the Muslim practice.[43]

During the rest of the year, when performing their daily prayer, Jews only use the postures of limited bowing (a slight genuflection and an inclination of the head), bending knees (moving only the upper part of the body), sitting while praying, standing in silent meditation (*'amidāh*), and laying face down in a submissive position (*taḥanūn*).

Washing before Prayer

Purity (Hebrew: *ṭaharāh;* Arabic *ṭahārah*), both physical and spiritual, is an essential part of worship in both Islam and Judaism. Before offering prayers, Muslims are required to perform an elaborate system of ritual ablution (*wuḍū'*). After declaring the intention of performing ablution, a Muslim worshiper goes through the following steps, the first five being repeated three times each:

1. Washing of hands up to the wrists
2. Rinsing of the mouth
3. Sniffing of water in the nostrils
4. Washing of the face from the forehead to the chin and from ear to ear
5. Washing the arms up to the elbow
6. Washing the head
7. Washing the feet up to the ankles

The biblical law prescribed that the priests in the Holy Temple in Jerusalem, who served in the Sanctuary, had to be in a state of physical and spiritual cleanness and therefore they washed their hands and feet before entering. They used a special laver, which stood between the Tent of the Meeting and the altar.[44] From this ceremony, the Rabbis derived the rule practiced today that one should wash one's hands before any of the statutory services. Synagogues therefore have special lavers at their entrance. Biblical passages often cited to support this custom are taken from the Psalms: "I will wash my hands in cleanliness, so I will compass Your altar, O Lord,"[45] and "Who may ascend the mountain of the Lord, and who may stand in the place of His sanctity? One with clean hands and a pure heart."[46] From this passage, it is inferred that washing of hands is required before performing any holy act. So, although complete ablution is prescribed, it is the purificatory washing that has survived most completely and is most practiced by contemporary Jewish worshipers. The hands must be washed before any meal of which bread forms a part, followed by a special blessing called *Neṭilāt Yadāyim* (Washing of the Hands), and for this purpose a special pitcher is used. Washing is also done after any unclean bodily function or after contact with any unclean object. Complete immersion is still done on Friday, when a Jew is required to bathe his entire body in warm water, in honor of the Sabbath. If he is unable to do so, he should at least wash his face, hands, and feet in warm water.[47]

Jewish laws of ritual purity require a woman, after her monthly period (Hebrew: *niddāh*), or a non-Jew who embraces Judaism through conversion according to the Jewish Law (*giyyūr ka-halakhāh*), to immerse in a *mikvāh* (meaning literally "a [water] gathering place"), a pool of water that meets specified qualifications and is normally attached to a synagogue.[48] Also, in some Islamic cultures, we find men customarily go to the *ḥammām*, a public steam bath, to wash and socialize. In Arabic the word means "spreader of warmth" and, like in Hebrew, it derives from the root verb *ḥ.m.m.*, meaning in both languages "to warm up." Ever since the conquering Arabs encountered Roman and Greek baths in Syria and Egypt, the *ḥammām* gained popularity and religious significance, and became an annex to the mosque, used to comply with the Islamic laws of hygiene and purification.[49]

The Laws of Circumcision

Circumcision is a positive commandment obligatory under Jewish law.[50] It is the very first commandment introduced as part of God's covenant with Abraham. According to the commandment, all sons of Jewish women are to be circumcised on the eighth day after their birth. This is why the Hebrew term for circumcision is ***brīt milāh***, which means "Covenant of Circumcision." The ritual of surgically removing the foreskin of the penis is performed by a trained religious expert called ***mohēl***, in the presence of relatives and friends. Circumcision is such a fundamental practice in the Jewish religion that it outweighs all other commandments prescribed in the Torah. It is therefore allowed to take place even on the Sabbath or on Yom Kippūr, two sacred days in which no work is permitted.

The Covenant refers to the pledge that God made to Abraham, during which God changed his name from "Abram" to "Abraham," and in which He promised to bless him, make him prosper and offer the Land of Canaan to his descendants: "And I will establish My covenant between Me and you and your seed after you throughout their generations for an everlasting covenant, to be a God to you and to your seed after you. And I will give to you and to your seed after you, the land of your sojourning, all the Land of Canaan, for an everlasting possession; and I will be their God."[51]

In turn, Abraham, to show his loyalty to God and to enter into this covenant with Him, was commanded as follows:

> And God said to Abraham: "And as for you, you shall keep My covenant, you and your seed after you throughout their generations. This is My covenant, which you shall keep, between Me and you and your seed after you: Every male among you shall be circumcised. And you shall be circumcised in the flesh of your foreskin; and it shall be a sign of a covenant between Me and you. And he that is eight days old shall be circumcised among you, every male throughout your generations, he that is born in the house, or bought with money of any foreigner, that is not of your seed."[52]

The rite of circumcision has served, since the time of Abraham, as the "sign of the Covenant" between God and the Jewish people, and has been universally observed by Jews all over the world. During the circumcision ritual, the baby's father makes the following blessing: "Blessed are You, Lord our God, King of the Universe, Who has sanctified us with His commandments and commanded us to enter him into the Covenant of Abraham, our father."

Circumcision is not mentioned in the Qur'ān, but it is highlighted in the ***ḥadīth*** (Prophet Muhammad's recorded words and actions), which every Muslim is expected to follow. It is called ***khitān*** in Arabic, meaning "cutting off," and sometimes ***ṭahārah***, meaning "purification." Muslims everywhere regard it as an introduction to Islamic faith and a sign of belonging to the Islamic community.

There is no consensus among scholars of *Fiqh* (Islamic jurisprudence) as to whether circumcision is obligatory. Some state that it is recommended; others that it is obligatory.[53] Some have quoted the *ḥadīth* to argue that the requirement of circumcision is based on the covenant with Abraham.[54] While endorsing circumcision for males, scholars note that it is not a requirement for converting to Islam.[55] Some scholars refer to *ḥadīth* that regards circumcision as an act of cleanliness.[56] Some refer to the example of Abraham, who circumcised himself at the age of 80,[57] and to the principle of following the religion of Abraham. We should remember that the biblical narrative relates the account of Abraham circumcising not only himself, but also all the men of his household, including his son Ishmael when he was 13 years old.[58] Many observant Muslims follow this tradition and circumcise their sons at the age of 13.

Dietary laws: Kosher and Ḥalāl

Jewish and Islamic dietary laws, respectively called Kosher (an Anglicization of the Hebrew word *Kashēr*) and *Ḥalāl*, meaning "permissible" in both traditions, are very similar. They can therefore help bring Jews and Muslims together, especially those who live as minorities in a majority secular or Christian society. The following comparison is not meant to be comprehensive, but merely to give a basic understanding of some of its similarities and differences.

In general, in both traditions, all the animals that may be eaten, birds and mammals included, must be slaughtered in accordance with their respective scriptural law. All blood must be drained from the meat or broiled out of it before it is eaten. Certain parts of permitted animals may not be eaten.

In detail, both Judaism and Islam have a wide variety of similar dietary laws, which are based on the Torah for the Jews and the Qur'ān for the Muslims. Here are some of them:

Torah: Any animal that "parts the hoof, and is wholly cloven-footed, and chews the cud, among the beasts, you may eat."[59]

Qur'ān: "O you who believe! Fulfill [all] obligations. Lawful to you [for food] are all four-footed animals, with the exceptions named. But animals of the chase are forbidden while you are in the Sacred Precincts or in pilgrim garb (*iḥrām*): For God does command according to His will and plan."[60]

Torah: "Whatever has fins and scales in the waters, in the seas, and in the rivers, them may you eat."[61]

Qur'ān: "Lawful to you is the pursuit of water-game (e.g. fish) and its use for food, for the benefit of yourselves and those who travel."[62]

Torah: The mammals and birds that may be eaten must be slaughtered in accordance with Jewish law.[63]

Qur'ān: "Eat of [the meat of the animals] on which Name of God has been invoked, if you are a believer."[64] "Eat not of [meat of animal] on which the Name of God has not been invoked: That would be [an act of] impiety."[65]

Torah: "You shall not eat of anything that died of itself (i.e., natural causes)."[66]

Qur'ān: "Forbidden to you [for food] are dead animals."[67]

Torah: Prohibits consumption of blood.[68]

Qur'ān: "Forbidden to you [for food] blood."[69]

Torah: "And the swine, because it parts the hoof and is cloven-footed, but does not chew the cud, is unclean to you."[70]

Qur'ān: "He has only forbidden you [...] the flesh of swine."[71]

The Qur'ān states that "the food of the People of the Book (i.e., Jews and Christians) is lawful to you and yours is lawful to them."[72] However, we find some food items that have been forbidden in the Torah, yet allowed in the Qur'ān because, according to Islamic Law, they do not cause harm or illness. Health is a central theme in the Qur'ān: "Eat and drink in health [as a reward] for your [good] deeds."[73] For example, the Muslims eat the flesh and milk of the camel, whereas the Jewish Law forbids it—the Torah says that "the camel, because he chews the cud but parts not the hoof, he is unclean to you."[74] On the other hand, as we have seen above, both Islamic and Jewish laws prohibit the eating of the swine (*ḥazīr* in Hebrew; *ḥanzīr* in Arabic).

Jewish dietary laws make a distinction between three "gender" foods: meat (religiously slaughtered and processed), dairy (taken from Kosher animals and processed from milk products), and pareve ("neutral" foods that are neither meat nor dairy, such as fish). It further commands the separation of meat and dairy in food, utensils, and processing equipment. These prohibitions do not exist in Islam. The explanation given by Islamic jurists is that they are self-inflicted prohibitions prescribed by human-made laws, which unfairly forbid the bounty and blessings from God. Thus, the Qur'ān says, "all food was lawful to the Children of Israel except that which Israel had forbidden to itself, before the Torah was revealed."[75]

In both Judaism and Islam, there is a special blessing before slaughtering. However, there is one major difference between Kosher and *Ḥalāl* related to animal slaughter. In Judaism, the killing of the animal must be done in a ritualistic slaughter performed by a professionally trained *shoḥēṭ*, or slaughterer. In Islam, any person having reached puberty is allowed to slaughter after saying the Name of God and facing Mecca. There is no restriction in Islamic Law to buy and eat meat that was slaughtered by the People of the

Book. In fact, many devout Muslims prefer to buy from a Jewish butcher, given Judaism's more restrictive laws. Observant Jews, on the other hand, will only buy Kosher food from certified Jewish markets and eat only in restaurants certified by rabbinic authorities. They will not even eat kosher food on utensils that have come into contact with non-Kosher food.

The Way of Greeting

Every group of people has a distinctive way of greeting others. Not in the case of the Jews and the Muslims; they both say "hello" the same way, with blessing, with the word "peace." In greeting people using the Name of God, Peace (*Shalōm* in Hebrew; *Salām* in Arabic), they invite God to be present in their midst. A Jew greets another Jew by saying, "*Shalōm 'Aleikhēm,*" meaning "may Peace be upon you." The Jew who is greeted, responds with "*'Aleikhēm Ha-Shalōm,*" meaning "may upon you there be Peace [as well]." Sometimes, the response is "*Shalōm 'u-Vrakhāh,*" which means "Peace and Blessing [upon you]."

Muslims use exactly the same exchange of greetings: "*As-Salāmu 'Alaikum*" and "*Wa-'Alaikum As-Salām.* If a Muslim is greeted with "*As-Salāmu 'Alaikum wa-Raḥmatu-llāh,*" which means, "may Peace and Mercy of God be upon you," they answer with a longer and more gracious greeting: "*Wa-'Alaikum As-Salām wa-Raḥmatu-llāhi wa-Barakatuhu,*" which means, "may Peace, Mercy of God and His Blessing be upon you." Says the Qur'ān: "When a courteous greeting is offered to you, you meet it with a greeting still more courteous, or [at least] of equal courtesy."[76] And "Whenever you enter any house, greet one another with a blessed, wholesome greeting as [it is] from God."[77]

Similarly, the Mishnah, the Jewish code of law, emphasizes the importance of taking initiative of greeting first—"Be the first to greet every person."[78] Jewish sages spoke about the reward for kindness toward fellow men, saying that "one who loves peace and pursues peace, and offers [the greeting of] peace and responds [with the greeting of] peace, the Blessed Holy One will make him inherit the life of This World and the life of the World-to-Come."[79] It was said about Rabbi Yohanan ben Zakkai, the outstanding leader of the Jewish community during the crucial years before and after the destruction of the Second Temple, that no man ever preceded him in offering a greeting, even an ordinary non-Jew in the market place.[80] This should not come as a surprise as the Mishnah prescribes the duty of showing, "for the sake of peace (*mipnēi darkhēi shalōm*), friendliness towards non-Jews."[81]

Final Thoughts

Obviously, there is a real similarity between Judaism and Islam in the ways their observant communities keep their scriptural law and conduct their worship. Jews and Muslims are close to each other because their religions, unlike Christianity, have a greater emphasis on law and commandments than on faith alone. Their traditions serve as a strong common basis, whereby members of their communities can easily relate to each other across the religious divide. But, for intercommunal and interfaith relations, it is the prescribed commandments "between man and his fellow" that should be more emphasized than the prescribed commandments "between man and God."

The Persian-born Sufi mystic and perhaps the world's greatest spiritual poet, Jalaluddin Rumi (1207–1273), whose poetry of love and friendship is highly popular in the West, wrote a delightful poem entitled "Moses and the Shepherd" that touches upon the subject. After Moses criticizes a shepherd for praying to God in his own simple language and not using the appropriate prayer lexicon, God rebukes him, saying:

> You have separated Me
> from one of my own.
> Did you come as a Prophet to unite,
> or to sever?
> I have given each being a separate and unique way
> of seeing and knowing and saying that knowledge.
> What's seems wrong to you is right for him.
> What is poison to one is honey to someone else.
> Purity and impurity, sloth and diligence in worship,
> these mean nothing to Me.
> I am apart from all that.
> Ways of worshiping are not to be ranked as better
> or worse than one another.
> Hindus do Hindu things.
> The Dravidian Muslims in India do what they do.
> It's all praise, and it's all right. It's not Me that's
> glorified in acts of worship.
> It's the worshipers!
> I don't hear the words
> they say. I look inside at the humility.
> That broken-open lowliness is the reality,
> not the language! Forget phraseology.
> I want burning, burning.
> Be friends

with your burning. Burn up your thinking
and your forms of expression!
Moses,
those who pay attention to ways of behaving
and speaking are one sort. Lovers who burn
are another.

The poem continues in describing Moses's self-realization and self-criticism. In Rumi's words:

The "wrong" way he talks is better than a hundred
"right" ways of others.
Inside the Ka'bah
it doesn't matter which direction you point
your prayer rug!
The ocean diver doesn't need snowshoes!
The love-religion has no code or doctrine.
Only God.

Inspired by God's vision and words, Moses then ran after the shepherd and, after long chase, finally caught up with him and said:

I was wrong. God has revealed to me
that there are no rules for worship.
Say whatever
and however your
loving tells you to. Your sweet blasphemy
is the truest devotion.
Through you a whole world is freed.
Loosen your tongue
and don't worry what comes out.
It's all the light of the spirit.[82]

Rumi, influenced by the great traditions, realized that for lovers of God there are no rules for worship. Didn't Prophet Muhammad say, "Righteousness is not that you turn your faces [in prayer] towards east or the west; but righteousness means that one believes in God,"[83] and that "We have prescribed each of you a [different] law and custom"?[84] Doesn't the Jewish prayer of *Shmonēh 'Esrēh* say that God hears "the prayer [that is coming out] of every mouth (*tefillāt kol peh*)?" God does not care for "phraseology," using Rumi's term. He listens to the murmurings of the human heart and prefers the pure in heart, as the Psalmist prays: "A pure heart create for me, O God,"[85] and tells us: "Who shall ascend into the mountain of the Lord? And who shall stand in His holy place? He who has clean hands and a pure heart; who has not taken My name in vain, and has not sworn deceitfully. He shall receive a blessing from the Lord."[86] Also the Qur'ān talks about the centrality of the pure, loving heart when it says, "Only those who come to God with pure heart [will be saved]."[87] But when the Sacred Books call to come to God and serve Him with a pure, loving heart, they also mean to recognize the Divine in every person and be in service of humanity with a heart that is sensitive and caring for every person regardless of his or her religion.

This universal approach that prefers human love to religious particularism is beautifully expressed by another famous Sufi poet, Ibn Arabi (1165–1240):

> There was a time when I used to condemn my friend if his religion was not close to mine. But now, my heart embraces any [religious] form: the pastureland of the deer, the monastery of the monks, the temple of the idol-worshipers, the Ka'bah for the [Muslim] pilgrim, the Tablets of the Torah, and the Book of the Qur'an. Love is my only religion, and wherever its chariot horses turn, there is my religion and faith.[88]

Part II

Two Communities, One Ancestor

Chapter 4

The Gate of Legacy

The Religion of Abraham—a Common Ground

Nowhere in the world can we presently experience the intensity of the Israeli-Palestinian conflict more than in Hebron, the city of Abraham. Hebron is regarded by the Jews as second in sanctity to Jerusalem, and by the Muslims as the fourth-holiest city after Mecca. In both traditions, the name of the city refers to Abraham, "the friend of God." The name Hebron is derived from the Hebrew word "*ḥavēr*," meaning "friend." So is the Arabic name for the city, "*Al-Khalīl*." In 1968, immediately after the Six Day War, the Jewish community of Hebron had reestablished itself just east of the city in a place called Qiryāt Arba', which carries the ancient name of Hebron.[1] And since 1979, a small group of settlers has also been living in *Shkhunāt Avrahām Avīnu* (Our Father Abraham's Neighborhood), an enclave located in the middle of an overwhelming Muslim community.

The relations between the neighboring Jewish and Muslim communities are imbued with hostility and deep mistrust. The conflict is centered on the Tomb of the Patriarchs, called by the Jews *Me'arāt Ha-Makhpelāh* (the Cave of the Doubled [Burials]) and by the Muslims *Al-Ḥaram al-'Ibrāhīmī* (the Sanctuary of Abraham). There, according to ancient tradition, the Patriarchs Abraham, Isaac, and Jacob, and the Matriarchs Sarah, Rebecca, and Leah are buried. Today the children of Abraham have bitterly been fighting each other to establish control over this holy place. As each side is attempting to appropriate Abraham as its own, no agreeable way has yet been found to demarcate what is holy to Jews from what is holy to Muslims.

When Abraham purchased the burial plot from a Hittite named Ephron, in order to bury his wife Sarah,[2] he had no intention to leave Beersheba in the south and reside in Hebron amidst a crowded Hittite population. Would he have proceeded in the transaction had he been able to foresee the bitter conflict between his children? Would he choose to be buried in a place that triggers such deep hostility and causes the basic tenets of his religion, as he practiced it, to be violated?

We have already seen in the previous chapters how Jews and Muslims trace their traditions and practices to their common ancestor, Abraham. What was his religion? What was his code of ethics? Can we find in his conduct a common ground where the two religions can meet? Is the essence of their faith one and the same, inherited from their common ancestor? What do the teachings of the Jews and Muslims say about him? Can we use him as a model for their future relations, as an inspiration for their reconciliation?

These questions must be seen within the context of Abraham as an archetype. Being "our father" means he is a prototype, a model from which we can learn about ourselves and about our relationship with others. The Jewish sages teach us that "the deeds of fathers are an augural sign for their children."[3] Meaning, whatever Abraham experienced, his descendents will. The ethical standards that guided him will be those that will guide his children forever. The Midrash tells us, "The Blessed Holy One said: 'Abraham, what do I have to tell you and what do I have to bless you? [...] only that *all* the children, who will descend from you, will be like you.'"[4] Thus, the Hebrew Prophet Isaiah appealed to the People of Israel, in the name of God, saying: "Listen to Me, you who pursue righteousness, you who seek the Lord; look to the rock from which you were hewn, and to the hole of the pit from which you were dug; look to Abraham your father, and to Sarah that bore you; for when he was but one I called him, and I blessed him, and multiplied him."[5]

"The Religion of Abraham" in the Qur'ān

Although leaving us without the details of Abraham's religious conduct that made him worthy of divine distinction, the Qur'ān regards him as a "man of Truth [and] a prophet [of God],"[6] His "friend" or *khalīl*,[7] "devoutly obedient and true in faith" or *ḥanīf*.[8] His faith in God was so strong that the Qur'ān treats his monotheistic "religion," which it calls *millat 'Ibrāhīm*, as the foundation of Islam. It says: "Abraham was indeed a model, devoutly obedient [to God] and true in faith."[9]

The Qur'ān even criticizes the Jews and the Christians for claiming the merits of Abraham while deviating from his pure, monotheistic, *ḥanīf* doctrine of personal submission to the One True God:

> They say: "Become Jews or Christians, if you be guided." Say you: "Nay! I would rather [follow] the religion of Abraham, the true in faith."[10]
>
> And who turns away from the religion of Abraham but such as debase his soul with folly? Him we chose and rendered pure in this world.[11]

According to the Qur'ān, the faith of Abraham was based on two dominant principles: belief in the unity (*tawḥīd*) of God and submission (*islām*) to His will. On one occasion, God is said to have commanded Abraham to "submit" and he promptly responded by declaring *aslamti*—"I have submitted!"[12] Therefore, the Qur'ān takes the view that only those who actually follow his ways of conduct are entitled to claim him as their ancestor: "The closest to Abraham are those who follow him."[13] Therefore, calls the Qur'ān: "Follow the ways of Abraham, the true in faith."[14]

To further define Abraham's "religion," the Qur'ān says that "God guided him on the straight path (*Ṣirāṭ al-Mustaqīm*)."[15] According to the following verse, his "religion" is, and can be, defined in the phrase: The straight path: "Say: 'As for me, my Lord has guided me along the straight path, the right way, the religion of Abraham, the true in faith.'"[16]

As previously mentioned, "the straight path" is a central principle in Islam. It is mentioned in the opening chapter of the Qur'ān and set in a form of invocation to God, appealing to Him to "guide us along the straight path."[17] Muslims are expected to distinguish "the straight path" from other paths. Thus, in another *sūrah*, Muslims are advised to abide by the so-called Ten Commandments, which, if followed, will guide them to "the straight path," the Way of God that leads to righteousness. Following other paths will separate them from Him. Here are the Commandments:[18]

> Say: "Come, I will recite to you what your Lord has forbidden you:
>
> I. You shall not associate anything with Him (i.e., commit idolatry);
> II. You shall do good to [your] parents;
> III. You shall not kill your children because of poverty—We provide for you and for them;
> IV. You shall not come near sins [of adultery], whether open or hidden;
> V. You shall not take [anybody's] life, which God has made sacred, except in the course of justice;
>
> These He has commanded you, so that you may understand.
>
> VI. You shall not touch the wealth of the orphan until he attains the age, except to improve it;

VII. You shall give full measure and full weight [when you trade] in all fairness—We do not burden any soul beyond its means;
VIII. You shall be absolutely just when you bear witness, even if it is [against] a close relative;
IX. You shall fulfill the Covenant of God.
These He has commanded you, so that you may bear in mind.
X. And [He commanded you, saying]: *The path of Mine is straight.* Follow it and do not follow [other] paths, which separate you from His path.
This has He commanded you, so that you may be righteous" (emphasis added).

The shortest distance between two points is a straight line. So is the recommended path, connecting man to God. Maulana Abul Kalam Azad (1888–1958), a modern commentator of the Qur'ān, writes that the term "the straight path" was chosen in the Qur'ān to signify the universal religion, *ad-Dīn*, or the Way. We may have a number of paths to reach a particular destination. But, explains Azad, there is only one path, the royal road that a traveler can complete his journey and reach his destination as quickly as possible and with safety. The Qur'ān says "the straight path" in religion likewise can be only one and not several. That is why the Qur'ān repeatedly styles "the straight path" as *ad-Dīn*.

Who are to be considered followers of "the straight path," the adherents of "the Religion of Abraham"? The Qur'ān answers: "All who obey God and the Messenger are those whom God has shown favor—the Prophets, the Righteous and the Witnesses, and the Good-doers; the best of company are they."[19]

In this verse, the Qur'ān refers to four categories of people on whom God has shown His favor: The Prophets (*nabbiyyīn*), who guide people in the Divine Truth; the Righteous (*ṣaddiqīn*), who love and live by the Truth; the Witnesses (*shuhadā'*), who bear testimony to Truth; and Good-doers (*ṣaliḥīn)*, who keep themselves and others on the path of goodness. According to Azad, the reference in this verse is to all followers of Truth and righteousness and is not confined to followers of any particular religion. The privilege is extended to all those who have shown those qualities and who have followed "the straight path." It is Azad's opinion that "the straight path" is the straight road to peace, both inward and outward.[20]

"The Religion of Abraham" in Jewish Tradition

In the Jewish sources—the Torah and Midrash—like in the Qur'ān, we find similar appellations given to Abraham. He was a "God-fearing man" (*yere' 'Elohīm*),[21] a "prophet" (*navī*),[22] "friend" (*yadīd*),[23] "whole-hearted" (*tamīm*),[24] "head of all the righteous" (*rosh kol ha-tzadiqīm*),[25] whose heart God found to be "faithful" (*ne'emān*).[26] Like in Islam, his religion is considered the basis of Judaism, as explained by Rabbi Shmuel David Luzzatto: "Moses was not sent to teach a new religion, but to confirm the correct views held since the days of Abraham and to establish laws and institutions designed to regulate the customs and keep within them the healthy ideas of the religion of Abraham."[27]

But, there is a problem. Despite the lengthy biblical narrative available to us about Abraham and his frequent contacts with and intimate counsels of God, we cannot find where he received any divine instruction to perform a certain religious commandment, conduct, or ritual, except that of circumcision, which was designed by God to set Abraham and his descendents apart from their idol-worshiping neighbors. There are two references, where God instructed him, as a condition for entering into a covenant with Him, to "walk before me and be whole-hearted," [28] and to "command his children and his posterity that they shall keep the way of the Lord *to do righteousness and justice* (*la'asōt tzedaqāh u-mishpāṭ*)."[29] But these instructions are vague and general, giving no explanation as to what is the "way of the Lord."

Some modern Jewish commentators, using citations from the Hebrew Prophet Jeremiah,[30] observed that the doing of righteousness and justice is synonymous with "the way of the Lord."[31] The Jewish standing prayer, *Shmonēh 'Esrēh*, identifies God as the "King who loves righteousness and justice," One Who reigns "with kindness and compassion, with righteousness and justice." In order words, Abraham was commanded to emulate God and establish His "way" on earth.

Only later did the term "the way of the Lord" receive a more specific definition. Starting with the book of Deuteronomy,[32] we see the frequent use of the saying, "And you shall do that which is right and good in the sight of the Lord." It is not enough to do "that which is right", that is, to act according to the strict letter of the Law, but also to do that which is "good" in one's relationship with the other fellow man. The opposite is "[to do] that which is evil in the sight of the Lord."[33] The Hebrew word "*yashār*" means right or straight. The Hebrew prophets picked up on this saying and began to use the term "the straight and good path"[34] or just "the straight path"[35] to denote "the way of the Lord."

Still, we are left with a lack of clarity. All we know is that the Bible attests to the fact that Abraham was a monotheist, a link in a chain of monotheists that goes back to Adam.[36] But it gives no details of his religion other than one creedal element (the belief in One God), one ethical element (righteousness and justice), and one ritual element (circumcision).[37] For these we need to consult some classical commentators and other Jewish traditions.

The sages of the Mishnah wrestled with the term "the straight path." In responding to the question, "Which is the straight path that a man should choose for himself," they suggested: "Any [path] that is an adornment to those who pursue it and that brings adornment from his fellow men."[38] What is the quality of "adornment," or *tif'ēret* in Hebrew, that they refer to? In Jewish mystical traditions, *tif'ēret* represents beauty, truth, peace, and harmony. Therefore, the people who walk "the straight path" are people of peace. They create peace both for themselves, that is, inner peace, and for others, that is, outer peace, exactly like Maulana Azad's interpretation.

Also Maimonides uses the concept of "the straight path" (*ha-dērekh ha-yesharāh*), which people should walk, but defines it as "the middle path" (*ha-dērekh ha-'emtza'īt* or *ha-dērekh ha-benonīt*), "a disposition that is equally distant from the two extremes in its class." Like in Islam, he called it "the way of the Lord, which Abraham our father taught to his children, as it is written" (in Genesis 18:19). He regards this optimal median virtue as the highway of human life and suggests that "whoever walks in this path, secures for himself goodness and blessedness" as Abraham did.[39] Rabbi Luzzatto argues against the dialectic Aristotelian philosophy of Maimonides. He suggests that Abraham's "way of the Lord" was "the way of love and loving-kindness" (*dērekh ha-ahavāh ve-ha-ḥēsed*), which "is expressed in the fulfillment of the social edicts, in other words love of fellowmen and justice"; it was not Maimonides's "way of intellect and reason" (*dērekh ha-sēkhel ve-ha-ḥeshbōn*).[40]

In his commentary on Genesis, the nineteenth-century sage, Rabbi Naftali Tzvi Yehudah Berlin, best known by the acronym Netziv (1816–1893), offers a similar definition for *dērekh ha-yashār*, "the straight path," which in his opinion is the proper treatment of another. The demand of Torah, he writes, is that *dērekh ha-yashār* applies not only in our relationships with those who abide by Torah but also with all other inhabitants of the world.[41] This is why Genesis is called, like the name of the well-known medieval apocryphal work, *Sēfer ha-Yashār*, for the stories of the Patriarchs are examples of this principle of uprightness. The Patriarchs are exemplary specifically because of the positive way they treated all people, even the idolaters that they encountered.

What did Abraham do that he deserved so many accolades and rewards from God? The Torah gives a clear answer: "God appeared to Isaac and said... 'I will keep the oath that I made to your father: I will multiply your descendants as numerous as the stars of the sky, and grant them all these lands. All the nations of the earth shall be blessed through your descendants. All this [I promise] because Abraham obeyed Me, and he kept My charge (Hebrew: *mishmartī*), My commandments (Hebrew: *mitzvotāi*), My statues (Hebrew: *ḥuqotāi*), and My laws (Hebrew: *torotāi*).'"[42]

Commenting on the above citation, the famed Jewish scholar and the most referenced biblical commentator Rabbi Shlomo ben Yitzhaq (1040–1105), usually known as Rashi, distinguishes the ways Abraham obeyed God and suggests that he knew the entire Torah, both the Written and the Oral. His exegesis of the above-mentioned passage is as follows:[43]

- "*And he kept My charge*"—These are the precautionary decrees instituted by the sages, which are intended to caution against violation of the biblical laws, such as certain prohibitions regarding the Sabbath.
- "*My commandments*"—These are the precepts which, had they not been written in the Torah, would have been required to be written, such as robbery and murder.
- "*My statues*"—These are decrees with no apparent rationale, such as prohibitions against eating swine and wearing garments woven of both wool and linen.
- "*And My laws*"—These are all the laws, the Written Law given to Moses from Sinai and the Oral Law.

Another famous biblical commentator and one of the greatest medieval Jewish scholars, Rabbi Moses ben Nachman (1194–1270), known as Ramban or Nachmanides, quotes Rashi, but offers his own commentary. He argues that Abraham, who learned the entire Torah (that already existed in Heaven) by *Ruaḥ Ha-Qōdesh*—meaning the Holy Spirit—fulfilled and observed it before it was given in Sinai. But his distinctions are different:[44]

- "*My charge*" refers to Abraham's absolute certainty that God exists, which led him to dispute the pervasive idolatrous beliefs of his day, and to guide his generation toward belief in One God.
- "*My Commandments*" refers to God's direct instructions to Abraham, such as God's commandment to leave his ancestral homeland and travel to an unknown destination (i.e., the Land of Canaan).
- "*My statues*" refers to Abraham's emulation of God by being merciful and compassionate, doing righteousness and making a judgment.
- "*My laws*" refers to Abraham's observance of the Seven Noahide Laws, which are incumbent upon all mankind, and his fulfillment of God's circumcision commandment.

The apocryphal chronicle of Genesis, *Sēfer Ha-Yovlīm* ("Book of Jubilees"), offers a more specific list of commandments. In recounting Abraham's last wishes for his sons and grandsons, it tells that he "commanded them that they should observe *the way of the Lord*; that they work righteousness, and love each his neighbor, and act on this manner amongst all men; that they should each so walk with regard to them as to do judgment and righteousness on the earth." He then lists a number of "red lines" that they must not cross.[45]

- They must circumcise their sons "according to the Covenant."
- They are not allowed to intermarry with the Canaanites.
- They must guard themselves from all sorts of "fornication and uncleanness."
- They should not serve or worship idols.

Instead, they were commanded to "love the God of Heaven and cleave to all His commandments [...] serve the most High God and worship Him continually and hope for His countenance always." His direction was clear: *Go straight*! "Do not deviate to the right hand or the left of all the paths which the Lord had commanded us";[46] an instruction that reminds us of "the straight path" rule common to both Judaism and Islam.

Abraham's Path—a Model to Follow

Although the ritual element of Abraham's religion seems to be meager, its ethical element is quite detailed. It can serve as a model of virtue for both Jews and Muslims to follow when seeking a common ground for their conflicting positions. We are told that to be true Jews or true Muslims, we need to strive to become disciplined children of Abraham. To be considered his followers, we need to travel the same path that he chose.[47]

The instruction in the Qur'ān to follow Abraham's model is supported by Maimonides. In response to a question by Rabbi Obadiah the Proselyte of Spain, whether as a proselyte he can utter the prayer "Our God and God of *our fathers*, he writes: "Abraham is also *your* father." His explanation was as follows:

> Abraham, our father, taught his contemporaries the belief in the Unity of God and left this legacy to his children and his descendants to the end of all generations, as it is written: "For I know him, that he will command his children and his household after him and they shall keep the way of the Lord" (Genesis, 18:19). Thus he who becomes a proselyte in any generation to the end of all generations and confesses the Unity of God, blessed be He, as taught in the Torah of Moses, is considered a disciple of Abraham and his household and is included in the testament he gave to his children and his household after him. In this sense, *Abraham is the father of his descendants who follow his ways* and of his disciples who are not from his descendants (emphasis added).[48]

Three centuries later, Abraham ben David Halevi (ca.1110–1180), also known as Ibrahim ibn Dāwūd, the Spanish-born historian and philosopher, wrote about emulating Abraham in his Arabic *Al-'Aqīdah al-Rafi'ah* ("The Sublime Faith"; later translated into Hebrew as *Ha-'Emunāh Ha-Rammāh*): "He [Abraham] gave himself over completely to the fulfillment of His command and believed that his knowledge was of no merit compared with that of God, and so he went forth obedient to the command of the Blessed Holy One. This attitude of Abraham's was not hidden from the Blessed Holy One, but *He wanted Abraham's conduct and the qualities he demonstrated to serve as an example to be followed by those who obey God, and as a model they might set before their eyes*" (emphasis added).[49]

From a Hebrew hymn written by an eleventh-century Jewish poet, Elijah ben Mordecai, we learn so much about how Abraham conducted his life:

He [Abraham] firmly discerned Your faith.
In an age when yet man knew not Your will.
He was delighted in You, and taught others how to revere You.
He rejoiced to make known Your glory unto all.
He led the erring to Your paths.
He was surnamed the father of his people.
He was careful to keep Your commandment.
He desired to find safety in the shade of Your Divine Presence.
He refreshed the wanderers with Your food.
He taught the penitent that there is none besides You.
He besought You because he believed in You.
He planted a grove to proclaim Your mighty deeds.[50]

Also in the Islamic text *Qiṣaṣṣ al-Anbiyā'*, we find the following poetic verse about Abraham's character:

Our Lord removed the veils
from the seven spheres of heaven and earth for him.
So Abraham saw everything
from the dust on earth to the high Throne of Heaven.

For the people Abraham established,
until the Day of Judgment,
the custom of entertaining guests,
slaughtering oxen, camels and sheep.

When about to sacrifice his son,
Abraham received on earth
the substitute ram from Gabriel,
which had been fattened by grazing in heaven.

> Abraham heaved the axe and hewed the idol
> on which the fox had urinated.
> Though hungry himself, he offered a meal of meat;
> he made himself a name and extinguished the fire.[51]

Abraham's code of ethics, particularly in human relationships, can be summed up as consisting of three primary principles:

1. Hospitality and Love of Humanity

Abraham is regarded as the classic exemplar of the ideal of hospitality. The Torah records the example of his model of hospitality in detail.[52] We are told that Abraham "lifted up his eyes and saw three men standing near him; and as soon as he saw them, he ran from the entrance of the tent to greet them and, bowing down to the ground, he said: 'My lords, if it please you, pass not away from your servant. Let now a little water be fetched, and wash your feet, and recline yourselves under the tree.'" Thereafter, the ceremonial hospitality is described in detail, every act and every gesture. The commentators point out to us that Abraham planned his elaborate feast and displayed wholehearted proactive hospitality, despite his physical pain (as he was recuperating from the circumcision) and his being in the middle of prayer to God. We are told that Abraham's tent was open in four directions to allow strangers to enter freely into his home. Thus, *Pirkēi Avōt* ("Sayings of the Fathers") teaches us to "let your house be wide open, and let the needy be treated as members of your household."[53]

The Talmud[54] explains that Abraham's treatment of his guests teaches us that the practice of hospitality takes precedence over welcoming and greeting God in prayer (*gedolāh hakhnasāt orḥīm mi-qabbalāt pnēi ha-shekhināh*). The Talmud made the observation that Abraham was addressing God, asking Him to wait until after he had welcomed the guests into his home. How can we apply this lesson to our everyday lives? Being kind to human beings takes first priority. God does not want us to neglect prayer. But He wants us to treat people honorably before appealing to Him in prayer.

The Testament of Abraham, a first century CE apocryphal work of Jewish origin, begins with a very detailed description of Abraham's practice of hospitality:

> Abraham lived the measure of his life, nine hundred and ninety-five years, and having lived all the years of his life in quietness, gentleness, and righteousness, the righteous one was exceedingly hospitable; for, pitching his tent in the cross-ways at the oaks of Mamre, he received every one, both rich and

poor, kings and rulers, the maimed and the helpless, friends and strangers, neighbors and travelers, all alike did the devout, all-holy, righteous, and hospitable Abraham entertain.[55]

2. Peacemaking

The Bible tells us about an interesting incident where the herdsmen of Abraham's cattle and the herdsmen of Lot's cattle quarreled. Recognizing the limited availability of good pastureland and their differences, Abraham was determined to resolve the quarrel peacefully. He said to his nephew Lot: "Let there be no strife between me and you and between my herdsmen and your herdsmen; for we are brothers." Then Abraham, out of generosity, gave Lot the first choice of selecting a dwelling land for himself: "Is not the whole land before you? Please separate yourself from me; if you wish to take the left hand, then I will go to the right; or if you take the right hand, then I will go to the left." Lot surveyed the Jordan Valley and found it lush and fertile. He compared it to the Garden of Eden in Mesopotamia and to the Egyptian Delta, both of which were irrigated by huge rivers, and "chose for himself all the plain of the Jordan." Thereafter, the biblical narrative completes the story by telling us, "Lot journeyed east; and they separated themselves the one from the other."[56]

We can only assume that Abraham regretted deeply the separation from Lot whom he considered as a son since their departure from their homeland. Though Lot sparked the dispute, Abraham was determined to settle it swiftly by offering a territorial compromise. Perhaps one may see this peaceful solution as foreshadowing—like the two-state resolution of the Israeli-Palestinian conflict (see Chapter 7). Abraham later encountered a similar problem with his southern neighbor Abimelech, the ruler of the Philistine land.

When a conflict arose between the rank and file of Abraham and the herdsmen of Abimelech, in their daily struggle to maintain adequate water supply and access to wells, Abraham approached Abimelech and pointed out the importance of maintaining friendly and respectful neighborly relations. Abimelech, who denied any knowledge of this water dispute, accepted Abraham's peace offer in the form of sheep and oxen, and they made a covenant. To commemorate the enforcement of the peace treaty, Abraham named the place where he and Abimelech took an oath, Beersheba (or in Hebrew, Be'ēr [well]-Shēva' [swore]). Thereafter, the biblical narrative made a point to tell that "Abraham sojourned in the land of the Philistines many days," obviously with Abimelech's blessings.[57] These peaceful relations continued into the days of Abraham's son, Isaac. When a sharp dispute erupted again over wells and pastureland, King Abimelech and his retinue came to Isaac to conclude a new covenant. Isaac made a feast for them and they departed from him in peace.[58]

3. Quest for Justice

Lot's separation did not mean a total divorce. When the four kings of the east occupied the land of Sodom and Gomorrah and took Lot as captive, Abraham did not hesitate to call upon his allies—he mobilized all their forces and set out to rescue Lot. He was motivated by his concept of justice and saving life, as the later Commandment demands, "[you] shall not stand idly by the blood of your neighbor."[59] After the war, the king of Sodom wanted to offer Abraham all the booty, if Abraham would turn over all the captives to him. But Abraham replied: "I have lifted up my hand unto the Lord, the Exalted God, Maker of Heaven and Earth, [and made a vow] that I shall not take a thread nor a shoe-latchet from anything that belongs to you, lest you proclaim [to the world]: I have made Abraham rich."[60] All Abraham wanted was to redeem the captives and restore their personal property. He was not interested in the spoils of the war.

Abraham is not a passive observer. God's move to destroy Sodom and Gomorrah turns him into a participant. Abraham was concerned with and sensitive to justice. He was, according to the Qur'ān, "without doubt, forbearing [of other people's sins], good-hearted, and seeking God [for repentance]."[61] He truly believed in the dictum of "justice and only justice shall you follow."[62] He did not believe that innocent people should suffer for the evil doings of others. Arguing on their behalf, he took a stand and, in the name of justice and morality, pleaded with God directly: "Far be it from You, doing such a thing, to slay the righteous with the wicked, equating the righteous and the wicked. Far be it from You! Shall not the Judge of all the earth deal justly?"[63] Abraham felt that if God wanted him "to do righteousness and justice,"[64] He should do the same. He held Him responsible for applying His own teaching. How could I, thought Abraham, command my children to follow this precept, if God goes to destroy Sodom and Gomorrah without justification? Abraham, who is completely overwhelmed by the fate that awaits those communities, asked for mercy upon them. God's reply was short and to the point: "If I find in Sodom fifty righteous within the city, I will forgive the entire place for their sake." But Abraham could not meet God's conditions and, in a back-and-forth dialogue, negotiated with Him all the way down to ten decent human beings. But Abraham could not find them and was unable to save these depraved communities from the wrath of God.[65]

The Bible recorded no angry response from God over Abraham's rebuke. On the contrary, the Teacher accepted His own teaching of justice. God accepted Abraham's rebuke because that rebuke did not represent a lack of faith in God but rather a proof of faith.

The Seven Noahide Laws as a Joint Foundation

Perhaps the most important legacy Abraham left for us is his straight path, or what the Jews designate as *Dērekh Ha-Yashār* and the Muslims as *Ṣirāṭ al-Mustaqīm*. When looking at the Qur'ān's basic commandments, often referred to as the Muslims' "Ten Commandments," which outlines the characteristics of the Muslims' "straight path" mentioned earlier, one is amazed by the similarities between these commandments and the Ten Commandments revealed to Moses on Mount Sinai on the one hand, and the Seven Noahide Laws, considered by the Jews as the Torah of the sons of Noah on the other.[66] All religions have moral codes that regulate human relations and prevent community life from degenerating into chaos. What's important here is that in the very basic rules of living, the three sets of codes resemble each other.

From a Muslim perspective, the basic commandments appear in the Qur'ān in the context of a dialogue between Prophet Muhammad and the Jews and Christians. As such, they represent God's basic universal message to humanity and lay the fundamental precepts that should be commonly acceptable to Muslims, Jews, and Christians.[67] From a Jewish perspective, the biblical Ten Commandments are prescribed for the People of Israel alone, whereas the Seven Noahide Laws are the basic injunctions given to Noah and are therefore binding upon all humankind, including Jews, Christians, and Muslims.[68] Abraham inherited these commandments and, therefore, from a Jewish perspective, they should be considered as the foundation upon which Jews and Muslims can establish their common "straight path." Jewish sages suggested that "there are righteous among the nations [who observe the Noahide Laws] and they do have a portion in the World-to-Come."[69]

The comparative chart (Table 4.1) displays the resemblance among the three sets of commandments. It should be noted that in the chart, the shaded areas represent typical injunctions unshared by other sets of commandments. However, the majority of the commandments are the same in all three doctrines. One of them is the prohibition of murder and sanctification of human life, an injunction that is violated today more than ever. If one can draw any conclusion from this, it is the urgent need to suspend violence and replace it with peaceful resolution instead.

Table 4.1 Comparison of Universal Sets of Commandments

Corresponding Commandments	Seven Laws of Noah	Judaism's Ten Commandments	Islam's Basic Commandments
A 2 I	A Prohibition against idolatry	1 I am the Lord your God	I You shall not associate anything with Him (i.e., commit idolatry)
B 3	B Prohibition against blasphemy	2 You shall have no other gods before me	II You shall do good to [your] parents
C 6 III+V	C Prohibition against murder	3 You shall not take the name of the Lord your God in vain	III You shall not kill your children
D 8 VI+VII	D Prohibition against theft	4 Remember the Sabbath day to keep it holy	IV You shall not come near sins [of adultery]
E 7 IV	E Prohibition against sexual immorality	5 Honor your father and mother	V You shall not take [anybody's] life
	F Prohibition against eating the limb of a living animal	6 You shall not murder	VI You shall not touch the wealth of the orphan
G 9 VIII	G Establish courts of justice	7 You shall not commit adultery	VII You shall give full measure and full weight [when you trade]
5 II		8 You shall not steal	VIII You shall be absolutely just when you bear witness
		9 You shall not bear false witness against your neighbor	IX You shall fulfill the Covenant of God
		10 You shall not covet your neighbor's house, wife, etc.	X Follow ["the straight path"] and do not follow [other] paths

The Straight Path Is a Direct Path

For Abraham "the straight path" meant also a direct path to God without intermediaries, a simple way of conversation with the Almighty. This theme finds lyrical expression in my poem entitled "Direct Line to Heaven":

Abraham
In mid-day
Sat on his stool meditating
At the entrance of his tent
Looked at the horizon
And saw
The angels of peace coming.

Isaac
In the afternoon
Went out barefoot to nearby meadow
Heard the trees moaning
Smelled the flowers' fragrance
And listened to the birds
Singing halleluiah.

Jacob
In the late evening
Placed his head
On a hard rock
Closed his eyes
And climbed his ladder
To meet the Creator.

So do I, see my heart
A temple without walls
A sanctuary wide open
A private holy of holies
Where God and I come together.
Everyone has a direct line to Heaven.

Abraham did not need mediation, which is considered in Judaism, and even more in Islam, as a form of idolatry. The sinful practice is called, in Islam, ***shirk*** or "association." The Qur'ān tells us: "Say: 'As for me, my Lord has guided me along the straight path, the right way, the religion of Abraham, the true in faith. And he [certainly] joined no associates (***mushrikīn***) with God.'"[70]

The Qur'ān is very critical of "associates," polytheists of all kinds, who attempt to take the place of God in offering a guide to His Truth. "Say: 'Can any of your *associates* guide one to Truth?' Say: 'It is God Who guides to Truth; is then He Who guides to Truth more worthy to be followed, than he who does not guide unless he himself is guided?'"[71]

Unlike Abraham, who sought and received direct guidance from God, we are now plagued by politically motivated and anger-filled preachers and all sorts of "truth-bearers" who attempt to show the believers in their community the right path to God or the path to His Truth. These extremely dangerous religious guides exploit the vulnerability of spiritual seekers and use it as a fertile ground to sow divisiveness and hostility between religions, peoples, and nations. They do it totally against the Qur'ān's teaching: "Do not take people among ourselves as patrons other than God."[72]

Judaism and Islam greatly stress the importance of reaching God directly, but their traditional authoritarian systems, by the nature of their existence, are being used by some to control or regulate the human relationship with God. Had their believers kept a direct and unmediated contact with the Divine, free of the divisiveness and political bias transmitted by many of their religious leaders and preachers, nothing would be standing in their way to overcome the religious differences between the children of Abraham. This is not a suggestion to get rid of those vitally important systems, but to encourage more self-criticism and embolden people to stand up against those community leaders who, in the name of God, spread rifts and disputes.

Final Thoughts

It is common nowadays for Jews, Christians, and Muslims to affectionately refer to Abraham as "our father." Given Abraham's biblical name, "the father of a multitude of nations,"[73] such a reference is completely understandable. The problem arises, however, when they, using their traditions and scriptures, seek to appropriate him as their own, and claim to be his true successors.

Abraham is considered the first proselyte to Judaism, and subsequently became the father of the Jewish people. It is, therefore, unsurprising that Jews throughout the generations have taken pride in their descent from Abraham. The Jewish sages, therefore, commonly referred to the first patriarch in their teachings as "Abraham our father" (*Avrahām Avīnu*).[74] They did not consider him as the father of the Jews alone. Expounding on this name, they agree that "in the beginning you were father to every man, and eventually you became the father of the whole world."[75] Maimonides went further by stating that "Abraham was the father of the whole world, because he taught them what faithfulness (*'emunāh*) is."[76]

The early Christians took issue with the Jewish reference to "Abraham our father." Saul of Tarsus, who was to become known to the world as Paul, the leading ideologist of early Christianity, made considerable use of the model of Abraham to justify the mission to the Gentiles. Pointing to the biblical verse (Genesis 15:6), "And he believed in the Lord; and He counted it to him for righteousness," Paul, in the fourth chapter of his Epistle to the Romans, argued that Abraham was said to be righteous by having faith in God before he was circumcised and therefore he is "the father of us all," the father of all believers.[77] For Paul, this verse proves that, in the case of Abraham, faith came before the Law, and therefore Abraham should not be considered as exclusively a Jewish figure. He calls the believers to "walk in the footsteps of the faith that our father Abraham had."[78]

Likewise, the Qur'ān suggests that Abraham was truly one of the original "submitters" or *muslims*, and that he could not be called a Jew or a Christian, as he lived before those religions came into being: "Abraham was not a Jew nor yet a Christian; but he was true in faith who submitted to God (*ḥanīfan musliman*)."[79] For the Muslims, God revealed Islam as the religion of the faithful, "the religion of your father Abraham."[80] But when the Qur'ān states that "the closest people to Abraham are those who follow him,"[81] it sends a clear message to all believers, inside and outside Islam, that being a lineal, physical descendant of Abraham is not a qualification or an entitlement. What the Qur'ān implies is that we need to be *spiritual* descendants of Abraham. We need to adhere to his values, like faithfulness, courage, determination, passion, humility, and generosity. We need to follow his ethical conduct—his pursuit of peace, his hospitality, his quest for justice, his belief in the sanctity of human life, and his kindness toward all humankind.

Abraham was "devoutly obedient to God and true in faith,"[82] but he was not a zealot; neither were his children. Zealotry means excessive intolerance and absolute denial of opposing views. A zealot would go about demonizing other people as absolutely evil and therefore deserving to be eliminated. Mainstream Islam and Judaism urge people to seek a balance and temper extremes by adhering to the happy medium, or what Maimonides terms as "Middle of the Road" (*Ha-Dērekh ha-'Emtza'īt*) mentioned earlier and what the Qur'ān defines as "the perfect [middle ground] in between."[83] Mainstream stresses interaction and integration rather than polarization and bifurcation. Mercy and compassion are median virtues that go hand-in-hand with moderation and tolerance. Thus, it is said in the Talmud that "anyone who is not compassionate to mankind cannot be truly a descendent of Abraham, our father."[84]

Prince Hasan ibn Talal of Jordan, an internationally renowned champion of interfaith dialogues, published an article in an Israeli newspaper, titled "The Descendents of Abraham Lost Their Way." In it, he appealed to both Jews and Muslims "to remember their common spiritual roots and recognize the foolishness of mixing religion and politics." "None of our communities," he argued, "has a monopoly of truth; but we have common values, such as the pursuit of truth itself, which we are forbidden to subject to political arbitrary caprices."[85]

Chapter 5

The Gate of Ancestry

Abraham and Ishmael—a Scriptural Reconstruction

It is very clear that the biblical narrative of Ishmael's life in Genesis is incomplete, fragmentary, and episodic. There are only two sections dedicated to his life. One is about his birth (Chapter 16). The second is about Isaac's birth by Sarah and the subsequent expulsion of Ishmael and his mother Hagar to the wilderness (Chapter 21). In between there is only one mention of Ishmael, relating to God's promises to Abraham and his family and to the Covenant, which was marked by the circumcision of Abraham's entire male household, including Ishmael (Chapter 17). The next time we hear about him is during Abraham's funeral, when Ishmael and Isaac join together to mourn their father and bury him; and this is just a brief comment (Chapter 25).

What happened to Ishmael during the period between the biblical account relating to his exile, when Abraham was 100 years old, and the last account about the death of Abraham, when he was 175 years old? There is a gap of about 75 years, which is not accounted for in the Bible. Is there a reason for the curtain of silence? Are we to deduce that Abraham had no relations or contact whatsoever with his elder son, whom he obviously loved as any father would love his son?

The Bible is not a conventional history textbook. It selects from all the deeds and events of its protagonists only what it needs, primarily religious and educational material. The omission of that period in the story can only be explained by the shift of the narrative's attention to Isaac, to whom Abraham "passed the torch" as his divinely sanctioned heir, and who now became the ancestor of the People of Israel. From this perspective, the rest of Ishmael's life is no longer relevant to the continuity of God's covenant and, therefore, is unnecessary to be told. The great Jewish scholar and philosopher Maimonides suggested that Isaac became "essential" (*'iqār*) and Ishmael became "unessential" (*ṭafēl*) in the story once God told Abraham to listen to his wife Sarah's request to expel Hagar and Ishmael, and explained that "because your [spiritual] descendents will be through Isaac; and I will also make the son of the handmaid into a nation, because he is your [physical] descendent."[1]

Unfortunately, the consequence of this omission is the implied delegitimization of Ishmael, who is revered by Muslims as their spiritual ancestor and regarded by them as a direct progenitor of Prophet Muhammad. Therefore, the absence of the name Ishmael from the long list of personal names given today to Jewish children should come to us as no surprise. The historical Jewish-Muslim dispute and the contemporary Arab-Israeli conflict only helped to define Ishmael's name as illegitimate for Jews.

But exceptions can be found in the long list of early rabbis, who carried the name Ishmael.[2] One of them is Rabbi Ishmael ben Elisha (90–135 CE), one of the greatest sages of the Talmud who formulated the Thirteen Principles of Torah Interpretation, one of the "Ten Martyrs" tortured to death by the Romans after the Bar-Kochba rebellion, and a grandson of the high priest of the same name[3]. Why would a highly respected rabbinic family name their son after "a wild man whose hand will be against every one, and the hand of every one against him?"[4] Why would they adopt Ishmael's name, when the Zohar, one of the fundamental texts of Jewish mysticism, bashes him? It tells us that, from the day Isaac was born, as long as Ishmael was in Abraham's house, he was called not by his name, but was called "son of Hagar," because "in a place where gold exists, refuse is not mentioned."[5] Perhaps there is more to biblical Ishmael, the rejected son of Abraham, than we truly know? Is it possible that, in naming his child Ishmael, definitely an undesirable personal name, the son of the high priest wanted to make a statement?

Outline of Ishmael's Life

The biblical narrative of Ishmael's life can be divided into four periods:

A. Ishmael's Birth to Hagar (Genesis, Chapter 16)

1. Sarah is childless; Hagar is Sarah's Egyptian maidservant (Genesis 16:1).
2. Sarah offers Hagar to Abraham, hoping to obtain a child by her (Genesis 16:2).

3. When Hagar conceived Ishmael, she became despised in Sarah's eyes (Genesis 16:4).
4. Hagar fled when Sarah dealt harshly with her (Genesis 16:6).
5. The Angel of the Lord named her son Ishmael, stating that he will be a "wild ass of a man," in conflict with everyone and dwelling among his brethren outside the Land of Canaan (Genesis 16:11–12).
6. Hagar bore Ishmael to Abraham when he was eighty-six years old (Genesis 16:16).

B. Ishmael—Part of Covenant with Abraham (Genesis, Chapter 17)

1. Abraham says to God, "Oh, that [at least] Ishmael might live before You!" (Genesis 17:18).
2. God replies, "No, Sarah your wife shall bear you a son, and you shall call his name Isaac; I will establish My covenant with him for an everlasting covenant, and with his descendants after him. And as for Ishmael, I have heard you. Behold, I have blessed him, and will make him fruitful, and will multiply him exceedingly. He shall beget twelve princes, and I will make him a great nation. But My covenant I will establish with Isaac, whom Sarah shall bear to you at this set time next year" (Genesis 17:19–21).
3. Abraham circumcises Ishmael at the age of 13 (Genesis 17:25).

C. Isaac is Born and Ishmael is Cast Out (Genesis, Chapter 21)

1. Isaac is born when Ishmael is 14 years old (Genesis 21:1–8).
2. Ishmael is caught scoffing at Isaac on the day he was weaned (Genesis 21:8–9).
3. Hagar and Ishmael are cast out, but God tells Abraham that He will make a nation out of Ishmael because he is of Abraham's seed (Genesis 21:10–13).
4. God hears Ishmael's voice in the wilderness and calls Hagar and tells her that He will make Ishmael into a great nation (Genesis 21:18–18).
5. God is with Ishmael while he grows up and lives in the wilderness and learns to be an archer (Genesis 21:20).
6. Ishmael dwells in the wilderness of Paran and Hagar takes a wife from Egypt for him (Genesis 21:21).

GAP

D. Abraham Passes Away (Genesis, Chapter 25)
1. Abraham leaves the inheritance to Isaac only (Genesis 25:5).
2. Ishmael and Isaac bury their father (Genesis 25:9).

Filling In the Gap

The use of scriptural reconstruction to explain the omission in the biblical narrative is by no means to suggest that an arbitrary textual emendation is employed. In the absence of a biblical account, we are compelled to fill in the gap and expand on the narrative by consulting extra-biblical sources—Jewish texts that were canonically excluded from the Bible. Two of these texts are classified as Apocrypha—excluded writings preserved by the early Christians, and another two books of Midrash—anthologies of interpretive teachings and homiletical expositions of the biblical text compiled from the fifth through the twelfth centuries CE:

1. *Sēfer ha-Yashār* ("Book of Jasher")—Apocryphal chronicle mentioned several times in the Bible.
2. *Sēfer ha-Yovlīm* ("Book of Jubilees")—Apocryphal chronicle of Genesis traced back to second-century BCE.
3. *Pirkēi d'Rabbi Eliezer*—An eighth-century CE Palestinian midrashic commentary on the Book of Genesis.
4. *Bereshīt Rabbāh*—One of a ten-part set of fifth and sixth century CE midrashic collection of homiletical and narrative material, known as *Midrāsh Rabbāh* covering the Book of Genesis.

These and other Jewish texts will help us fill in the gap and shed new light on Ishmael, son of Abraham. Here is some of what these sources reveal.

Expulsion of Hagar and Ishmael[6]

> And Abraham rose up early in the morning, and took bread and a bottle of water. He sent her away with a bill of divorcement, and he took the veil, and he bound it around her waist, so that it should drag behind her to disclose the fact that she was a bondwoman. Not only this, but also because Abraham desired to see Ishmael, his son, and to see the way whereon they went.

Hagar and Ishmael in the Wilderness[7]

> And they [Hagar and Ishmael] dwelt in the wilderness of Paran with the inhabitants of the wilderness, and Ishmael was an archer, and he dwelt in

the wilderness a long time. And he and his mother afterward went to the land of Egypt, and they dwelt there, and Hagar took a wife for her son from Egypt, and her name was Meribah. And the wife of Ishmael conceived and bore four sons and two daughters, and Ishmael and his mother and his wife and children afterward went and returned to the wilderness. And they made themselves tents in the wilderness, in which they dwelt, and they continued to travel and then to rest monthly and yearly. And God gave Ishmael flocks and herds and tents on account of Abraham his father, and the man increased in cattle. And Ishmael dwelt in deserts and in tents, traveling and resting for a long time, and he did not see the face of his father.

Abraham's Visits of Ishmael[8]

After three years, Abraham went to see Ishmael his son, having sworn to Sarah that he would not descend from the camel in the place where Ishmael dwelt. He arrived there at midday and found there the wife of Ishmael. He said to her: "Where is Ishmael?" She said to him: "He has gone with his mother to fetch the fruit of the palms from the wilderness." He said to her: "Give me little bread and a little water, for my soul is faint after the journey in the desert." She said to him: "I have neither bread nor water." He said to her: "When Ishmael comes, tell him this story, and say to him: A certain old man came from the land of Canaan to see you, and he said 'Exchange the threshold of your house, for it is not good for you.'" When Ishmael came [home], his wife told him the story. A son of a wise man is like half a wise man. Ishmael understood. His mother sent and took for him a wife from her father's house, and her name was Fatimah.

Again after three years, Abraham went to see his son Ishmael, having sworn to Sarah as on the first occasion that he would not descend from the camel in the place where Ishmael dwelt. He came there at midday, and found there Ishmael's wife. He said to her: "Where is Ishmael?" She replied to him: "He has gone with his mother to feed the camels in the desert." He said to her: "Give me a little bread and water, for my soul is faint after the journey of the desert." She fetched it and gave it to him. Abraham arose and prayed before the Blessed Holy One for his son, and [thereupon] Ishmael's house was filled with all good things of the various blessings. When Ishmael came [home] his wife told him what had happened, and Ishmael knew that his father's love was still extended to him.

Ishmael returns to his Father with his Wife and Children[9]

And Ishmael then rose up and took his wife and his children and his cattle and all belonging to him, and he journeyed from there and he went to his father in the land of the Philistines. And Abraham related to Ishmael his son the transaction with the first wife that Ishmael took, according to what she did. And Ishmael and his children dwelt with Abraham many days in that land, and Abraham dwelt in the land of the Philistines a long time.

Isaac and Ishmael's Conversation, the Offering of Isaac Foretold[10]

And Isaac the son of Abraham was growing up in those days, and Abraham his father taught him the way of the Lord to know the Lord, and the Lord was with him. And when Isaac was thirty-seven years old, Ishmael his brother [who came from the wilderness of Paran to visit] was going about with him in the tent. And Ishmael boasted of himself to Isaac, saying, "I was thirteen years old when the Lord spoke to my father to circumcise us, and I did according to the word of the Lord which he spoke to my father, and I gave my soul unto the Lord, and I did not transgress his word which he commanded my father." And Isaac answered Ishmael, saying, "Why do you boast to me about this, about a little bit of your flesh which you did take from your body, concerning which the Lord commanded you. As the Lord lives, the God of my father Abraham, if the Lord should say unto my father, Take now your son Isaac and bring him up an offering before me, I would not refrain but I would joyfully accede to it." And the Lord heard the word that Isaac spoke to Ishmael, and it seemed good in the sight of the Lord, and he thought to try Abraham in this matter.

God's Commands Abraham with the Sacrifice[11]

And God tested Abraham. And He said to him: "Take your son." [Abraham] said: "I have two sons." [God] said: "Your only one." [Abraham] said: "But this one is an only son to his mother, and the other is an only son to his mother." [God] said: "The one whom you love." [Abraham] said to Him: "Both of them I love." [God] said: "Take Isaac."

Ishmael Participates in the Sacrifice[12]

And Abraham went with Isaac his son to bring him up as an offering before the Lord, as He had commanded him. And Abraham took two of his young men with him, Ishmael the son of Hagar and Eliezer his servant, and they went together with them. While they were walking in the road the young men spoke these words to each other. And Ishmael said to Eliezer, "Now my father Abraham is going with Isaac to bring him up for a burnt offering to the Lord, as He commanded him. Now when he returns he will give unto me all that he possesses, to inherit after him, for I am his first born." And Eliezer answered Ishmael and said, "Surely Abraham did cast you away with your mother, and swear that you should not inherit any thing of all he possesses, and to whom will he give all that he has, with all his treasures, but unto me his servant, who has been faithful in his house, who has served him night and day, and has done all that he desired me? To me will he bequeath at his death all that he possesses."

Abraham Remarries Hagar (a)[13]

Rebecca first saw Isaac as he was coming from the way of Be'ēr-Lahai-Roi, the dwelling-place of Hagar, whither he had gone after the death of his mother, for the purpose of reuniting his father with Hagar, or, as she is also called, Keturah.

Abraham Remarries Hagar (b)[14]

[Keturah] This is Hagar. Because we learn that, after Hagar separated from Abraham and went astray following her father's idolatry, she repented and did good deeds; therefore her name changed to Keturah, which alludes to her connection to good deeds. Keturah means connected, and this is why Abraham sent for her and took her for a wife. Thus, the name change atones for sins, and therefore her name was changed to Keturah in order to atone for her sins.

Abraham's Last Words to his Children and Grandchildren[15]

And in the forty-second jubilee, in the first year of the seventh week, Abraham called Ishmael, and his twelve sons, and Isaac and his two sons, and the six sons of Keturah, and their sons. And he commanded them that they should observe the way of the Lord; that they should work righteousness, and love each his neighbor, and act on this manner amongst all men; that they should each so walk with regard to them as to do judgment and righteousness on the earth. That they should circumcise their sons, according to the covenant which He had made with them, and not deviate to the right hand or the left of all the paths which the Lord had commanded us; and that we should keep ourselves from all fornication and uncleanness. And if any woman or maid commit fornication amongst you, burn her with fire, and let them not commit fornication with her after their eyes and their heart; and let them not take to themselves wives from the daughters of Canaan; for the seed of Canaan will be rooted out of the land. And he told them of the judgment of the giants, and the judgment of the Sodomites, how they had been judged on account of their wickedness, and had died on account of their fornication, and uncleanness, and mutual corruption through fornication.

Isaac, Ishmael and Jacob join in Festival with Abraham for the Last Time[16]

And it came to pass in the first week in the forty-fourth jubilee, in the second year, that is, the year in which Abraham died, that Isaac and Ishmael came from the Well of the Oath [i.e., Beersheba] to celebrate the Feast of Weeks [i.e., Shavu'ōt]—that is, the feast of the first fruits of the harvest—to Abraham, their father, and Abraham rejoiced because his two sons had come. For Isaac had many possessions in Beersheba, and Isaac wanted to go and see his possessions and to return to his father. And in those days Ishmael came to see his father, and they both came together, and Isaac offered a sacrifice for a burnt-offering, and presented it on the altar of his father, which he had made in Hebron. And he offered a thank-offering and made a feast of joy before Ishmael, his brother. And Rebecca made new cakes from the new grain, and gave them to Jacob, her son, to take them to Abraham, his father, from the first fruits of the land, that he might eat and bless the Creator of all things before he died. And Isaac, too, sent by the hand of Jacob to Abraham a best thank-offering, that he might eat and drink. And he ate and drank, and blessed the Most High God, Who has created heaven and earth, and given them to the children of men who have made all the fat things of the earth, that they might eat and drink and bless their Creator.

[Abraham's last prayer:] "And now I give thanks unto You, my God, because You have caused me to see this day: behold, I am one hundred three score and fifteen years, an old man and full of days, and all my days have been unto me peace. The sword of the adversary has not overcome me in all that You have given me and my children all the days of my life until this day. My God, may Your mercy and Your peace be upon Your servant, and upon the seed of his sons, that they may be to You a chosen nation and an inheritance from amongst all the nations of the earth from henceforth unto all the days of the generations of the earth, unto all the ages."

The Death and Burial of Abraham[17]

And he placed two fingers of Jacob on his eyes, and he blessed the God of gods, and he covered his face and stretched out his feet and slept the sleep of eternity, and was gathered to his fathers. And notwithstanding all this Jacob was lying in his bosom, and knew not that Abraham, his father's father, was dead. And Jacob awoke from his sleep, and behold Abraham was cold as ice, and he said: "Father, father!" but there was none that spoke, and he knew that he was dead. And he arose from his bosom and ran and told Rebecca, his mother; and Rebecca went to Isaac in the night and told him; and they went together, and Jacob with them, and a lamp was in his hand, and when they had gone in they found Abraham lying dead. And Isaac fell on the face of his father, and wept and kissed him. And the voices were heard in the house of Abraham, and Ishmael his son arose, and went to Abraham his father, and wept over Abraham his father, he and all the house of Abraham, and they wept with a great weeping. And his sons Isaac and Ishmael buried him in the Cave of the Doubled [Burials], near Sarah his wife, and they wept for him forty days, all the men of his house, and Isaac and Ishmael, and all their sons, and all the sons of Keturah in their places, and the days of weeping for Abraham were ended. And he lived three jubilees and four weeks of years, one hundred and seventy-five years, and completed the days of his life, being old and full of days.

Why Was Ishmael Banished?

According to the famed biblical commentator, Nachmanides, it was all about a power struggle within the Abraham household. He makes an unusual criticism of both Sarah and Abraham for causing this. Sarah, he writes, was jealous of Hagar's pregnancy, and when she complained to Abraham, he in turn responded, "Here is your maidservant, do what you like with her; and Sarai afflicted her and [Hagar] fled from her" (Genesis 15:6). Nachmanides expounds on this verse saying, "our matriarch [Sarah] committed sin by this affliction [of Hagar] and so did Abraham by permitting her to do so. And God heard her affliction and gave her a son, who would be 'a wild ass of a man' (Genesis, 16: 12) to afflict the seed of Abraham and Sarah with all kinds of affliction."[18]

In other words, Nachmanides, seeing the first banishment of Hagar as future history in the making, blames the enmity between the descendents of Ishmael, the Arabs, and the descendants of Isaac, the Jews, on the harshness of Sarah toward Hagar and the callousness of Abraham. Thus, when Sarah gave her handmaid, Hagar, to Abraham for a wife, and Hagar conceived, the seeds of the Arab-Israeli conflict had been planted. Perhaps Nachmanides was aware of the commentary by David Kimhi (1160–1235), an earlier medieval rabbi and biblical commentator who is known by his Hebrew acronym RaDak. Criticizing Sarah's affliction of Hagar, RaDak writes that "it is inappropriate for a person to do whatever he wants to another person under him," and suggests that we ought to learn from our ancestors' experience and that this story is in the Bible for a reason: "So that man acquires good traits and distances himself from the bad ones." In other words, the affliction of Hagar is an example of what one should not do.[19]

The second banishment of Hagar, this time with her son Ishmael, took the struggle over the inheritance to a higher level of confrontation. The following dispute between two important rabbis, Rabbi Akiba and Rabbi Shimon Bar Yohai, is quite revelatory. In this dispute, Rabbi Akiba represents the majority view that the banishment of Ishmael at the request of Sarah was justified given Ishmael's many transgressions. These transgressions, which were detailed in the Midrash literature,[20] were picked up by the famed commentator Rashi, who listed heinous crimes such as idolatry, adultery, and attempted murder (of Isaac).[21] Rabbi Shimon Bar Yohai represents the virtually silent minority view that the banishment of Ishmael had nothing to do with his bad behavior or evil ways, but with a power struggle within Abraham's family over inheritance. Here is the dispute:

> And [Sarah] said to Abraham: "Cast out this bondwoman and her son" (Genesis, 21:10). This verse, says Rabbi Akiba [offering a list of sources], teaches us that Sarah Our Mother saw Ishmael building altars, hunting grasshoppers and engaging in idolatry. She said: "Should I allow my son to learn such things and practices and then have the Name of Heaven be desecrated?" [Abraham] said to her: "After we do something for someone aren't we indebted

to him? After we make her [Hagar] a mistress and elevate her to fame, are we just going to banish her? What will people say? There is no evidence that the Name of Heaven was desecrated." She answered: "If that's what you say, let God judge between my words and yours."

Said Rabbi Shimon Bar Yohai: "This is one of four cases where Rabbi Akiba and I interpret differently and my interpretation seems more acceptable than his. I say: Heaven forbid that such be in the house of such a righteous one. Is it possible that he for whom it was written, 'For I have known him, to the end that he may command his children and his household, etc.,' (Genesis, 18: 19), to engage in idolatry in his house? The word (*tzḥōq*), 'mocking', that appears here is but an allusion to the inheritance. When Isaac was born to Abraham everyone rejoiced, saying: 'A son was born to Abraham! A son was born to Abraham, he will inherit the world!' So Ishmael [hearing that] mocked and said: 'Don't be fools, don't be fools! I am the firstborn and am entitled to a double portion [which is the firstborn's right]'. From the verse, 'And she [Sarah] said unto Abraham: Cast out this bondwoman and her [son]; for he shall not be heir, the son of this bondwoman, with my son, with Isaac' (Genesis, 21: 10), you learn that 'mocking' refers to inheritance. And my interpretation therefore seems more acceptable than that of Rabbi Akiba."[22]

Nachmanides quotes this dispute and another important source, Rabbi Abraham ibn Ezra, who accepts the literal interpretation that "*tziḥūq*" means "scoffing," "mimicry," or "playing frivolously," as is normal for every boy, and suggests that Sarah was simply jealous of Ishmael's seniority. But Nachmanides adds his own interpretation. He submits that the "*tziḥūq*" incident appears to take place during the feast or on the day that Isaac was weaned, when he was 24 months old. So how can Ishmael be blamed to be a bad influence on such an infant?[23]

We can only understand the dispute between Rabbi Akiba and Rabbi Shimon Bar Yohai against the background of the legal system in force during Abraham's time. For this we need to consult Deuteronomy[24] that lists, among others, the laws of domestic life, three of which refer to the situation at issue: marriage with a female war captive, the inheritance rights of the firstborn, and the punishment of a disobedient son. The juxtaposition of these three laws in that order may implicitly support the argument that Abraham's act in the Hagar-Ishmael affair was in accordance with the laws of his time.

The first law rules that a female war captive, once brought into the captor's household and married to him, must enjoy the full rights and duties of a wife, must not be dishonored and reduced to the level of a bondwoman, and must not be cast out unless formally divorced.[25] Although Hagar was not a war captive but Sarah's bondwoman, this law applied in her situation. Once given to Abraham as a wife, she seemed to enjoy spousal rights until the conflict with Sarah erupted. Once Sarah demanded that Hagar be banished, the latter received a formal divorce paper from Abraham.

The second law rules that in the case of a two-wife family, one beloved and the other hated, where the firstborn son was given birth by the hated one, the double portion due to him given his seniority is inalienable, even though his mother was the one less loved. [26] Based on this law, Ishmael was right in demanding the double portion, unless he clearly violated the next law.

This next and third law rules that a disobedient son, a delinquent who throws off the authority of his parents and God, deserves a harsh punishment, even death, "so [that] you shall put away the evil from your midst," and "that you shall not defile the land which the Lord your God has given you for an inheritance."[27] Based on this law, if indeed Ishmael was a rebellious son, Abraham had the right to disentitle him from the inheritance of his property. This is why the majority of Jewish sources, in justifying the banishment of Ishmael, refer to his alleged heinous crimes.

Still, the big question is whether he committed this, or any, crime. It seems the position taken by Rabbi Shimon bar Yohai in this controversy is much more acceptable, as he refutes the allegation of Ishmael's deplorable crimes and suggests that this argument may only cause the defamation of his parents, who raised a "juvenile outlaw" in their home for 14 years. This is not the type of education Abraham would have given his children. There is nothing in the biblical text to substantiate the heavy accusations leveled against Ishmael in the *midrashīm* that are quoted by Rashi. They seem to be more a propaganda campaign aimed at justifying the severity of Sarah's action and fulfilling certain political and theological needs by bashing the "other" son of Abraham.

Abraham's Visits of Ishmael in the Hijaz

The biblical narrative records Abraham's journeys throughout the Land of Canaan in response to God's command, "Arise, walk through the land in the length of it and in the breadth of it; for unto you will I give it."[28] Abraham "conquered" the Promised Land with his feet, walking from one place to another, from Shechem in Samaria via Beth El, Jerusalem, and Hebron in the Judean Hills down south as far as Beersheba in the Negev, and built there altars to acknowledge and pray to God.[29] Scholars identified the busy north-south trade route as "The Patriarchs' Route" (Hebrew: *Dērekh ha-Avōt*).[30] But, when necessary, Abraham journeyed beyond the Land of Canaan. When there was famine in the land, he went with his family down to Egypt.[31]

Similarly, when Abraham needed for obvious emotional reasons to reunite with his banished son, he did it by journeying far beyond the Land of Canaan. The Midrash even tells us that, when Abraham sent Hagar and Ishmael away to the southern desert, he tied a veil around Hagar's waist so that it would drag behind not only to disclose her bondwoman's status, "but also because Abraham desired to see Ishmael, his son, and to see the path they have taken."[32] And indeed Abraham later visited him, a story related in detail by both the Midrash and Islamic exegesis (see above).[33] For Ishmael, the visits by his father meant that "his father's love was still extended to him."[34]

Abraham's visits of Ishmael can also be understood within the context of his traveling practice.[35] The north-south trade route, used by merchants and travelers of his time, continued into Arabia and passed through Mecca. Within this context, the Qur'ān's account of Abraham's visits of Ishmael in Mecca in the Hijaz and his mission to spread monotheism by building there a House of God converges with the biblical narrative. The Qur'ān relates the words of God as follows:[36] "Remember We made the House [of God, i.e., the Ka'bah] a place of assembly for men and a place of safety; and take you the Station of Abraham as a place of prayer; and We covenanted with Abraham and Ishmael, that they should sanctify My House for those who circumambulates it, or use it as a retreat, or bow, or prostrate themselves [therein in prayer]. And remember that Abraham and Ishmael raised the foundations of the House [with this prayer]: 'Our Lord! Accept [this service] from us: for You are the All-Hearing, the All-Knowing.'"

Qiṣaṣ al-Anbiyā' devotes a longer account of Abraham's building of the Ka'bah, where the First Adam erected his "Well-appointed House." After God commanded Abraham and Ishmael to build the House of God, and after they had finished it, the account continues, God ordered Abraham to get on one corner and call on the people to perform the pilgrimage to Mecca.[37] Ever since this dramatic event, the pilgrimage to Mecca, the *Ḥajj*, became one of the Five Pillars of Islam. Following the injunction of the Qur'ān, every Muslim who can afford the journey should attempt to perform it at least once in a lifetime, because "the pilgrimage thereto is a duty men owe to God."[38]

Final Thoughts

From the above texts that fill in the gap in the biblical narrative, one can easily draw two important conclusions:

1. The relations between Abraham and Ishmael continued without interruption.
2. Ishmael and Isaac maintained close brotherly relations.

The very last text describes in detail the death and funeral of Abraham, and mentions what Genesis records only briefly: "And Isaac and Ishmael *his sons* buried him."[39] Two things can be learned from this verse. One, that this is the only time that the biblical narrative speaks of them together, calling both of them "his sons," meaning that the death of Abraham finally brought them together and signaled a new era of direct relationship. Two, what Rashi explains, that we learn that "Ishmael repented and permitted Isaac to precede him [at the funeral] and this is [a sign of] a good old age that was [previously] attributed to Abraham."[40] The Midrash expresses the same view, relating to the fact that Ishmael took a long journey from the far end of the desert to give respect to his deceased father and gave precedence to Isaac.[41] In other words, Ishmael, against the protocol of seniority and out of humility, insists that Isaac become first. With one small act, Ishmael demonstrates, according to Jewish sources, his total transformation from a "wild man" to a pious man. Rashi, commenting on Genesis' remark that Ishmael "expired and died," elevated him to the level of a righteous man, explaining that the term "expiration" is used only in reference to righteous people.[42] The Talmud goes even further, suggesting that Ishmael repented not at the end of his days, but during the lifetime of Abraham, which may explain why the father and son would continue their relationship without interruption. It says:

> And whence do we know that Ishmael repented while Abraham was still alive—From the discussion, which took place between Rabina and R. Hama b. Buzi, when they were once sitting before Raba while he was dozing. Said Rabina to R. Hama b. Buzi: "Do your people really maintain that wherever the term 'expiring' [*gevi'āh*] is used in connection with the 'gathering in' [*asifāh*] of any person, it implies that that person died righteous?" "That is so," he replied. "But, what then of the generation of the Flood?" [he asked.] "We only make this inference," he replied, "if both, 'expiring' and 'gathering in' are mentioned." "But," he rejoined, "what of Ishmael, who is said both to have 'expiring' and 'been gathered in'?" At this point Raba awoke and heard them. "Children," he said, "this is what R. Yohanan has said: 'Ishmael repented in the lifetime of his father'. [We know this] because it says, 'And Isaac and Ishmael his sons buried him' [Genesis, 25:9]. But perhaps the text arranges them in the order of their wisdom? If that were so, then why in the verse, 'And Esau and Jacob his sons buried him' [Genesis 35:29] are they not arranged in the order of their wisdom? What we have to say is that the fact that the text placed Isaac first shows that Ishmael made way for him, and from the fact that he made way for him we infer that he repented in Abraham's lifetime."[43]

Furthermore, the fact that Abraham's story ended with the non-accidental comments, "now these are the chronicles of Ishmael, son of Abraham,"[44] and shortly later, "now these are the chronicles of Isaac, son of Abraham,"[45] clearly shows that, despite Ishmael's misrepresentation in the Bible, he is regarded at the very end as a son in the total sense of the word, as equal a son as Isaac; not "son of Hagar" anymore, but "son of Abraham." Interestingly, the biblical story concludes with the naming of the 12 sons of Ishmael and stating: "These are the sons of Ishmael, and these are their names, by their villages, and by their encampments; twelve princes according to their nations," paralleling the 12 tribes of Israel.[46] In the final book of the Bible, the Chronicles that gives concise annals of humanity, we see the following citation: "Abram is the same as Abraham. The sons of Abraham: Isaac and Ishmael."[47] Short and to the point: Isaac and Ishmael are equal sons.

Expounding on the phrase "Abram (Hebrew: Avrām) is the same as Abraham (Hebrew: Avrahām)," the Talmud explains: "At first he became father to Arām and finally, he became father to the whole of the world."[48] The change of name implies a complete transformation. The original Hebrew name Avram sounds like a combination of two words, *Av-Arām* and means literally "father of Arām," referring to Arām Naharāyim, which is literally "Arām of the two rivers," that is, Mesopotamia. But, when God told Abram: "Go forth out of your country, and from your kindred, and from your father's house, unto the land that I will show you," he wanted him to ultimately shake off the narrow confines of tribal particularism and adopt the universal idea of "father of the whole of the world." This came about when God established his covenant with him and changed his name to Abraham: "Neither shall your name any more be called Abram, but your name shall be Abraham, for the father of a multitude of nations have I made you."[49] The new Hebrew name *Avrahām* is assumed to be composed of two parts *Av* (father) and *Hamōn* (multitude). With this new name, Abraham became the father of all mankind. Therefore, the next citation in the Chronicles, "The sons of Abraham: Isaac and Ishmael," brings closure to the ancestral issue—Abraham is the father of both Isaac and Ishmael, and his descendants can refer to him as "our father" (*avīnu* in Hebrew; *abūna* in Arabic). This affirms the sublime idea of a universal unity (represented by Abraham) in diversity (represented by the two sons)—the vision of peaceful coexistence of nations.

This perhaps explains why Elisha, the son of the high priest, who lived during and immediately after the destruction of the Second Temple, was proud to name his child Ishmael.

The primordial relationship of Abraham to his sons, Ishmael and Isaac, impacts the current Muslim-Jewish equation. In the union of Abraham and Hagar we find the genesis of the Arab nation and the Islamic faith. From a Jewish perspective, the Arab nation, brought forth by Abraham and Hagar, is one-half Jewish. Likewise, from a Muslim perspective, the Jewish people brought forth by Abraham and Sarah are one-half Muslim. The Islamic belief that Abraham is the first Muslim has an ironic implication; it makes Isaac, not only Ishmael, a Muslim too. Perhaps, Muslims and Jews reject each other not because they are different, but because they are—like the step-brotherly relationship between Ishmael and Isaac—the same and different. They don't accept the other because the other is part of one's self. As you will see in a later chapter, language is quite revelatory. It speaks its own truth. Jews adopted Abraham's name *'Ivrī* עברי ("Hebrew" in English) as their modern name. It is not by accident that, in the Hebrew language, an Arab is called *'Aravī* ערבי—a perfect anagram, a word play that reproduces the same letters in another order, like mirror images of each other. How ironic!

Chapter 6

The Gate of Morality

The Sacrifice of Isaac/Ishmael—Some Forgotten Lessons

No other scriptural story can be found where Jewish and Islamic traditional sources take such a completely divergent course and around which conflicting religious views and traditions have evolved, than that of Abraham's near-sacrifice of his son.

According to Jewish and Christian traditions, Isaac, with whom God's covenant with Abraham was established, is the son who went through a near-sacrifice on Mount Moriah, an act known as the *'Aqeidāh*, or "Binding." This chilling event became a central component of Jewish theology and liturgy. No other single event, with the exception of the awesome drama of the giving of the Torah at Mount Sinai, had such an overwhelming effect on the emotionality of the Jewish people. The fact that this perplexing biblical account—the twenty-second chapter of the Book of Genesis—is recited at the opening of the Jewish daily morning prayer and is read every Rosh Ha-Shanāh, the Jewish New Year celebration, at the time when the first blow of the Shofār was sounded, should not come to us as a surprise. The Shofār, a Hebrew word for "horn," represents the horns of the sacrificial ram that served as a substitute for Isaac. The recalling of the awesome trial of Abraham and his triumphant affirmation of his faith in God reminds Jews that God blesses those who submit to a divine calling without reservation, and sets the stage for the worshiper to plea to God to extend His forgiveness to them and all transgressors.

The Islamic tradition, on the other hand, identified Isaac's older brother, Ishmael, as the "*Dhabīḥ*," or "Sacrificed," and built around it both the ritual

Ḥajj to Mecca, a momentous event in the life of every Muslim devotee and one of the prescribed Pillars of Islam, and the festive *'Īd al-Aḍḥā* ("Feast of the Sacrifice") that commemorates the attempted sacrifice of Ishmael by slaughtering hundreds of sheep, cows, and camels and donating portions of the meat to the poor and the needy. The Islamic version of the sacrifice is very real in the minds of Muslims, especially given their solemn belief that the Prophet Muhammad was a descendent of Ishmael.

The terms used in Hebrew and Arabic for "sacrifice" are etymologically related, deriving from the same linguistic family. The root *'a.q.d.* appears in both languages denoting "to bind" or "to tie." The root *z.v.ḥ.* in Hebrew and the root *dh.b.ḥ.* in Arabic stem from the same source meaning "to sacrifice" or "to slaughter."

In both traditions, the scriptural story points to Abraham's complete obedience and faithfulness to God. This is the only point of agreement between Judaism and Islam about this story. Perhaps, instead of arguing about who is the son that was sacrificed, or intended to be sacrificed, by the Patriarch Abraham, Jews and Muslims should shift their focus to properly appreciating the moral teachings of this controversial incident. This shift in context may bring them to the realization that the lessons to be learned from this ancient human drama can bring them together as members of the human commonwealth. Perhaps this shift will help them realize that the fatal rescuing of Abraham's sons by God ultimately allowed the establishment of two separate genealogical lines that have created Judaism and Islam, not as contenders for the Truth, but as two sprouts sprung from one stem by God's design. Both Ishmael and Isaac went through a near-sacrifice and their lives were spared because they had their own destiny to fulfill. In the case of Ishmael, his life was spared and then he had to be banished along with his mother Hagar to the far-southern desert so that he could go about creating his Arab nation, which he might not have done had he stayed with his father. Perhaps, Islam would not have been created. In the case of Isaac, his life was spared so that he could go about fulfilling God's promises to his father and build the Hebrew nation.

Egypt's president, Anwar Al-Sadat, the first Arab leader to sign a peace treaty with Israel, saw Abraham's attempted sacrifice of his son as a source of inspiration for his "trip of peace," as he called it, to Jerusalem. In his address to the Knēsset, Israel's parliament, on November 20, 1977, he said: "When Abraham—peace be upon him—great-grandfather of the Arabs and Jews, submitted to God; I say when God Almighty ordered him, and to Him Abraham went, with dedicated sentiments, not out of weakness, but through a giant spiritual force and by a free will, to sacrifice his very own son, prompted by a firm and unshakable belief in ideals that lend life a profound significance."[1] For implementing a noble idea whose time had not yet come, this courageous leader was assassinated. But this idea—the commonality found in the shared ancestry represented by Abraham and the blood tie that justified the making of peace—was not killed.

The Story of the 'Aqeidāh

On the surface, God's command of Abraham to sacrifice his son seems to be an offense to our common morality, and, even more to the spirit of His own teaching. After all Abraham was instructed to do something that is contrary to the new message he introduced to mankind—that there is One God in the universe Who, in His love and mercy for mankind, desires to do good to man and does not desire to see him harming himself or the people around him. But, the fascinating story of the *'Aqeidāh* has a deeper level. It begins with the revelatory verse "And God tried Abraham."[2]

Pirkēi Avōt tells that "our father Abraham, peace be upon him, was tested by ten trials (pl. *nisyonōt*), yet he stood firm through all of them, to make known how great was the love our father Abraham, peace be upon him, [for God]."[3] Based on the chronology of the Torah narratives, Maimonides details the ten trials as follows:[4]

1. He was commanded to leave the land of his birth for an unspecified land.
2. He encountered famine in the Land of Canaan and had to flee to Egypt.
3. He faced the abduction of Sarah by Pharaoh.
4. He was forced to battle the four kings to save his nephew Lot.
5. He took Hagar for a wife after giving up hope to bear a child through Sarah.
6. He was commanded to circumcise himself at an old age.
7. He faced the abduction of Sarah this time by the King of Grar.
8. He faced the banishment of Hagar when she was pregnant.
9. He was asked to expel Hagar and his son, Ishmael, to the wilderness.
10. He was commanded to offer his son Isaac as a sacrifice.

Pirkēi d'Rabbi Eliezer, which devotes a whole section under the title "The Trials of Abraham," also lists ten trials.[5] Although basing the first two on the Midrash, the very last one is also the *'Aqeidāh*:

1. He was forced to hide underground for 13 years when Nimrod sought to kill him.
2. He was put into prison for ten years and then thrown into a burning furnace by Nimrod.

3. As #1 above
4. As #2 above
5. As #3 above
6. As #4 above
7. He encountered God in the vision of the Covenant between the Parts.
8. As #6 above
9. As #9 above
10. As #10 above

From the above listings, one can easily see that, on ten separate occasions, God tested Abraham with exceedingly severe trials, with the last one, the *'Aqeidāh,* being the ultimate, most severe test. From a Jewish perspective, the intended sacrifice by Abraham of Isaac, the long-sought son whom God repeatedly promised him and Sarah to be born at their very late age and become his progeny that inherits his legacy and continues his cause of promoting awareness of the One God, was the hardest trial to endure.

So what does the biblical narrative tell us about the *'Aqeidāh*?[6] It tells us how God, without giving Abraham any prior hint or warning and without revealing His intention, demanded him to take his son Isaac to a mountaintop in the land of Moriah "and offer him there as a burnt-offering." Thereafter, Abraham, in complete faithfulness to God, set out with Isaac and two men to the designated place, where he was ready to slay his son on an altar he built for that purpose. But, at the last minute, God's angel intervened and called him to desist, whereupon Abraham offered up a ram he sighted nearby "caught in the thicket by his horns" as a burnt-offering in substitution of his son. According to Rashi,[7] God did not "change His mind" at the last moment, and spare Isaac's life. Rather, He never intended that Isaac be slaughtered in the first place. It was His last trial of Abraham. When he passed it, God spoke through the angel, declaring, "For now I know that you are a God-fearing man, seeing that you have not withheld your only son from Me," and repeating God's promise to Abraham, "I will bless you greatly, and increase your offspring like the stars of the sky and the sand on the seashore. Your offspring shall inherit their enemies' gate. All the nations of the world shall be blessed through your descendants; all because you obeyed Me."

We are told in the story that it was not only Abraham who carried out the perceived will of God, but also Isaac. This willing self-sacrifice on the part of Isaac has become a paradigm of martyrdom in Jewish tradition, a complete willingness to give up one's life for one's beliefs, to die *'al qiddūsh Ha-Shēm*, "in sanctification of God's Name." This story also gave rise to the Jewish concept of the animal scapegoat that found expression in a slaughter ritual during the days of the Holy Temple in Jerusalem, and, even today on the eve of Yom Kippūr, when many Orthodox Jews still observe the archaic rite of *kapparōt*—a vicarious sacrifice of "atonement" (*kapparāh,* the singular form) for the sins committed during the year gone by—by performing the "scapegoat rooster" ritual.

The Story of the Dhabīḥ

The Qur'ān writes that "Abraham was tried by his Lord with certain commands,"[8] but it makes a very short reference to Abraham's sacrifice of his son and omits the identity of the son and the place of sacrifice. It says: "Then, when [the son] reached [the age of serious] work with him, he [Abraham] said, 'O my son! I see in a vision that I offer you in sacrifice, now let's see what your view is!' [The son] said, 'O my father! Do as you are commanded, you will find me, if God so wills, one practicing patience and constancy!' So when they had both submitted their wills [to God], and he had laid him prostrate on his forehead [for sacrifice], We called out to him, 'O Abraham! You have already fulfilled the vision!' Thus, indeed do We reward those who do right. For this was obviously a trial. And We ransomed him with a momentous sacrifice, and We left [this blessing] for him among generations [to come] in later times—'Peace and salutation to Abraham!'"[9]

According to the Islamic tradition, Abraham's vision took place near Mecca. Some would identify it with the valley of Minā, six miles north of Mecca, where a commemoration sacrifice is annually celebrated as a rite of the *Ḥajj* on the tenth of Dhū al-Ḥijjah, the "Feast of the Sacrifice," in memory of the sacrifice of Abraham of his son. Others say the original place of sacrifice was near the hill of Marwah, the companion hill to Safā, where Ishmael was raised.

More problematic, however, is the question of the identity of the son who was sacrificed. Early Muslim exegetes disagreed as to whether the son, unnamed in the Qur'ān, is Isaac or Ishmael. *Qiṣaṣ al- Anbiyā'* admits that "among the religious scholars there is a difference of opinion as to who is the sacrifice,"—Ishmael or Isaac—and devotes a broad discussion to this question.[10] Abu Ja'far Muhammad ibn Jarir Al-Tabari (c.839–923), one of the greatest historians of early Islam, presents in his *Ta'rīkh al-Rusul wal-Mulūk* the two arguments in details, but believes that Isaac is actually the sacrificed son.[11]

Over many years, the Islamic commentary literature was engaged in a debate as each school presented its own sources and proofs in support of one argument against the other. But by the ninth or tenth century, Muslim scholars had reached a consensus that Ishmael, increasingly associated with Mecca and identified as the ancestor of the Arabs, was the *Dhabīh* or the "sacrificed."[12]

So what does the Islamic tradition tell us about the *Dhabīh*? *Qiṣaṣ al-Anbiyā'* presents a detailed account of the story.[13] Abraham, it tells, was dreaming that God said, "Oh Abraham, arise and present the sacrifice!" At dawn, Abraham took one hundred ewes and sacrificed them. The next night he again dreamt that he heard God's words, "Oh Abraham, arise and present the sacrifice!" Abraham asked "But what am I to sacrifice? What sacrifice? What is my sacrifice? What am I to sacrifice?" God said, "If there is someone besides Me whom you love, sacrifice him." Then He said, "Sacrifice your son." Abraham realized that he was meant to sacrifice Ishmael. That morning he told Hagar: "I have a dear friend who asks for this boy and says: 'Bring him, that I may see him.' Now wash Ishmael's head and hair, then I will take him." When Hagar washed Ishmael and dressed him in clean clothes, Ishmael looked very beautiful. Ishmael's mother gazed upon his face and embraced him. Abraham then took a rope, put it in his sleeve, along with a knife, and set out for the mountains. Hagar remarked, "You say that you are going on a visit. But what will you do with the rope and the knife?" Abraham said, "Perhaps I will bring a sheep on my way back." Abraham walked ahead and told Ishmael to follow after him. And so Ishmael began walking behind Abraham.

Satan, disguised as a man, approached Ishmael and said, "Do you know where your father is taking you?" Ishmael answered, "He is taking me to a friend of his." Satan said, "He is talking you away to sacrifice you." Ishmael said, "What father ever sacrificed his son?" Satan replied, "He says he is going to sacrifice you at God's command." Ishmael said, "Should it be that a command has come from God, I will sacrifice my life if it is necessary." Thus Ishmael gave his consent. Satan thought, "I cannot influence this boy. I will go to Hagar." And Satan went off thinking, "Women are weaker." So he went to Hagar and said, "Do you know where Abraham is taking Ishmael?" She replied, "To a friend of his." Satan said, "He is taking him away to sacrifice him." Hagar replied, "What father has ever sacrificed his son?" Satan said, "God has ordered it." Hagar said, "Oh foolish one, if it be God's command, a thousand lives may be sacrificed." Satan lost hope and went after Ishmael again. He set about tempting him. But Ishmael called his father and said, "An old man has come who is offending me." Abraham replied, "That is Satan. Throw stones at him so he will go away." Ishmael picked up seven stones and threw them, and so throwing stones at that place has become a custom performed by the *Ḥajj* pilgrims in Mecca.

Then Abraham reached the top of the mountain. He threw the knife down on a stone and began to weep. Ishmael asked, "Why are you weeping?"

Abraham replied, "Oh son, in my dream I saw myself slaughter you." Ishmael said, "Oh father, you are soliciting the friendship of God; can a man who solicits God's friendship be asleep? If you hadn't been asleep, you wouldn't have seen that dream." Again Ishmael spoke, "Whatever God has commanded, carry it out! You may have lost your son, but I will have lost my life. Please perform your task." Abraham said, "Oh my son, how will you be able to bear it?" He replied, "If God, the mighty and glorious, so wishes, He will make me one of the steadfast." Then Ishmael spoke again, "Oh father, why didn't you tell me at home? I would have cast myself at my mother's feet and taken leave of her. Her beloved countenance would have remained before my eyes. In any case, I have three last wishes: first, that you bind my hands and feet tightly lest when I feel the pain of the knife, I writhe and my blood stains you garment; second, put my face downward, lest you behold my face and, moved by a father's compassion, are unable to wield the knife; third, take my shirt and my hair to my mother as a memento."

Thereupon, Abraham bound Ishmael's hands and feet and laid him face down on the earth. He held the knife at his throat, but it didn't cut. As much as he tried, the knife wouldn't cut. Seven times Abraham drew the knife, but it wouldn't cut into the flesh. Abraham threw down the knife, cursing it. Then a voice came forth from the knife, "Oh Friend of God, you tell me to cut, but the Glorious One tells me not to cut." We are told that the angels made a request of God to spare his life, after seeing from the Preserved Tablet that Prophet Muhammad will come from the line of Ishmael. Then a heavenly voice was heard: "Oh Abraham, your dream has come true...you have fulfilled your promise." As a reward, he was asked, "Take this ram and sacrifice it; your son remains safe." Then Abraham saw Archangel Gabriel bringing a ram, and rejoiced, "God is great! Praise be to God!" Thus came down the tradition of pronouncing the *takbīr*—announcing "*Allāhu Akbar*"—on the Feast of the Sacrifice.

Where Is Mount Moriah?

According to the biblical narrative in Genesis, the *'Aqeidāh* took place on a mountaintop in the land of Moriah (meaning literally, in Hebrew, "God's myrrh"). Jewish sages attributed significant importance to the exact identity of the place. During the times of King David and King Solomon, the site was identified as being in northern Jerusalem. It was purchased from a Jebusite by the name of Araunah by King David who built and turned the place into an altar. Because of the sanctity of the place, King Solomon built the First Temple there, the construction of which was completed in 957 BCE. Ever since then, Jews traditionally identify the location as Temple Mount.

One should know, however, that there was no consensus regarding the location of Moriah. When King Solomon died in 922 BCE, the Hebrew kingdom broke up into two states—Israel, with its capital at Samaria, and Judah, under the house of David, with its capital in Jerusalem. In those days, the royal house of the northern kingdom of Israel identified Moriah as Mount Gerizim. The small ancient community of the Samaritans (Hebrew: *Shomronīm*) still keeps this tradition—that the *'Aqeidāh* took place on Mount Gerizim, a location near Shechem. This is why they built their temple and still celebrate Passover there. As we have seen above, the Muslims identified Marwah, a mountain near Mecca, as Mount Moriah. Both names phonetically resemble each other.

We can only draw the conclusion that each nation wanted to have its own Moriah. They believed that the one who possesses it also appropriates Abraham and "owns" his legacy. They treated the relationship to Adam, the primordial man, in the same way. They believed that whoever established a historical connection to Adam made a causal connection to the beginning of human history. Jewish Midrashic texts identify Moriah with the Garden of Eden, where Adam and Eve were created.[14] Muslims, too, believe that their most exalted and venerated object, the set-in-gold Black Stone ("*Al-Ḥajar al-Aswad*") fell from heaven to show Adam where to build an altar and offer a sacrifice to God. Abraham, who found the Stone at the original site of Adam's altar, ordered his son Ishmael to build a new temple in which to imbed the Stone. This new temple is the Ka'bah.

We should all be reminded that, throughout history, man has favored the idea of mountains as a site of sacredness and their peaks as a place for divine revelation. For any devotee, a mountain is a place of awe and inspiration, where earth and heaven meet. Thus, the Psalmist writes, "I lift my eyes to the mountains—from where shall my help come? My help comes from the Lord, Who made heaven and earth."[15]

It was on a mountaintop in Beth El, near Jerusalem, that the Patriarch Jacob experienced his Ladder Dream and the presence of the House of God. It was on Mount Horeb (Hebrew: *Ḥorēv*), depicted as "Mountain of God," where Moses encountered God, who warned him as he was approaching the Burning Bush to "remove your shoes from your feet, for the place whereon you stand is holy ground."[16] In this calling, God made a clear statement that every spot on earth where God has manifested His presence, is holy ground. Thus, one of God's Names in Jewish tradition is "Ha-Maqōm," meaning, literally, "The Place." And for everybody, "The Place" is on the top of mountains. This is why Moses climbed Mount Sinai to receive

God's revelation. This is why Jesus delivered his sermon on a mount in Galilee, and why Muhammad delivered his last sermon on Mount Arafat. Therefore, the desire of every group to have its own Mount Moriah is totally understandable.

A Two-Part Story

The fact that the Qur'ān omits the identity of the son whom Abraham offered as sacrifice shows us that the name is not as important as the moral and educational lessons we can learn from this episode. In the discussion of the identity issue, *Qiṣaṣ al-Anbiyā'* even quotes traditions suggesting that Prophet Muhammad has stated, "I am the son of two sacrifices,"[17] meaning that both Ishmael and Isaac were sacrifices. Although Muhammad has always identified himself as a descendent of Ishmael, this statement suggests a clue that perhaps early Muslims believed that not only was Isaac sacrificed, but also Ishmael when he was banished to the wilderness.

Perhaps in making the *'Isrā'*[18] the night journey from the Sacred Mosque in Mecca, where Ishmael was sacrificed by Abraham according to Islamic tradition, to the Farthest Mosque in Mount Moriah in Jerusalem, where Isaac was sacrificed according to Jewish tradition, Prophet Muhammad wanted to connect the two versions of the sacrifice and send us a reconciliatory message—that he is indeed "the son of the two sacrifices," Isaac and Ishmael, and that the two sacrifices represent one story.

To accept this line of thought, we may need to question the basic supposition that Isaac was sacrificed because he was the only son Abraham loved, and suggest another one—that Abraham was actually asked to sacrifice the two children he loved. It is not by accident that both biblical stories in Genesis—the banishment of Ishmael (Chapter 21) and the sacrifice of Isaac (Chapter 22)—appear one after the other, and that they are listed as the last two out of the ten trials of Abraham. It shows that they were two parts of one story of a father who sacrificed both his sons, and from their perspectives, a story of two brothers who went through the same near-death experience in which their own father was the executioner. In the case of Ishmael, the banishment to the desert with bread and a bottle of water was a potential death, whereas the attempted sacrifice of Isaac was a sure death. Luckily, they both survived the ordeal.

To see the accounts of Ishmael and Isaac as a two-part story, the reader needs to look at it as one contextual unit with many literary similarities.[19] In both accounts, the divine demand for a sacrifice from Abraham is the same. In the case of Ishmael, God told Abraham, "Do not be troubled because of the boy and your slave," whereas in the case of Isaac, God told

Abraham, "Take your son, your only son you love, Isaac." Indeed, in the case of Ishmael, when Abraham showed agony and displeasure with the command, God told him not to question his wife's demand, despite the fact that this act seemed horrendous. Yet, in the case of Isaac, Abraham's anguish was not even reported. Obviously, Abraham learned the lesson. Since God told him not to question Sarah's demand, how could he now question God's command to perform a similarly horrendous act with his other son? In other words, to test Abraham with the sacrifice of Isaac, God wanted to prepare him for it by experiencing the sacrifice of Ishmael. They were two interrelated, consecutive events; two parts of one story.

In both cases, Abraham responded promptly and quickly. In the case of Ishmael, "And Abraham got up early in the morning, and took bread and a skin of water, and gave it to Hagar, placing it on her shoulder, and sent her away with the boy." In the case of Isaac, "And Abraham got up early in the morning, and saddled his donkey, and took two of his young men with him, along with his son Isaac; and he cut wood for the offering, and set out." In both accounts, the reader is convinced that the death of the child is imminent. In the case of Ishmael, his mother Hagar "set the boy under one of the bushes. She walked away, and sat down facing him, about a bowshot away; for she said, 'Let me not see the boy die.' And she sat there facing him, and she wept in a loud voice." In the case of Isaac, it is written, "And Abraham reached out and took the slaughter knife to slay his son." In both accounts, we see the divine intervention: in the case of Ishmael, "And God heard the boy weeping; and God's angel called to Hagar from heaven, and said to her, 'What's the matter, Hagar? Do not be afraid, for God has heard the boy's voice there where he is.'" In the case of Isaac, "God's angel called him from heaven and said, 'Abraham! Abraham!' He said, 'I am here,' 'Do not harm the boy. [the angel] said, Do not lay your hand upon him.'" In both accounts, the parents suddenly see a way out. In the case of Ishmael and Hagar, "God opened her eyes, and she saw a well of water. She went and filled the skin with water, giving the boy some to drink." In the case of Isaac, "Abraham then looked up and saw a ram caught by its horns in a thicket. He went and got the ram, sacrificing it as an all-burnt offering in his son's place." In both accounts, God ended with a blessing to the parent through the son. In the case of Ishmael, he promised Hagar, "I will make of him a great nation," and in the case of Isaac, he promised Abraham, "I will bless you greatly, and increase your offspring like the stars of the sky and the sand on the seashore."

The consistent parallels in the two accounts show that it is one story of two events of *'Aqeidāh*, where Abraham was commanded by God to commit an immoral act that was not meant to materialize. In both cases, the act was so inhumane that only God could "suspend" the trial by sending His angel to save Ishmael and Isaac from death. The two brothers, who kept contacting each other (see chapter 5), obviously realized that the acts of sacrifice were not of their father's making and that they were only separated in order to fulfill different missions sanctioned by the same God they worshiped.

Some Forgotten Lessons

What moralistic conclusions can we draw from this morally troubling story? God definitely had a purpose in orchestrating this dramatic act. After all, this harsh command of killing one's son stands in conflict with the Ten Commandments prescribed by both Judaism and Islam. God would not demand Abraham to face such a horrific challenge unless He had a purpose—to guide us, to teach us some rules of behavior, some codes of ethics. What could they be? Are there messages that are being conveyed here? Can Jews and Muslims learn from them to improve their relationship and life in general on this planet?

1. Honoring Others' Myths

To begin with, let's talk about the story. Honoring each other's truth-based scriptural narratives is fundamental in interreligious understanding. Judaism and Islam each has an elaborate system of religious myths, sacred stories, and rituals based on its own scripture that differentiates it from other religions. The different stories in the Bible and the Qur'ān of Abraham's sacrifice of his son, be it Isaac or Ishmael, is just one example. Such a system encourages the believers to follow the faith of their ancestors, to hold onto the time-honored truths, and to get a sense of meaning, identity, and continuity. The term "myth" has suffered tremendous confusion and misunderstanding.[20] It has been observed that theologians, clergies, and all kinds of religious authorities often use the ill-defined word "myth" to characterize sacred stories, beliefs, and rituals other than their own. While trivializing others' stories as invented ones or fables, they consider that their stories are a critical history or collection of facts. In doing that, they only help expand the gulf between religions and societies.

There is no sense in resorting to such a shameful game of shattering other peoples' myths or stories. On the contrary, there is a lot of sense in studying them, in searching for the ethos of faith behind them, and in continuing recording, reconstructing, and differentiating the beautiful myths that make us all proud of our unique traditions. As the great mythologist

Joseph Campbell was quoted to have said, "A myth is a mask of God, a metaphor for what lies behind the visible world."[21] To explore this world—whether it is Jewish or Muslim—it is crucial to study and honor its myths and truths. It can only contribute to interreligious understanding.

2. Trials in Life

Trials and tests are a necessary part of life. They reveal our character and the genuineness of our faith. Trials and tribulations are part of one's existence. Without them we would not become stronger and more resilient. Moreover, trials are self-teaching opportunities, buried treasures. Human beings are on a quest to encounter life's trials and find buried treasures, things of value that we can learn from and integrate into our lives. The trials may be big or small; they always give us an opportunity to grow. The Qur'ān tells us that "God thus put you to the test to bring out your true conviction and to test what is in your heart, and God is fully aware of your innermost thoughts."[22]

It is said that "life is a succession of lessons, which must be lived to be understood" (a phrase attributed to Ralph Waldo Emerson, Helen Keller, and others). Other people may be there to teach us, guide us along the path of life, but the lessons to be learned are always ours. Like the ten trials of Abraham, we all go through our own trials. They are of God's making. Nachmanides provides a fundamental perspective on God's purpose in testing man. He writes that the testing of man derives from his absolute free choice. God tests man in order to create opportunities for him to actualize his potential to act righteously and thereby earn the greater reward for righteous actions, rather than for righteous thought alone. For this reason, divine tests are solely for the benefit of man, rather than for God Who already knows the moral character of the individual being tested. Divine tests solidify our true level of morality by translating thoughts into actions.[23] The Midrash, playing with the Hebrew word "*nes*," which means both "miracle" and "banner," writes that God conducts miraculous test after test in order to elevate a person to a high level of moral character, to prominence, like "a highflying ship's mast."[24]

Our purpose, as human beings, is to find out what is the divine purpose for us. Once we begin to learn our unique purpose for these tests, we will be able to live life to the fullest and also remain standing through any storm of life. Whatever the situation, whatever the test, whatever the hardship we face, we trust God. "Even if I will walk in the valley of the shadow of death," says the Psalmist, "I will fear no evil, for you are with me." It is my journey, my walking staff, yet, the Psalmist continues "Your rod and Your staff, they will comfort me."[25]

Both Jews and Muslims are familiar with the biblical story of Job (Hebrew: *Iyōv*; Arabic: *Ayyūb*), the trials he had to face, and the hardships and misfortunes he had to endure.[26] He suffered greatly, yet he was still able to exalt the Name of God and give praise to Him throughout his ordeals. His life has stood as a testimony to the faithfulness to God, as an example of human victory, and as a model of encouragement as we go through our own trials of life. When his wife advised him, seeing him in great suffering, "Blaspheme God, and die," he answered her, "You speak as one of the vile women speak. What? Shall we receive good at the hand of God, and shall we not receive evil?" Ultimately, despite all his ordeals, it is written, "After all of this Job did not sin with his lips." Like Abraham, he passed all his trials and tests.

3. Prohibition of Human Sacrifice

Still another moralistic conclusion, perhaps the major one, to be extracted from the climactic resolution of the story is that God chose a unique way to demonstrate His prohibition of human sacrifice. The story of the angel preventing Abraham from sacrificing his son shows that human sacrifice is not what God is interested in. Rashi, the greatest Jewish commentator, understood it and interpreted God's command of Abraham as "offer him up [but He] did not say slaughter him" (*ve-ha'lēhu lo' 'amār lo shḥaṭēhu*).[27] Had Abraham proceeded with the slaughter, he would not have passed his trial. The story validates the shift taking place during that period from human sacrifice to animal sacrifice and the cardinal belief in the sanctification of the human soul. In both Jewish and Islamic narratives, it is God Himself Who ordered Abraham to sacrifice his son and it is His angel who prevented him from doing it. What do we learn from that? When it comes to committing murder, killing a human being, only God may command such a horrific act. The Qur'ān says that "it is God Who gives life and death."[28] On the other hand, an angel, a lesser being in the heavenly hierarchy, is sent by God to fulfill other missions, such as the annulment of God's commandments. Killing of a human being by another human being, even for the sake of God, is a severe violation of the fundamental, universal laws prescribed by both Jewish and Islamic laws.

This leads us to the whole question of suicide bombers sent nowadays by Muslim militant groups on missions of killing innocent people. This phenomenon reminds us of Abraham's sacrifice of his son "in the name of God," because in almost all cases the suicide bombers are blindly obedient youth sent on a "Godly sanctioned" mission by older people, who, strictly defined, are committing filicide. Those brainwashed youth and their approving parents believe that, by committing this homicidal act, they will be rewarded in heaven. Jewish sages have a clear notion in this regard, stating that "the disciples of Abraham our father enjoy This World and inherit the World-to-Come."[29] In other words, one can inherit the World-to-Come, the heavenly paradise, only if one knows to live his life fully and serve God in This World. Sacrificing someone's life on this earth and "sending" him to hell in order for oneself to get a ticket to paradise is not the way Abraham lived his life; neither should his disciples, whether they are Jews or Muslims.

Filicide, the deliberate act of a parent killing his child, speaks to each of us as parents. Abraham lived a long childless life of agony, until he was blessed at an older age with two children. Without them, his life was meaningless. Had he killed them, the ethical ideas he had brought to the world would die with them. Ishmael and Isaac were meant to carry his ideological torch to the next generations. Eternality of life is what made Abraham's life meaningful. What kind of parenthood do we seek and what motivates us to be parents at all? When we give birth and raise children, we do it in order to continue our lives and make them worthy. Killing these children is not only contrary to the code of ethics of Abraham whom we, Jews and Muslims, are being asked to follow; it also acts contrary to nature, where life—human, animal, or tree—continues by bearing fruits from which a new cycle of life begins. It is also contrary to our humanity. Those who still commit filicide for political and ideological reasons, such as those fringe Muslim militants who send their youth on suicide-bombing missions to find fulfillment as martyrs and their parents who bless them beforehand, should remember this fundamental law of life: although you give birth, the moment God's spirit was blown into the child's mouth, you are not allowed to cut off his life; it is not in your hands anymore, as the Angel of God warned Abraham, "do not lay your hand upon the boy";[30] not yours and not anyone else's.

The greatness of Abraham our father was not only in his submission to God when he took his son for sacrifice, but also in his final moment when he did not lay hands on him. At both times, when Abraham and Isaac set out to Mount Moriah and when they returned back home to Beersheba after the attempted sacrifice ordeal, the Bible makes a point to tell us that "*together* they set out." The lives of the father and son were bound forever; a true "Binding," or *'Aqeidāh*. They readily consented to the sacrifice and were in concert in submission to God's will. When they returned home, they were both transformed people adhering to a new faith, according to which a person who kills another human being is not a man of God, but an abominable creature about which the Bible writes "You shall utterly detest it and you shall utterly abhor it, for it is a taboo."[31] The words for taboo—in Hebrew *ḥērem* and in Arabic *ḥarām*—etymologically derive from the same root; they refer to an offensive and shameful act that is absolutely unforgivable. The act of murder is classified in Islam as one of the gravest sins, or *kabā'ir*.

A message to all of us: you cannot end evil, but you can stop participating in it. It is not a prejudice against your coreligionist to express outrage against anyone who fosters the wish for martyrdom by children, or by anybody, and advocates the destruction of human lives. When you know that someone considers committing such an offense, or when you witness your neighbor doing it, or when you hear your preacher quoting the scriptures to support it, remember what the Hebrew prophet Micah writes and ask yourself, "Shall I give my first-born for my transgression, the fruit of my body for the sin of my soul?"[32] Remember God's covenant with Noah and one of His universal laws, "He who sheds man's blood shall have his blood be shed by man, for God made man with His own image."[33] Remember how the Jewish sages valued human life when they said, "Whoever causes the loss of a single soul is as though he caused the loss of a whole world, and whoever saves one is as though he saved a whole world."[34] The Qur'ān sends exactly the same message: "If anyone slew a person . . . it would be as if he slew the whole mankind; and if anyone saved a life, it would be as if he saved the life of the whole mankind."[35] It prohibits apotheosis of death and homicide in clear terms, saying, "Take not life, which God has made sacred, except by way of [the court of] justice and law,"[36] and forbids suicide, saying, "O you who believe! [. . . do not] kill yourself, for truly God has been to you Most Merciful. If any do that in rancor and injustice, soon shall We cast him into the Fire."[37] The Qur'ān does allow excessive fighting: "Fight in the path of God against those who fight you, but do not go beyond the limits. God does not love those who go beyond the limits."[38] No question, exaltation of glorious death, homicide and filicide are acts that "go beyond the limits."

4. The Perils of Obedience

Unlike his reaction to God's wish to destroy Sodom and Gomorrah, when he questioned God's decree and pleaded directly with him, Abraham was silent throughout the sacrifice affair. Possibly, in his personal life he was totally obedient to God, while in public matters he was not hesitant to argue with Him. Nevertheless, one would expect to see him defying God in an attempt to rescue his beloved son. Instead, he did not even question the rightness of His command, but simply hastened to obey His extremely harsh demand. Abraham's obedience to God was complete.

This kind of reaction raises the whole question of obedience. When most people think of the word "obedience," they think of something close to slavery, something negative and wrong. Obedience occurs when people obey commands or orders from others to do something. People in general are more willing to obey people who are in authority, that is, from higher-ranking people within an organization. It is like the army, where military officers shout out commands that they expect to be followed without question. The problem is that there can be tragic consequences of obedience if it is used in the wrong way. One of the most horrific forms of obedience can occur when it is blind obedience. Such as what happened during the Holocaust, in the Second World War, when blind obedience was carried to the extreme by the Nazis. They established death camps where soldiers and even prisoners obeyed commands to systematically murder millions of innocent victims. The main line of defense by Nazi commanders in the postwar trials was "I was following orders."

The problem is that blind obedience often occurs when a society as a whole is captive to a collective consciousness created by a totalitarian regime, such as in Nazi Germany. Jewish Law has a clear prohibition against "following the herd" in the case of evildoing. It says, "You shall not follow the majority to do evil."[39]

Blind obedience is not the only peril of obedience. One of the issues we may consider in the case of Abraham is the practice of sacrifice as a way to show obedience to God. Indeed, the Israelites were commanded to give offerings to God as Prophet Isaiah states, "And I will bring them to My holy mountain, and make them joyful in My house of prayer; their burnt-offerings and their sacrifices shall be acceptable upon My altar."[40] But many Hebrew prophets, starting with Samuel, argued that obedience to God's moral precepts is more important than the observance of ritual sacrifice, but does not exclude it. It is written that "Samuel said, 'Has the Lord as great a delight in burnt-offerings and sacrifices, as in hearkening to the voice of the Lord? Behold, to obey is better than sacrifice, and to hearken than the fat of rams.'"[41] Prophet Hosea made a similar argument, saying, "For I delight in loyalty rather than [animal] sacrifice, and in the knowledge of God rather than burnt-offerings."[42] Also the writer of Proverbs says, "To do righteousness and justice is desired by the Lord rather than [animal] sacrifice."[43] In other words, what God is saying through His prophets is that He wants a change in our moral behavior rather than mere performance of a religious observance. This is not to say that sacrifices are not important, because they are. However, sacrifices as an expression of obedience and faithfulness to God without living a moral life is just a facade, "putting on a show," a pretense of living righteously. That's not what God wants. This is a lesson for all of us, Jews and Muslims alike, who have their own prescribed set of rituals. Yet without being accompanied by moral convictions, such as love of human beings, any act of worship is empty and meaningless.

5. Love of God vs. Fear of God

When God saw that Abraham was ready to sacrifice his son, He said, "For now I know that you are a God-fearing man (Hebrew: *Yere' 'Elohīm*), since you have not withheld your son, your only son, from Me."[44] Why did God use the word "to fear" and not "to love"? Would Abraham's obedience in this episode stem from "fear" (Hebrew: *yir'āh*)? Does the Islamic narrative make the distinction between fear and love of God?

Qiṣaṣ al-Anbiyā' narrates a dialogue between Abraham and Ishmael, where Abraham tells his son that he dreamed of sacrificing him. Ishmael, who sees his father weeping, confronts him, telling him that what he was doing is not dreaming but soliciting the friendship of God, and such a solicitation could not be done while asleep. "Have you not heard," asked Ishmael, "what God has revealed to some of His prophets, 'How can someone claim that he loves Me, when the night overwhelms him and both his eyes are open?'" *Qiṣaṣ al-Anbiyā'* then makes a poetic remark questioning whether Abraham was asleep, "How odd it is for a lover [of God] to be asleep! All sleep is forbidden to a lover...The seeker of Paradise does not sleep...The man who loves someone is forbidden to sleep."[45] It appears as if the narrator suggests that Abraham may not have been fully awake, like the Qur'ān's reference to Abraham's saying to Ishmael, "I see in [my] sleep"[46] (Arabic: *manām*, which can be translated as a dream). Therefore, it seems that Abraham has not done it truly out of love of God, but out of fear of Him, which explains his weeping. He rather did it as an act of obedience, of submission (Arabic: *islām*), as the Qur'ān writes, "So as they [Abraham and Ishmael] both submitted to Him [God]."[47] A Jewish prayer recalls that "Abraham our father suppressed his mercifulness (*kavāsh 'et raḥamāv*) for his only son to do Your will with his whole heart,"[48] which suggests that Abraham subdued his emotions to allow himself to go through this awful experience.

While the Bible makes many references both to love of God and fear of God, Jewish commentary attempts to distinguish between the two.[49] It seems that in the case of Abraham, like in the case of Job who was also described as "a God-fearing man,"[50] fear—fear of punishment or fear of the consequences of wrong doing—was perhaps the motivating force, not fear of reverence and awe. One cannot love God unless he loves human beings, who were created in His image. They are different sides of the same coin of love. It is not humanly possible that Abraham, who obviously loved his son very much, could have attempted to slaughter him out of his love of God. He feared God and feared for the life of his son. In sending His angel to stop Abraham from proceeding with his human sacrifice, God also sent mankind an important message—you may fear Me, but to have a true relationship with Me, you must also love me, as it is written, "You shall love the Lord your God with all your heart, with all your soul, and with all your being,"[51] and love human beings as well, as it is written, "Love your fellow man as yourself."[52] Our God is a God of Love. The more you love God, the more capacity you develop to love others, your spouse, your children, your country, and your fellow human beings. It is ultimately the love of God that validates the love of human beings.

6. Sacrifice of Our Egotism

The attempts by Satan, as related not only in Islamic but also in Jewish sources,[53] to sway Abraham, Isaac (in the Jewish tradition), and Ishmael (in the Islamic tradition) from proceeding with the sacrifice, offer us insight into the psychological dimension of the act. Human beings are given the power of free will to choose between right and wrong, between doing good and doing evil. The sacrifice story of Abraham can be understood metaphorically as the inner struggle human beings experience between the higher "self" and the lower "ego," or between the heavenly voice in the story that represents the "good inclination" (*yētzer ha-ṭōv*) and the Satan that represents what Jews term "evil inclination" (*yētzer ha-rāʿ*) and what the Muslims call *shayṭān* (from the root sh.ṭ.n. denoting "to go astray" or "to act devilishly"). In Islamic theology, the *shayṭān* and his minions are "whisperers," who whisper into the hearts of men and women, urging them to commit sins (see Surāt an-Nās, p. 33). The Qur'ān says, "The Satan's plan is [but] to cause enmity and hatred between you."[54] For us, Abraham represents the ideal man, one who confronted Satan, his ego, and rejected the "evil inclination" within him, thus allowing the "good inclination" to take over and believe in God. According to the Qur'ān, "Whoever rejects evil and believes in God has grasped the firmest handle that will never break."[55]

We are often led by our pure ego that thrives on power, domination, control, and separation rather than by our spiritual heart that delights in its empathy, compassion, generosity, and love. We are led by our allegiances and ideologies rather than our compassionate heart, forgetting the old slogan, "arms are for hugging." We ought to surrender the will of our own ego, our self-sense of separateness, to our loving heart that sees no boundaries, the same way we submit to the will of God. The world would then look totally different.

Final Thoughts

The horrific story of the sacrifice is particularly relevant today, when religious fanaticism plagues the world. Unlike the worldview of the fanatics, who are convinced that killing human beings to serve their cause is what God wants them to do, we find in both Jewish and Islamic narratives of the story a different thinking about a God Who does not want the death of human beings as a sign of obedience and submission to His will, a God that does not want us to die for Him, but rather desires that we live for him.

Surrounded by people who still perform ritual sacrifice of their children to the Moloch (Hebrew: *Mōlekh*), the pagan bloodthirsty idol, God wanted Abraham to know that He despised this popular practice, saying, "Do not worship God your Lord with such practices. In worshiping their gods, [these nations] committed all sorts of perversions hated by God. They would even burn their sons and daughters in fire as a means of worshiping their gods."[56] God wanted Abraham to replace Molochism, which violates two of the Seven Noahide Laws—murder and idolatry—with ethical monotheism, where concepts of loving-kindness, compassion, and peace prevail. He wanted him to learn a lesson through a traumatic experience, a transformative one, one that leaves its imprint forever. God tested Abraham to see how far he would go to serve Him and then stopped him. He knows the animalistic nature of human beings and warns us, through this event, to show self-restraint. In testing Abraham, God tests all of us. In preventing Abraham from slaying his son, He wanted to send all of us a clear message—that human life is sacred and that human sacrifice is a twisted form of worship that should be eradicated from the face of the earth. He wanted to send us a message of life over death, teaching over ignorance, consensus over polarization, and peace over destruction.

Tragically, the struggle between Molochism and Monotheism is still alive today. In the face of this ongoing struggle, we must tell the precautionary story of the sacrifice in our schools and places of worship. We must join forces to deplore the death of innocent people, to end violence, and stop killing "in the name of God." To be the true disciples of Abraham, who are supposed to have learned the lesson, we need to display the sacrificial ram every place in this sad world, in order to warn against fanatics who raise the knife to slay their fellow human being. This is the way God would have wanted us to remember our common ancestor, Abraham. This is the way we ought to commemorate the scriptural account of the attempted sacrifice of Ishmael/Isaac.

We are told in the Bible that the ram, which Abraham sighted immediately after the attempted sacrifice, became stuck in the hedge by its horns. This detail is extremely instructive. Because the substituted ram became stuck in the hedge, Abraham had to go after the trapped ram in order to sacrifice it. It did not conveniently fall into his lap. So is the case with us; we cannot wait for reality to change unless we do something about it, unless we take action. By going after the target, change will occur. Thus, the writer of Proverbs teaches us regarding peacemaking, "Seek peace and pursue it."[57] This metaphor suggests another angle. The ram got stuck by its horns, which emanate from the head. We, as human beings, are often stuck in our heads, in our rigid ideologies and belief systems that emanate from the head, and forget to be human with love and compassion that emanate from the heart. It is up to us, metaphorically speaking, to cut off our outgrowing horns that stand in our way of being human and "go public" by blowing them with powerful sounds of love, peace, and reconciliation across the Jewish-Islamic divide. This self-expression of human emotion that objects to the helplessness and complacency of the world is the way we can make the scriptural account of the attempted sacrifice relevant to us, Muslims and Jews. We need to recognize that we are all on the same planetary ship. We are going to either succeed in hoisting its sails together and charting a course that fulfills God's covenant with Abraham to make him "the father of a multitude of nations" living side by side in peace, or we will all go down with the ship.

Part III

Two Issues, One Resolution

Chapter 7

The Gate of Peace

Rights to the Holy Land—a Theological Reexamination

The contemporary bone of contention between Jews and Muslims and the poisonous stem that constantly inflames their relationship is the Arab-Israeli conflict.[1] At the root of this historical dispute are the conflicting claims of Jews and Arabs to possession of a territory east of the Mediterranean, which the Jewish people regard as 'Ēretz Yisraēl, or the Land of Israel, and the Arab people call Filasṭīn, or Palestine. This land became a distinct geographical, historical, and political entity for the first time when the Israelites settled there about 3,000 years ago. Later, during the eleventh and tenth centuries BCE, they founded a kingdom with Jerusalem as the site of the First Temple and King Solomon's capital. In 70 CE, the Romans destroyed the Jewish state and the Second Temple and most of its Jewish inhabitants were killed or exiled.

Thereafter, for nearly 2,000 years, this land was ruled by a succession of foreign conquerors that treated it as a tiny, remote, colonial province in their empire. Five centuries after the destruction of the Jewish kingdom, with the Arab conquest in 638–640 CE, a good part of the country's population was Arabized and Islamized. Then, the Jewish community, which survived the exile, became a minority in their own land. This status has dramatically changed in the late nineteenth and the early twentieth century with the large-scale immigration of Jews to their ancient biblical homeland and its British occupation from Turkish Ottoman hands in 1918. Thereafter, Allied promises to the Arabs bore fruit with the creation of independent states in Egypt, Saudi Arabia, Yemen, Iraq, Syria, Lebanon, and the unexpected formation in 1921 of the Kingdom of Transjordan. Consequently, nearly four-fifths of the territory that was to have been the Jewish homeland, granted by the Balfour Declaration of 1917, was handed to the Arabs. What remained of 'Ēretz Yisraēl / Palestine was now about 10,000 square miles shared by both Arab and Jewish communities. With the final creation of the State of Israel in 1948, the relations between these neighboring communities turned into a full-blown conflict that has yet to be resolved.

The emergence of a Jewish state in the very heart of the Arab-Muslim world has resurrected old antagonisms, the most ancient of which are the conflicting claims to the disputed land of 'Ēretz Yisraēl / Palestine. What makes this conflict so bitter is its theological foundation, where the two antagonists, the two children of Abraham, hold on to uncompromising divine-sanctioned ideologies. The radical among them, who are blind to any possibilities of peaceful resolution, are entrenched in positions that are grotesque and delusional—the annihilation of their neighboring enemy. Unfortunately, zealotry sets the tone and dominates the scene.

Although the conflicting traditions have inherent divergences associated with this historical conflict, is it possible to converge the traditions into a place of understanding and mutual respect? What are the Jewish claims to the Land? What is the Qur'ān's position? Is a reasonable compromise feasible? To answer these questions, we need to navigate through history, from modern back to ancient times.

The Rights to the Land—the Jewish View

The question of who has the right to the Land has always been in dispute. The claim of the Jewish people to the Land is based on six arguments: legal validity, historical attachment, occupation through wars, settlement and conquest, contractual purchase, and divine promise. The following review is instructive given the official position of the Palestinians that denies any Jewish historical links and Jewish sovereign rights to the Land. Let's review the Jewish arguments:

1. Legal Validity—International legal recognition of the Jewish claim was granted on four separate occasions: The first is the Balfour Declaration of 1917, when the British declared "sympathy with Zionist aspiration" and committed themselves to support the creation of a "National Home" for the Jewish people in Palestine. The second one is when The League of Nations Mandate adopted the Balfour Declaration and incorporated it into the Mandate Agreement. The third one took place in 1947, when the United

Nations General Assembly adopted a resolution calling for the partition of Palestine into Jewish and Arab states. The fourth and last event took place in September 1949, when the State of Israel was recognized as a member of the United Nations and the overwhelming majority of the world's nations recognized its legitimacy.

2. Historical Attachment—The history of the Jews in the Land is well described in The Declaration of the Establishment of the State of Israel, called "The Scroll of Independence," on May 14, 1948. It declares that "'Ēretz Yisraēl [the Land of Israel] was the birthplace of the Jewish people. Here their spiritual, religious and political identity was shaped. Here they first attained statehood, created cultural values of national and universal significance and gave to the world the eternal Book of Books [the Bible]. After being forcibly exiled from their land, the people kept faith with it throughout their dispersion and never ceased to pray and hope for their return to it and for the restoration in it of their political freedom. Impelled by this historic and traditional attachment, Jews strove in every successive generation to re-establish themselves in their ancient homeland."[2]

3. Occupation through Wars—Since its establishment, Israel has survived constant military threats, most notably attacks by Arab states in the Six-Day War of June 1967, and the Yom Kippur War of October 1973. In each of these large-scale wars, the Arab armies were defeated and some of their territories were captured. Sinai was returned to the Egyptians in 1979, the Gaza Strip (captured from the Egyptians) and a small territory in northern Samaria were taken over by the Palestinians in 2005, as part of Israel's disengagement policy. Israel still retains the West Bank territories (captured from the Jordanians in 1967) and the Golan Heights (captured from the Syrians in 1967).

4. Settlement and Conquest—The implication derived from God's promises of the Land to the Patriarchs is the commandment to settle the Land and conquer it if necessary. From the very beginning, Abraham was commanded by God to traverse the entire Land that is destined to belong to his descendents and take possession of it: "For all the land which you see, to you will I give it, and to your descendents for ever"; therefore "arise, walk through the land in the length of it and in the breadth of it; for unto you will I give it."[3] Nachmanides cites the Midrash and says that "The Blessed Holy One gave Abraham a sign that whatever has happened to him will happen to his children,"[4] and suggests that it is for this reason that the Bible narrated at great length the account of the journeys of the Patriarchs, the digging of the wells, and other events.[5] The territorial conquest of the Land by Joshua in the thirteenth century BCE and the settlement of the Israelites there was an extension of the works of the Patriarchs and a fulfillment of God's oath to them. Thus, the revered Jewish master Rabbi Menachem

Mendel Schneerson argues that "although the Blessed Holy One promised and gave the Land of Israel to Abraham our father, so that the Land of Israel belongs to the Children of Israel for ever, the Blessed Holy One wanted the Children of Israel to receive the Land of Israel actually and openly through war (as it actually took place through Joshua's conquest)." Rabbi Schneerson distinguishes between two types of land ownership: general and private. General ownership stems from Joshua's occupation of the Land and suggests that it belongs to the entire People of Israel, whereas private ownership stems from actual settlement and possession of the Land and suggests that every Jew holds an individual portion of it.[6]

5. Contractual Purchase—*Shulḥān 'Arūkh*, the book of Jewish code, rules that a land can be acquired by means of either payment (*kēssef*), a deed (*shṭār*), or a physical act of possession (*ḥazaqāh*).[7] According to the Bible, the Jews have been holding the deeds of three key sites of the Holy Land that were purchased so that they would never be in dispute, or as the Midrash phrased it, "So that the nations of the world can never castigate [the People of] Israel and say 'you are occupying stolen territories.'"[8] These are the Tomb of the Patriarchs in Hebron purchased by Abraham,[9] Joseph's burial site in Shechem purchased by Jacob,[10] and the Temple Mount purchased by King David.[11] Likewise, during the late part of the nineteenth century and the first half of the twentieth century, when Jewish masses flocked to the Land, Jewish individuals and institutions purchased great tracts of land from various owners.

6. Divine Promise—From all the arguments Jews have been using to base their claim to the Holy Land, there is only one that stands out, that is the most profound premise from which all other arguments flow. It is the divine promise of the Land to the descendents of Abraham through Isaac, that is, to the Jewish people, as an everlasting covenant. It is the Word of God Himself, the One God Who is acknowledged by all three monotheistic religions—Judaism, Christianity, and Islam. Because of the divine promise, the Land was occupied by Joshua, taken over by the Jews who returned from the Babylonian exile under the leadership of Ezra the Scribe, and restored in modern times by the Jews who reestablished there the State of Israel. What made the Jews sanctify the Land and identify it as their Holy Land, or *'Ēretz ha-Qōdesh*, is this chain of historical events triggered by a divine promise.[12] This primary argument merits an extended elaboration.

The Divine Promise

The biblical story started with the divine call to Abraham, his first revelation from God: "Get out of your country, from your birthplace and from your father's house, to the Land which I will show you. [There] I will make you into a great nation, and I will bless you, and make your name great, and you will [enjoy the fruits of] blessing."[13] Thereafter, the Bible tells us, Abraham and his family left their home, in what is now Iraq, and headed to the Land of Canaan. Upon his arrival, God revealed himself again to Abraham and said: "I will give this land to your descendents."[14] Shortly after, as a reward for his loyalty, God struck a sacred agreement with him, known as the Covenant between the Parts (Hebrew: *Brit bein ha-Betarīm*), which promised him the inheritance of a very large territory for his descendents. The promise says: "I have given this land to your descendents, from the river of Egypt as far as the great river, the Euphrates river, the [lands of] the Kenites, the Kadmonites, the Chitites, the Perizites, the Refa'im, the Amorites, the Canaanites, the Girgashites, and the Jebusites."[15]

At this point, according to most Jewish sources, God made a binding agreement for eternity concerning the Jewish ownership of the Land of Israel. But, the Genesis account, two chapters later, tells about God's new revelation to Abraham and His Covenant of the Circumcision. There, the divine promise speaks of a more defined territory—the Land of Canaan west of the Jordan River: "I will establish My covenant between Me and you and your descendents after you throughout their generations as an everlasting covenant—to be your God and the God of your descendents after you. And I will give you, and your descendents after you, the Land in which you reside, the entire Land of Canaan, as an everlasting possession. And I will be God to them."[16]

What caused the change? Why was the territory re-specified in such a short period of time? Because a dramatic event took place between the two promises, one that changed the history of the region—Abraham gave birth to Ishmael. God, knowing of the upcoming birth of Isaac, did not change His "mind." He kept His promise fully, though the large territory had now to take two children into consideration. The first promise speaks of a large land to be inherited by the descendents of Abraham, that is, Ishmael and Isaac. The second promise speaks of a specific land to be given to Isaac, yet to be born, a territory that covered the entire Land of Canaan, between the Jordan River and the Mediterranean Sea. How do we know that the second promise of the Covenant of the Circumcision refers to Isaac? Because the promise speaks specifically for the first time of "your descendents *after you*," that is the son that inherits Abraham's spiritual legacy. The expression "after you," in reference to Isaac, will continue to be used in the following biblical accounts.

The promise was subsequently reaffirmed to Abraham's descendents. God said to Isaac: "Settle in this Land, and I will be with you and I will bless you. For I will give all these lands to you and to your descendents, and I will uphold the oath that I swore to Abraham, your father."[17] This oath was then given to Jacob: "The Land that I gave to Abraham and Isaac, I give to you, and to your heirs after you will I give the Land."[18] And Jacob reaffirmed the oath to his son Joseph,[19] and then he in turn did the same to his brothers.[20] The oath carried so much weight that God repeated it to Moses,[21] and even the fifth out of the Ten Commandments, revealed to the People of Israel at Sinai, mentioned it: "Honor your father and your mother, in order that you may long endure on the land that the Lord, your God, is giving to you."[22]

The borders of the inherited Land of Canaan are described in Exodus, as the Children of Israel were approaching Canaan. It was God's words to Moses: "And God spoke to Moses, saying: 'Command the Children of Israel and say to them: When you arrive in the Land of Canaan, the following is the Land that will fall to you as an inheritance, the Land of Canaan according to the borders thereof.'"[23] Thereafter God gave a very detailed description of the borders.[24] The detail can only indicate God's intention to distinguish the exact territory in order to avoid a future conflict over its borders. This territory included all the land from the "River of Egypt" in the south. In the broad definition by some scholars this river is the Nile, and in the narrow and most acceptable definition it is the Brook of El-Arish located at northeastern frontier of Egypt and at the southwestern tip of the Negev desert, where the unpopulated wilderness started. This territory stretched all the way to the Amanos Mountain in the north and Euphrates River in the northeast, and included the entire land of Syria.[25]

The Beginning of the Conflict

The Jewish sages were fully aware of the power struggle in the Abraham household and were highly concerned with Ishmael's bid for ownership of the entire Promised Land. They knew that Ishmael wanted "a double portion," the western Land of Israel (covered by the second promise) and the territory beyond (included in the first promise). They knew that the biblical story is a mirror upon which history reflects itself. They realized that Genesis is the beginning of the bitter conflict between the children of Abraham and that the Promised Land may turn into a disputed land. The Zohar, in its account on Abraham, made an even more striking prediction, suggesting that the Arabs will do their utmost to prevent the return of Jews to their Holy Land. It writes: "Once the years have completed... then, all your brethrens will be [gathered] from among all the nations to bring sacrifice to God, and the children of Ishmael will then be woken up together with all other peoples of the world to wage war upon Jerusalem."[26]

Commenting on the difference between Isaac's and Ishmael's right to the Land, the Zohar relates another episode about a leader of the descendents of

Ishmael, who complained regarding why God should give Isaac the Land as inheritance, if Ishmael had also been circumcised and therefore fulfilled the Covenant of Circumcision. The Zohar suggests that Ishmael's connection to the Covenant and the Land is only secondary and external—entitling him and his descendents to custodianship, not ownership, over the Land and only during the Jews' absence from that Land. It goes on saying that the Jewish People, the descendents of Jacob, have a primary and inner bond to the Land, and are entitled to ownership upon their return to the Land. Thus, the Zohar states so long ago: "In the future, the children of Ishmael... will rule over the Holy Land for many years when it is desolate and uninhabited. And they will hinder the return of the children of Israel to their places, until Ishmael's merit runs out."[27]

This early premonition eventually came true in the end of the nineteenth century, when Jews began pouring into the Land and establishing there the State of Israel.

The Psalmist devoted a special psalm on the real concern over the historic enmity exhibited by the nations of the world, including the children of Ishmael and Hagar, against the People of Israel. Perhaps, the Hebrew designations *Ishma'ēlīm* (descendents of Ishmael) and *Hagarīm* (descendents of Hagar) denote any nomadic desert people, as suggested by some scholars.[28] They nevertheless represent for the Psalmist the concern for the Land of Israel from their disputing cousins:

> O God, do not keep Yourself silent; be not peaceful, and be not still, O God. For behold, Your enemies are in uproar; and those who hate You have raised their head. Against Your people they plot deviously, and take counsel against Your treasured ones. They have said: "Come, and let us cut them off from being a nation; that Israel's name may not be remembered any more." For they have consulted together unanimously; they strike a covenant against You—the tents of Edom and the Ishmaelites; Moab, and the Hagrites, Gebal, and Ammon, and Amalek; Philistia with the inhabitants of Tyre. Even Assyria joined with them; they became a strong arm to the children of Lot. Selah. Do to them as to Midian, as to Sisera, as to Yabin at the Brook Kishon, who were destroyed at Ein-Dor; they became as dung for the earth. Make their nobles like Orev and Zeev, and all their princes like Zevah and Tzalmuna, who said, "Let us take to ourselves in possession the habitations of God."[29]

The Talmud records an episode concerning that historical dispute. It tells about descendents of Ishmael and Keturah, who came forward to claim their equal share in the Land of Canaan.

> And it happened again that the descendants of Ishmael and the descendants of Keturah summoned [the People of] Israel before Alexander of Macedonia, saying to him: the Land of Canaan is ours and yours, for it is written (Genesis,

> 25: 12) "And these are the generations of Ishmael, son of Abraham." And it is further written (Genesis, 25: 19) "And these are the generations of Isaac, son of Abraham." Gbiaha ben Pesisa requested the sages' permission to be [Israel's] advocate in front of Alexander of Macedonia, saying: Should they win, say you defeated an uneducated person among us, and should I win say the Torah of Moses Our Father defeated you. He received the permission and went ahead to confront them. He said to them: What evidence do you bring, and their answer was: From your Torah [Genesis 25: 12 and 19], which shows that Ishmael as well as Isaac were Abraham's children. And he then also brought his evidence from the same [ibid., 25: 5–6]: "And Abraham gave all that he had unto Isaac, but unto the sons of the concubines that Abraham had, Abraham gave gifts; and he sent them away from Isaac his son." If a father made a bequest to his children, while he was still alive, and sent them away from each other, can they have any claim upon the other thereafter? Assuredly not.[30]

The Talmud raises an important question: Why would Abraham give birth to more children through Keturah, if he ultimately would banish them the way he had Ishmael banished? He did it in order to fill up the vast land stretching between "the River of Egypt" and "the Euphrates River." Ultimately, the holy Land of Canaan promised at the Covenant of the Circumcision was to be inhabited by Isaac alone, whereas the rest of the land promised at the Covenant between the Parts was to be inhabited by the rest of his children. In other words, the children of Keturah and the children of Ishmael are not treated in the Bible like any other nations. They had the legitimate rights to settle throughout the vast land, but *only outside the Land of Canaan*. Thus, the Bible relates the story that Abraham, "while still alive" just before his death, made sure to leave behind a legacy that is clean of sibling quarrels. To Isaac he "gave all that he had" and to "the sons of the concubines" he gave gifts and sent them "eastward, to the east country (Hebrew: *'ēretz qēdem*)," to the desert east of the Gilead Mountains, far away from the Land of Canaan.[31] The Midrash was even more specific: "Seeing that Keturah's sons were thorns in the field of Isaac, Abraham built them a big city, around which he erected iron walls. Then he said to them, 'Dwell in this city so that you will be far from my son Isaac.'"[32] We are already told in Genesis that Ishmael was banished south, where "he dwelled in the wilderness of Paran," in the Sinai desert.[33] The Qur'ān identifies Ishmael's habitat even farther south, as far as Mecca in the Arabian Desert, where Abraham helped him to build the Ka'bah. So all the sources are very clear—as divinely promised, the Land of Canaan was granted to Isaac, who resided there all his life; whereas his step-brothers, later recognized as the progenies of the Arabs, wandered outside the borders of Canaan and absorbed the culture of the lands where they resided.

We learn from the Bible that Ishmael did not defy his father but accepted his decision wholeheartedly. In concluding the story of Ishmael, it lists Ishmael's sons and writes: "These were Ishmael's sons and this is how they were called in their towns and their walled cities. There were twelve princes for their nations. These were the years of Ishmael's life, [a total of] one hundred and thirty seven years. He expired and died, and he was gathered to his people [who] lived between Ḥavilāh and Shūr, which borders Egypt, as you go toward Ashūr, [where] he perished in the presence of all his brethren."[34]

In this account, the Bible alludes to the place of Ishmael's burial. He died at the age of 137 and brought to burial, not in the Tomb of the Patriarchs, the family vault of Abraham in Hebron, but among his own people, who lived as nomads "between Ḥavilāh and Shūr." We are told that King Saul pursued the Amalekites "from as you go to Shūr that is facing Egypt."[35] Scholars place this region, where Ishmael's 12 descending tribes dwelled, either in the Arabian desert or in the wilderness extending from northern Sudan to the northeastern border of Egypt,[36] unquestionably far away from Canaan.

Obviously, Ishmael knew about the Tomb of the Patriarchs, because he buried his father there. He could have instructed his children, as his last will and testament, to be buried there. But, accepting his father's request, he chose to give up on the Land of Canaan and end his life in the "east country" among his brethren. This narration is crucial as far as the rights of the descendents of Ishmael over the Land of Canaan. Control of the Cave meant the control of the Land. Once Ishmael gave up on the rights over the Cave, he gave up on the rights over the Land. Only the Patriarchs, Abraham, Isaac, and Jacob, who inherited the Promised Land, chose to be buried there along with their wives,[37] and thereby sent a clear message to their next generations—the Land belongs to the descendents of the last Patriarch to be buried there.

So Whose Land Is It?

Judaism, consistent with the Patriarchs' basic faith, always had three essentials: The Oneness of God, the Covenant, and the Land. God is the One God, the eternal God of Abraham, Isaac, and Jacob. The Covenant is the exclusive, everlasting "contract" between God and Isaac and his descendents. The Land is the Land of Israel, the physical vessel that contains Jewish life, like the body-soul relationship.[38] God says in the Bible: "And I will establish My covenant between Me and you and your descendents after you throughout their generations for an everlasting covenant, to be your God and the God of your descendents after you. And I will give unto you, and to your descendents after you, the land of your sojourning, all the Land of Canaan, for an everlasting possession; and I will be their God."[39]

As God is eternal, so are the election of the People (thus called "The Chosen People"—*Ha-'Am ha-Nivḥār* or *'Am ha-Beḥirāh*) and the gifting of the Land (thus called "the Chosen Land"—*'Ĕretz ha-Beḥirāh*). Thus, the eternal bond between the People and the Land became inseparable from the biblical conception of history and creation,[40] as clearly stated across the Bible:

> Behold, to the Lord Your God belong the heaven, and the heaven of heavens, the earth, with all that therein is. Only the Lord had a delight in your fathers to love them, and He chose their descendents after them, even you, above all peoples, as it is this day.[41]
>
> You are the Lord, you alone made the heaven, the heaven of heavens, with all their host, the earth and all things that are thereon, the seas and all that is in them, You preserve them all; and the host of heaven bows to You. You are the Lord, the God, who chose Abram, and brought him forth out of Ur of the Chaldees, and gave him the name of Abraham; and found his heart faithful before You, and made a covenant with him to give the land of the Canaanite, the Hittite, the Amorite, and the Perizzite, and the Jebusite, and the Girgashite, even to give it unto his descendents, and kept Your words; for You are righteous.[42]

Indeed, the Bible is cited to indicate that the land belonged to God and the People of Israel were merely tenants:

> And the land shall not be sold in perpetuity; for the land is Mine; for you are strangers and settlers with Me.[43]
>
> How manifold are your works, O Lord! In wisdom have You made them all; the earth is full of Your possessions.[44]
>
> You shall be Mine own treasure from among all peoples; for all the earth is Mine.[45]

But the Jewish sages explained that although the land belongs to God, He gave generously of his creation by retaining both Abraham and the Land of Israel for Himself as His own possessions:

> Five possessions did the Holy Blessed One make His very own in His world, and they are: Torah is one possession, heaven and earth is one possession, Abraham is one possession, [the People of] Israel is one possession; the Holy Temple is one possession.[46]
>
> When the Blessed Holy One created days, He set aside the Sabbath. When He created months, He set aside the festivals. When He created years, He chose Sabbatical years for Himself. When He created Sabbatical years for

> Himself, He chose the years of Jubilee for Himself. When He created the nations of the earth, he chose the Nation of Israel for Himself. When He created the Nation of Israel, He chose the Levites for Himself. When He created the Levites, He chose the priests for Himself. When He created the lands, He set aside the Land of Israel as a heave-offering from all other lands, as it is written, 'The earth is the Lord's and its fullness' (Psalms 24:1).[47]
>
> Three good gifts did the Blessed Holy One give to [the People of] Israel and He did it only with agony. They were the Torah, the Land of Israel and the World-to-Come.[48]

In reference to the last verse, the revered Jewish Bible scholar Nehama Leibowitz suggests that the exile of the People of Israel from its Land was not a punishment for their sins but perhaps an education through experiencing agony. In order words, *galūt* (exile) was destined for the purpose of *ge'ulāh* (redemption).[49]

Given the centrality of the Land of Israel in their thinking and their keen observation of historical processes, the sages expressed concern over the future struggle over that Land. It is, therefore, not surprising to see that Rashi, the greatest biblical exegete, begins his commentary of the very first verse of Genesis, "In the beginning," with immediate reference to the Land of Israel.

> R. Yitzchak said: [strictly speaking] the Torah should have begun with [the verse] "This month shall be to you [the beginning of months] (Exodus 12:2)," which is the very first commandment given to Israel. Why then, did [the Torah] begin with [the verse] "In the beginning"? Because of the power of His works He declared to His People in giving them the inheritance of the nations (Psalms, 111: 6). So, if the nations of the world would say to [the People of] Israel: "You are robbers, because you have conquered the lands of the seven nations"; they [the people of Israel] can answer them, "The entire earth belongs to the Blessed Holy One; He created it, so He can give it to whomsoever He wills. He desired to give it to them, and He desired to take it away from them and give it to us."[50]

In other words, Rashi argues, the creator of the world is *ipso facto* owner and ruler of the world (Hebrew: *Mēlekh ha-'Olām*), and therefore His gift to the People of Israel confers title.[51] God's covenant with Abraham and the promise of the Land to him and his descendents are so crucial in the Jewish heritage that the Jewish Morning Prayer on Sabbath begins with the following Psalm:

> Offer praise to the Lord, proclaim His Name, make His Deeds known among the nations [. . .] Remember His wonders, which He has done, His marvels, and the judgments uttered by His mouth; O descendents of Israel His servant,

> children of Jacob, His chosen ones, He is the Lord our God, His judgments extend over the entire earth. Remember His covenant forever, the word which He commanded to a thousand generations; [The covenant,] which He made with Abraham, and His oath to Isaac; and He established it for Jacob as a statute, for Israel for as an everlasting covenant; saying, "To you I shall give the Land of Canaan, the lot of your inheritance," when you were but a few men in number, and sojourners in it. They wandered from nation to nation, and wandered about from one kingdom to another people. He permitted no one to do them wrong and admonished kings, saying "Do not touch My anointed ones, and do not harm My prophets."[52]

It is clear that God's covenant with Abraham and his promise of the Land to his descendents through Isaac did not come without a price. From the very beginning, He wanted to see a continuity of three generations residing in the Land without interruption. Since God's Covenant of the Circumcision, when the promise of the Land was made, until the departure of Jacob and his sons to Egypt, we cannot see even one occurrence where at least one Patriarch did not reside in the Land. Initially, God did allow Abraham to leave for Egypt, because of the severe famine in the Land.[53] But He disallowed Isaac from doing the same. Here is what the Bible says: "And there was a famine in the Land, beside the first famine that was in the days of Abraham. And Isaac went unto Abimelech, King of Grar. And the Lord appeared unto him, and said: 'Go not down unto Egypt; dwell in the Land, which I shell tell you off. Settle in this Land, and I will be with you, and I will bless you; for I will give all these lands to you and to your descendents, and I will uphold the oath that I swore to Abraham, your father."[54]

After the death of Abraham, Ishmael left the Land for good and Isaac established himself there. Fearing his twin brother, Esau, Jacob was forced to flee the Land. But all this time, when Jacob dwelled abroad, Isaac continued residing in the Land. Only after Jacob's return, did Isaac die. The uninterrupted possession of the Land was a divine condition for the inheritance of the Promised Land.

When the descendents of Jacob were forced to live under slavery in Egypt, away from the Land, God did not forget His covenant. The Bible clearly states: "And I have also established My covenant with them, to give them the Land of Canaan, the land of their sojourning, where they dwelled. And I have also heard the cry of distress of the Children of Israel, whom the Egyptians are holding in bondage, and I have remembered My covenant."[55]

What precipitated thereafter are God's intervention and the miraculous exodus of the descendent of Jacob from Egypt, followed by their conquest of the Land of Canaan. This historical event repeated itself once again in a form of massive Jewish immigration to the Land that began in the last quarter of the nineteenth century and continued throughout the first half of the twentieth century, leading to the creation of the State of Israel in 1948. Thus, after many centuries of exile, the Children of Israel returned to what they have always believed to be their Land and established there a national home for themselves. From a Jewish perspective, God has never forgotten His covenant.

The Qur'ān's Position

The Qur'ān, in two different citations, amazingly uses the same argument, almost word by word:

> Say: O God! Possessor of the dominion (*al-mulk*), You give the dominion to whom You will, and You take the dominion from whom You will, and You endue with honor whom You will, and You humiliate whom You will. In Your Hand is all good. Verily, You have power over all things.[56]
>
> Said Moses to his people, "Pray for help from God, and be patient, for the earth is God's to give as inheritance to such of His servants as he pleased."[57]

In other words, the earth belongs to its Creator. He decides whom to give it, and it so happened that in the case of the Land of Israel, he gave it to the People of Israel. The Qur'ān further says, "[Said Moses to the People of Israel,] 'O my people! Enter the Holy Land, which God assigned to you."[58] Telling about the death of Abraham, *Qiṣaṣ al-Anbiyā'* writes clearly that "Abraham appointed Isaac as his successor in the Land of Syria (i.e., Canaan), and Ishmael in the Hijaz (i.e. in the Arabian desert)."[59]

The Qur'ān makes a clear distinction between Abraham, Isaac, and Jacob on the one hand, and Ishmael on the other: "Remember our servants Abraham, Isaac, and Jacob, who possessed both power and vision. Verily, we did choose them specifically as proclaiming the message of the Hereafter. In our sight, they were truly of the chosen (*min al-muṣṭafīn*) and the excellent. Remember Ishmael, Elisha and Dhu'l Kifl, each of whom was among the excellent."[60]

According to this verse, the Patriarchs are described as "the chosen and the excellent," whereas Ishmael was counted "among the excellent." The "chosenness" of the three Patriarchs is clearly related to the Covenant and the divine promises of the Land of Canaan. Consistent with these promises, the Qur'ān recognizes the Covenant of the Children of Israel with God and stresses the uniqueness of the People of Israel and its entitlement to the Promised Land:

> We did save the Children of Israel from humiliating punishment, inflicted by Pharaoh, who was arrogant [even] among inordinate transgressors. We chose them [the People of Israel] aforetime above the nations, knowingly, and granted them signs, which contained a manifest trial.[61]
>
> We did grant the Children of Israel the Book [Torah], the power of command and provided them with wholesome things, and prophethood [...] and We favored them over the nations.[62]
>
> O Children of Israel! Remember the favors that I bestowed upon you and [the fact] that I preferred you to all others.[63]
>
> And remember when We took your Covenant and We raised above you the Mount [of Sinai], Saying "hold firmly to what We have given you and remember what it contains, so that you may do your duty."[64]
>
> Remember what Moses said to his people: "O my people! Remember God's favor towards you when He produced prophets among you and made you kings, and gave you what He had not given to any other among the nations. O my people! Enter the Holy Land, which God has assigned to you; do not turn your backs on it, lest you be sent away as losers."[65]
>
> We settled the Children of Israel in a beautiful dwelling place, and provided them with wholesome things.[66]

The Qur'ān recognizes the eternity of God's promises and sees the return of the People of Israel to its land, after two exiles, as a divine plan. God carries His plan in full, and no power, whether the Babylonians or Romans, can stop His plan:

> With the help of God, He helps anyone He wishes, and He is Powerful, Most Merciful [Such is] God's promise; God does not break His promise (*lā yukhlifu allāhu wa'dahu*); even though most men do not realize that. They recognize but the outer things in life, while they are heedless of the eventuality.[67]
>
> When the first of the warnings came, we sent Our [Babylonian] servants to inflict severe violence upon you. They rampaged through your homes, and it served as a warning which was acted upon. Then we granted you the return as against them, and we reinforced you with wealth and children, and granted you more manpower. If you did well, you did well for yourself; if you committed evil, it was towards yourselves as well. So when the second warning came along [We permitted your Roman enemies] to trouble your people, to enter your Temple, as they [the Babylonians] had entered it before, and to visit with destruction anything they seized. Perhaps your Lord will have mercy upon you.[68]

The Prophets' Call for the Restoration of Israel

One of the Books of Maccabees, a postcanonical chronicle of the Maccabees dynasty in the second and first century BCE, makes a revelatory observation, suggesting that the Land of Israel was chosen by God for the People of Israel, not vice versa: "The Lord did not choose the nation for the sake of the holy place, but the place for the sake of the nation. Therefore, the place itself shared in the misfortunes that befell the nation and afterward participated in its benefits; and what was forsaken in the wrath of the Almighty was restored again in all its glory when the great Lord became reconciled."[69]

Indeed, as evidenced in modern history, the Lord did show mercy to the People of Israel, when He allowed them to return to their inherited land. The very Hebrew prophets, who threatened the People of Israel with captivity followed by exile from their homeland, have always reassured their people with the message that their exile was the expiation for their sin and would terminate when God deemed the penalty to have been exacted. They promised that God would restore them to their land. Such a prophecy was given, for example, by Isaiah, Jeremiah, Amos, and Zachariah as follows:

> Comfort you, comfort you, My people, said your God. Bid Jerusalem take heart, and proclaim unto her, that her time of service is accomplished, that her guilt is paid off; that she has received of the Lord's hand double for all her sins.[70]
>
> For thus said the Lord: "After seventy years are accomplished for Babylon, I will remember you, and perform My good word toward you, in causing you to return to this place [...] And I will be found of you, said the Lord, and I will restore you from your captivity, and gather you from all the nations, and from all the places where I have driven you, said the Lord; and I will bring you back unto the place from where I caused you to be exiled."[71]
>
> In that day will I raise up the tabernacle of David that is fallen, and close up the breaches thereof, and I will raise up his ruins, and I will build it as in the days of old...And I will restore my People of Israel from captivity, and they shall build the waste cities and inhabit them; and they shall plant vineyards, and drink their wine; they shall also till gardens and eat their fruits; and I will plant them upon their land, and they shall no more be uprooted from their land, which I have given them, said the Lord, your God.[72]
>
> Thus said the Lord of Hosts: "Behold, I will save My people from the east country, and from the west country; And I will bring them, and they shall dwell in the midst of Jerusalem; and they shall be My people, and I will be their God, in truth and in righteousness."[73]

The Prophet Isaiah, in one of his prophetic orations, connects God's promise to Abraham and the restoration of Zion as the fulfillment of that promise: "Look unto Abraham your father, and unto Sarah who bore; for when he was but one I called him, and I blessed him and multiplied him. For the Lord has comforted Zion; he has comforted all her waste places, and has made her wilderness like Eden, and her desert like the garden of the Lord."[74]

None of the four prophets mentioned above are recorded in the Qur'ān, although two of them—Jeremiah and Zachariah—are related in *Qiṣaṣ al-Anbiyā'*. But, we should all be reminded of the injunction in the Qur'ān warning to not to make any difference between the prophets.[75] Accordingly, all prophets are to be recognized by Muslims and their messages are to be accepted indiscriminately.

Here, on the other hand, is what we read in some of the Psalms of David, whom the Qur'ān regards as a prophet, a divine "vicegerent on earth" and whose scripture, Zabūr, as a message to mankind:[76]

> And [the Lord] gave their land for a heritage, for His mercy endures forever. A heritage unto Israel His servant, for His mercy endures forever. Who remembered us in our low state, for His mercy endures forever and has delivered us from our enemies, for His mercy endures forever.[77]
>
> He remembered His covenant forever—the Word which He commanded to a thousand generations—[the covenant] that He made with Abraham, and His oath to Isaac. Then He established it for Jacob as a statute, for Israel as an everlasting covenant; saying: "To you I shall give the Land of Canaan, the lot of your inheritance." When, they were but few in number, hardly dwelling there; and they wandered from people to people, from one kingdom to another people; He allowed no man to do them, and He rebuked kings for their sake.[78]
>
> You shall arise, and have mercy upon Zion, for it is time to be gracious unto her, for the set time is come. For Your servants take pleasure in its stones and love her dust. So the nations shall fear the name of the Lord, and all the kings of the earth Your glory. When the Lord shall build up Zion, He shall appear in His glory.[79]
>
> By the rivers of Babylon, there we sat down, yea, we wept, when we remembered Zion. Upon the willows in their midst we hanged up our harps. For there they that led us captive asked of us words of song, and our tormentors asked of us mirth, "Sing us one of the songs of Zion." How shall we sing the Lord's song in a foreign land? If I forget you, O Jerusalem, let my right hand whither. Let my tongue stick to my palate, if I cease to think of you, if I do not keep Jerusalem in memory even at my happiest hour.[80]

This famous oath, composed during the first exile in Babylonia, in the sixth century BCE, is traditionally recited by Jewish devotees at the beginning of their Grace After Meal and is used, perhaps more than any other biblical phrase, to convey the Jewish deep and sacred loyalty to the Land of Israel.

A New Vision of Peace

The biblical narrative of Genesis, the story of Patriarchs in particular, teaches us that the Land of Israel has never been "a land of milk and honey." Because of its special physical and spiritual characteristics, it has always encountered problems that needed to be resolved—the scarcity of territory that causes disputes over pastureland; the scarcity of natural resources, such as water that frequently causes famine; the precarious geopolitical strategic location that attracts neighboring empires to invade; the actual and potential conflicts between the recipients of the Covenant, that is, Abraham and its descendents, and the natives of the Land; and the power struggle within the family of Abraham over covenantal promises. We inherited these problems. Was the Land both blessed and cursed? It looks like that, on the surface. On the deeper level, God seemingly made His promises and they are now in the hands of the inheritors of the Land to peacefully resolve the issues associated with their implementation. Or perhaps, God wanted us to know that the Land's bitter adversaries are not the people who inhabit it, but the inherent scarcity and shortage in resources, which should only unite the people in their search for solutions.

When Abraham made a covenant with Abimelech, the Philistine King of Grar in the south (see Chapter 4), he in fact gave up the Land of the Philistines (Hebrew: *'Ēretz Plishṭīm*), which was part of the territory of the Land of Israel. He did it despite the divine promise of the Land to his descendents because he wanted to ensure the perpetuity of his family within a territory that he perceived to be inherently suffering from natural calamities.[81] This peace initiative by Abraham should be regarded as an example for us to follow, or as the Jewish sages suggested, "the deeds of fathers is an augural sign for their children."[82]

The moral and historical rights of the Jews to the Land of Israel, as rightful as they can be, cannot ignore the realty on the ground—specifically the national aspirations of the Palestinians to self-determination. Clearly, the destiny of the Israelis and Palestinians is interconnected by virtue of the common land they live in. They need to accept the unavoidable—that the constraints of Middle Eastern geography and demography necessitate cooperation and compromise. They also need to embrace the inevitable—that their historical aspirations and dreams of maximizing their territory must be compromised so that the two peoples can share the disputed land of historical 'Ēretz Yisraēl / Palestine. However, the collapse of the ill-designed Oslo process (1993–2000) and the 2006 violence on the northern and southern borders of Israel, despite the withdrawal by Israel of its military forces from Lebanon in 2000 and the unilateral disengagement from Gaza in 2005, show that the old mutually agreed upon principle of "land for peace" is not a sufficient basis for a political settlement. This compromising concept has not been convincing enough, because the two sides are driven by conflicting national interests shaped by different historical narratives.

To resolve their conflict, the Israelis and Palestinians need to recontextualize it, reframing it in terms of sharing the land rather than dividing it. This is not just semantics. Language is a form of behavior. The distinction of *sharing* is part of the vocabulary of peace, whereas *dividing* is part of the lexicon of war. Conflicts arise from the illusionary perception or misconception that there is not enough. The key for the Israelis and the Palestinians is to recognize each other on the basis of their mutual interests and the assets they share, despite the religious, national, and cultural differences that divide them. They must acknowledge their interdependence, even when they have already gained or still seek independence. The recognition of this fundamental commonality leads to the creative solution of the conflict.

Thus, the struggle over the historical British Mandate of 'Ĕretz Yisraēl / Palestine, now divided between Israel, Jordan, and the territories in between, where the Palestinians seeking statehood live, can be possibly resolved, not by a mere territorial partition, but rather by confederative arrangements.[83] Accordingly, this region will be politically transformed into a trilateral confederation, a system that combines self-rule with shared rule. It will be composed of three distinct, independent, sovereign states: the Jewish State of Israel, the Arab State of Palestine, and the Hashemite Kingdom of Jordan, and run by a Jerusalem-based confederal authority "on the top of the mountain." Such a political arrangement may be the best form of government for the resolution of the heart of the Arab-Israeli conflict and the key for a full normalization of the relations between Israel and all Arab states.

One word of clarification should be offered to the concerned traditional nationalists in both societies: confederation does not mean *more* supranationalism and *less* nation-state, or that it is a model of transnational organization that may reduce the sovereignty of its member-states, ultimately subjugating them to a central power and turning them into a single polity. All stakeholders must accept that historical 'Ĕretz Yisraēl / Palestine is a community of peoples, not only of states, and that the glue that binds them together is not a shared identity, but rather a shared destiny. Their sense of belonging to a regional group is not based on who they are, but of what they can accomplish together for the common good. They have to recognize the need for a community of projects with shared objectives that will use the vast human and natural resources of the region to the pursuits of peace.

Within this new context of a confederation "superstructure," out of a wholehearted commitment to a new vision of peace, partnership, mutuality, and cooperation, a Palestinian state can safely emerge west of the

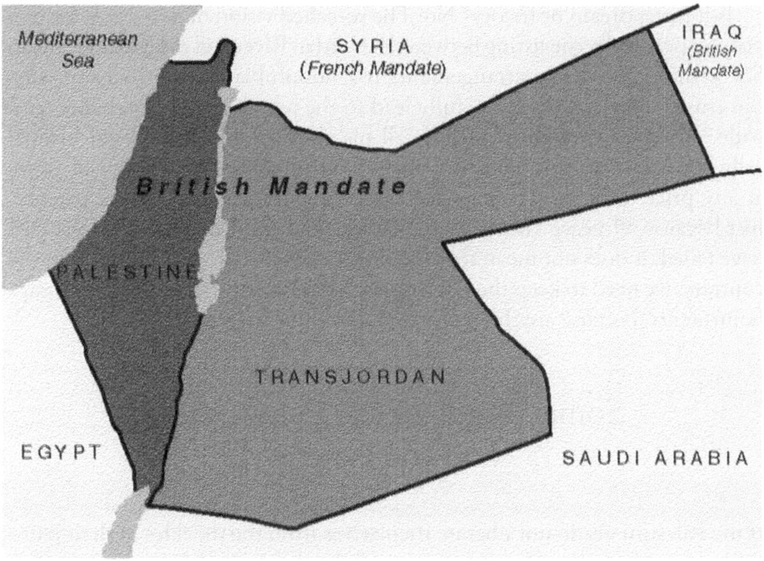

Figure 7.1 Map of the British Mandate of Palestine.

Jordan River, which might resolve the fundamental issue of viable economic well-being for the Palestinians and all other thorny core issues of a final peace agreement (including security, final borders, Jewish settlements, Palestinian refugees, Jerusalem, holy sites, and water problems).

The focus could shift altogether to a shared infrastructure of peace that enthusiastically harnesses the resources, talents, and imaginations of the peoples in the entire region, and effectively involves the international community in a new economic Marshall Plan–like recovery program. The Israeli-Palestinian-Jordanian confederative infrastructure could also expand its partnership to neighboring countries and together create a larger regional open space that is connected to the Mediterranean and Europe with multiple economic cooperative agreements and a concrete program of international financial support.

A successful model to follow is the Benelux union in western Europe that comprises three neighboring countries, Belgium, the Netherlands, and Luxembourg, and is run by a Secretary-General located in Brussels. Although Benelux represents only a cultural, economic, financial, and geographic grouping, its structure—an economic union with an Interparliamentary Consultative Council and a Committee of Ministers—demonstrates what's possible for an Israeli-Palestinian-Jordanian confederation.

Is it just a dream or theory? No! The so-called vision of two states for two peoples peacefully coexisting between the Jordan River and the Mediterranean Sea within confederate arrangements is a nonutopian vision that everyone can trust—one that may hopefully lead to the rebuilding of Abraham's tent, wide and open enough to include all his children who have been historically connected to this land. But this vision presented here is not of peace at any price. It is only a vision for those who seek peace with coexistence. Just because all peace efforts by the Israelis and the Palestinians in the past have failed, it does not mean that the future contains no possibilities. On the contrary, we need to keep the peace process alive despite the consistent disappointments, because anything else is tantamount to insanity.

Some Words to the Palestinians and the Israelis

If the Palestinians do not liberate themselves from the shackles of their painful past and from the "inner occupation" that has been ruining their society from within; if they resort to violence and terror as a policy and modus operandi against the State of Israel; if they are unable to govern themselves as civil society does and are incapable of producing a responsible and courageous leadership that shows up as a true and capable partner for peace; if they refuse to publicly and unambiguously recognize the right of the Jewish people to a sovereign state of its own in its historical homeland; if they do not think and speak in terms of a Palestinian state with defined boundaries along the side of Israel; if they keep raising demands that are inconsistent with a true desire to bring an end to the conflict—they cannot expect the Israelis to cede to their hands territories of the Land of Israel.

If the Israelis do not liberate themselves from the political paradigm where "peace through security" supersedes "security through peace"; if they do not stop treating the Israeli-Palestinian conflict with conflict management tools and adopt conflict transformation and resolution methods instead; if they neglect to speak of Prophet Isaiah's vision of peace and act according to it; if they are unable to produce a powerful leadership team that is capable of enrolling the people behind a shared vision of peace and lead them into a new era of reconciliation with the Palestinians; if they fail to recognize that peace is achievable only when they grant self-determination to the Palestinians, who have a legitimate claim to it; if they do not come to the realization that relinquishing substantial territories to allow a viable Palestinian state within a genuine peace agreement is inevitable—they cannot expect the Palestinians to end their fight against Israel.

Rabbi Ovadia Yosef, formerly the Sephardi Chief Rabbi of Israel and one of the greatest religious scholars in our generation, wrote an encouraging study titled, "Ceding Territory of the Land of Israel in order to Save Lives."[84] Based on a halakhik ruling he published in August 1979, he argues that "if it can be determined beyond all doubt that ceding territory will lead to a genuine peace between us and our Arab neighbors, and on the other hand, the threat of war is eminent if the territories are not returned to them—the territories should be returned, as nothing stands in the way of [the halakhic principle of] *piqūaḥ nēfesh* (saving life)." In order words, in his opinion, territories could be ceded in order to prevent loss of life and as long as the relinquishment will lead to a genuine peace. It would be helpful to see a similar ruling coming out of the hands of an important Muslim cleric.

Final Thoughts

There is a Middle Eastern folktale that has both Hebrew and Arabic versions about a special kind of brotherly relationship.[85] It tells about God traveling to the four corners of the world in search of the perfect site to build a holy temple. Somewhere in the mountains of the Holy Land, He came upon a large barley field shared by two brothers whose selfless love was greater than any love on earth.

The story relates that the two brothers grew barley together in this field and shared equally in the harvest. Each brother had his own house. The older brother was married and had children. The younger brother lived alone. One night, during the harvest, the older brother could not sleep. He was worried about his younger brother, thinking to himself, "My younger brother is all alone, while I have a wife and children. When I am old my children will take care of me. I must give some of my barley to my brother so he may save for his old age." On the same night, the younger brother tossed and turned in his bed worrying about his older brother. He thought to himself, "My brother has a family to feed and I only need to feed myself. I must give some of my barley to my brother." Quietly, and in secret, each brother loaded his arms with barley and carried it to his brother's storage area. The brothers did this for three nights. On the following mornings, when the brothers would check their piles of barley, they remained the same in size. Each wondered, "How could this be? I know I am putting more barley in my brother's pile." On the fourth night, when the moon was full, each brother again rose up. Each filled his arms with barley and made his way to his brother' storage area. Then, suddenly by the light of the moon, the two brothers met in the middle of the field. Each realized what the other had been doing. The put down their armfuls of barley and hugged each other.

The Jewish tradition tells us that God chose this spot to build the Holy Temple of Jerusalem. The Arab version of the story tells that in the morning, each brother was amazed to find the heaps still equal, until Allah sent a prophet who informed them that their unselfish love was pleasing to God. What made the relationship between these two brothers so special that it attracted God's attention? What can we learn from this story?

We learn a simple lesson of history. It was the love between two brothers that caused Jerusalem, the City of Peace, to be built, and it is hate that may cause its destruction. God chose this site of brotherly love in the hope that the love emanating from the Temple would bring brothers and sisters from around the world to the same level of caring and sharing as demonstrated by those two brothers in the Judean Hills.

Yet, there is another story about two brothers that ended tragically. This is the biblical story of Adam and Eve's sons, Cain and Abel. Each made an offering to God, but God favored that of Abel. So out of jealousy, Cain killed him.[86] *Qiṣaṣ al-Anbiyā'* adds its own account: "After Cain had killed Abel, the earth shook for seven days and nights. Abel's blood sank into the earth the way water sinks downward [. . .] Ever since that day, blood doesn't sink into the earth. On that spot hawthorns and tamarisks sprang up; the ground there became salty. The wild birds and beasts fled into the mountains because brothers no longer showed mercy to one another. Adam and Eve wept bitterly. Adam mourned and recited the following poem. Adam was the first person on earth to recite a poem."[87] Then, *Qiṣaṣ al-Anbiyā'* presents us a poem written by Adam, the first poem ever written by man, according to this Islamic tradition:

> The country and the people have changed,
> The face of the earth has become ugly and dusty.
> All that has color and taste has changed,
> And the good cheer of the pretty face has become rare,
> Because Cain has murdered his brother Abel.
> Alas! What regret for that beautiful face!
> The earth has replaced bounty with scarcity,
> While in Paradise, rivers are sad.
> Is there anything left for me in life but wailing?
> And will I ever have comfort in this life?
> Alack, alas for Abel, my son
> Who has been murdered and now lies in his grave![88]

Cain and Abel are metaphorical figures. Like today's religions that compete for God's favor, they each build their own altars, believing that their offering is the one to be accepted by God. And they are willing to kill for it. The poem, although a lamentation by the mythological Adam over his son Abel, can appeal to modern leaders in the face of what's going on in the world.

During the days of the Patriarchs, every one of our forefathers continued to build his own little altar to find favor in God's eyes. God later forbade the use of altars and instructed the People of Israel to designate one place, one Holy Temple. After its destruction, and the emergence of new religions out of the Jewish stem, Jerusalem became a center of many altars. Christian and Muslim shrines now stand side by side with the remains of the old Temple.

The two stories should be studied in every school and delivered to both Israeli and Palestinian diplomats before they negotiate peace, so that they are reminded to recognize each other as brothers and sisters who wish to repair the fractured spiritual legacy of their common ancestor, Abraham. Brotherhood should cross all religious and national boundaries. "Reconciliation (*iṣlāḥ*) between people,"[89] prescribed by the Qur'ān, should preside over the religious and national conversation in both Israel and the Palestinian territories. Remember the Qur'ān's verse, "But if the enemy inclines towards peace you [also] incline towards peace, and trust in God."[90] And if the Israelis and Palestinians finally reach an agreement, we should all be reminded of the Qur'ān's words, "Do not mischief on the earth, after reconciliation has been reached,"[91] a warning especially against the "spoilers" on both sides who consistently cause "mischief" (*fasād*) in order to disrupt any progress in the peace negotiations. The Qur'ān makes a clear distinction between "those who do evil" (*al-mufsidīn*), of whom we need to beware, and "those who do good" (*al-muḥsinīn*), who we need to support.[92] And "if a person forgives and reconciles," adds the Qur'ān, "his reward is due from God."[93] In the same vein, The Mishnah prescribes a special reward for a few deeds; one of them is "bringing peace between man and his fellow man," a precept "the fruits of which man enjoys in This World while the reward remains in the World-to-Come."[94]

Achieving a real peace that fulfils Prophet Hosea's words, "And I will break the bow and the sword and the battle out of the land,"[95] will demand an extreme act of faith from both Israelis and Palestinians, a belief in a shared vision of peace that can bridge the wide gap separating their historical narratives. Perhaps, like the brotherly sharing of crops in "The Tale of Two Brothers," sharing land for peace may be an alternative. But, unless we believe that peace is possible, the so-called peace efforts or peace talks will lack vision, and "where there is no vision, the people perish"[96] on both sides. But, where there is vision, the people flourish.[97] Unless we offspring of Abraham—children of Ishmael and Isaac—view the historical dispute through the right lenses, seeing us both live alongside each other rather than against each other, no resolution of the conflict will ever happen. Such is the lyrics of the following Israeli song by Hemi Rodner:

> How long, my God, shall I beseech you in prayer?
> And how long, my God, shall we look at each other
> through the sight of a rifle?
> No more will Ishmael be banished to the desert.
> Every morning we will get up to the side of Hagar's son
> and Israel will not be thrown out to the sea.
> This is the simple truth for the children of Abraham.
> (Author's translation from Hebrew)

Within the paradigm of consistently seeing the enemy "through the sight of a rifle," there are three etymologically related Hebrew words: *dām* (blood), *adām* (man) and *adamāh* (land). The linkage between them—"man" sheds "blood" over "land"—has a devastating effect on the Israeli-Palestinian conflict. Instead, we need a new paradigm, where man is guided by the ethical principle that the value of blood, or life, is greater than the value of land. Let's pray that this powerful transcendent vision of peace, where both nations are willing to end the bloodshed and share the land in order to enjoy the blessings of peace, will be an inspiration for their negotiating leaders.[98]

Chapter 8

The Gate of Humanness

The Problem of Truth—the Truth of the Problem

The most fundamental contemporary issue confronting the relations between Judaism and Islam, and consequently the relations between Israelis and Arabs, is the precedence their creeds give to Truth (with a capital T), the absolute truth, over all other ethical virtues. The common dictum, "All Truth is God's Truth," has become the main source of conflict, as each religious group upholds to and propagates its own absolutist version of God's Truth. In so doing, they "religiously" fall into two traps, both at the same time: first, the "relativity trap"—when each group rejects the view that all truths are relative to time, place, and culture. Second, the "exclusivity trap"—when each asserts in absolute terms that there is only one moral law, one code, one standard, one way, and "ours is the right one, because it is God's." Each group is convinced from its divine prerogatives that they are the only true religion, and claim that "we are right because we possess the Truth; if you differ from us, you are a nonbeliever or heretic, and you are in error."

The problem of Truth is the truth of the problem in Jewish-Muslim relations. As long as one faith insists on wearing its truth as divine certainty and depicts the other as representing a deviation from it, there is no chance for interreligious reconciliation. On the contrary, the "best" way to perpetuate the Jewish-Muslim rift, or any other intergroup dispute, is by making it a holy war, a conflict between truth and falsehood.

The problem is not whether there is absolute truth or not—there is. The problem arises when individuals and groups claim to possess the absolute truth—their own version of Truth. The problem is that they collapse the word "truth" with a position they believe in, whether political or ideological. The problem is that truth contains both a statement and its contradiction. Thus, for a belief system to be "true," all the other systems must be "false." This absurd stand, taken historically by various brands of fundamentalism and totalitarianism, has been disastrous in its consequences to the internal well-being of each individual religious group, and has been even more disastrous in its impact upon interreligious relations.

We must accept the notion that one's truth is that which corresponds with one's reality. It is a subjective truth because it corresponds with a subjective reality. The Truth, the absolute truth, is the collective body of many truths. When Muslims and Jews, Arabs and Israelis, embrace the notion that the Absolute has to be something other than *my* absolute, then free communication and enhanced understanding among them will become possible. When religions and nations begin to recognize the need to overcome their "religious egos" and "national egos" respectively—the way human beings overcome their individual egos—they will forge the path toward a new universal civilization, in which a culture of love and compassion dominates.

We all must live by and relate to each other in accordance with the phrase "the truth, the whole truth, and nothing but the truth," used in English law courts, but changing the last word from singular "truth" to plural "truths." The shift from the global context of One Truth to a new context of many truths will allow us to move toward theological connectedness and bring the diverse religious traditions together to respond to the challenges we now share in common. In this new context of higher consciousness, our task is to awaken everyone to the ultimate truth that there is only One and that we are all that One.

The Concept of God's Truth

The concept of God's Truth pervades the scriptures of both Judaism and Islam and dominates their entire belief systems as the concept of One God does. In both religions, Truth is God, and therefore His word is absolutely True.

Being one of God's chief attributes, Truth (Hebrew: *'emēt*) is considered in the Bible and Talmud as one of the greatest values. The idea of divinity as "the God of Truth" and His words as "the Law of Truth" is spread throughout the Psalms.[1] The virtue of truth is also seen throughout the teachings of the rabbinic sages, such as the first chapter of *Pirkēi Avōt* ("Sayings of the Fathers"), which includes the following statement by Rabbān Shimon ben Gamliel, the last *Nasī'* (chief) of the *Sanhedrīn* (the Great Assembly of Jewish judges in ancient Israel), "The world rests upon three things, on justice, on truth, and on peace."[2] Another sage, Rabbi Ḥanina, stated: "Truth is the Seal of the Blessed Holy One."[3] The Midrash gives the following explanation: "'What is the seal of the Blessed Holy One?' Our rabbi said in the name of Rabbi Reuven, 'Why is *'Emēt*, the Hebrew word for Truth?' Resh Lakish replied, 'Because it [אמת] is spelled *Aleph* (א) *Mem* (מ) *Tav* (ת). *Aleph* is the first letter [of the Hebrew alphabet], *Mem* is the middle letter, and *Tav* is the last letter. God thus says (in Isaiah 44:6), 'I am first, and I am last.'"[4] Meaning, the word *'Emēt*, Truth, was chosen by God as His seal because it represents the entire Hebrew language, the "holy tongue," His Word. Among the 16 virtues of the Word of God (the Torah) recited in the Jewish prayerbook, *'emēt* is listed as the very first one and defined as the master attribute from which all other virtues stem.

One point of clarification is needed. The chosenness of the People of Israel is an unfortunately misunderstood theological idea. The Torah's Truth that "the Lord your God has chosen you [the People of Israel] to be His own treasure, out of all peoples that are upon the face of the earth,"[5] is mistakenly understood by gentiles in qualitative and hierarchal terms and perceived by them as signs of Jewish proclamation of superiority.[6] It must be pointed out that while Judaism does not stop anyone from joining its ranks, it does not wish to convert the world nor does it want to become a world religion. It believes in a pluralistic universalism based on the cardinal principle that all human beings are God's children created in His image, and hopes, as expressed by the *'Aleinu* prayer, "to perfect the world under the sovereignty of the Almighty," meaning the establishment of a human commonwealth in which the belief in the Oneness of God, a world peace, interpersonal mercy and Divine Providence dominate.[7] The practice by Jews to make the ritual blessing before reading the Torah in Sabbath, "Blessed are You, Lord our God, King of the universe, who has chosen us from among all the nations and given us His Torah," is not a Jewish proclamation of their superiority; it is merely an acknowledgement of the role chosen for them by God.

In Islam, Truth (Arabic: *ḥaqq*) is also associated with God, the ultimate in truth, whose Name is "The Truth,"[8] and whose message, the Qur'ān, sent by God through Prophet Muhammad, is regarded as "the Truth."[9] For Muslims, their Holy Book is a book of Truth, "the way that is most right,"[10] a fully guarded Word of God that "no falsehood can approach it,"[11] one that "stands out clear from error."[12] Anchored in the Qur'ān, as the last, conclusive, perfect "words of living God," Muslims believe that ever since it was revealed to Prophet Muhammad, Islam has been destined to be superior over the other religions, as the Qur'ān says, "You are the best nation (*'ummah*) that has ever been raised up for mankind, enjoining what is right and forbidding what is wrong, and believing in God,"[13] and "It is He Who has sent His Messenger with guidance and the Religion of Truth, to proclaim it over all religions."[14] Thus, the preceding scriptures, the Torah (Old Testament) and the Gospels (New Testament), are held by Muslims as genuine divine revelations, which had become corrupted in their handing down, a deliberate change that necessitated the giving of the Qur'ān to Prophet Muhammad to correct this alleged distortion of the Word of God. Indeed the Muslims believe that their faith is related to that of Abraham of the Torah. But they also believe that their Prophet is "The Seal" (*Khātim an-Nabiyyīn*), who came to bring God's final law for the guidance of all humanity, that he supersedes all the previous prophets of Israel and that their religion is "The Religion" (*Ad-Dīn*), the only true religion in the universe. For that reason, they claim for themselves the exclusive truth.

The Arabic root of "truth" and "law" *ḥ.q.q.* can be found in Hebrew. There, it forms two related verbs "to legislate" (*le-ḥoqēq*) and "to engrave" (*la-ḥaqōq*). The Jewish Morning Prayer reminds us that "[Your] Word is good and eternal in truth and trustworthiness, a Law that will never be abrogated." Etymologically, divine Law (*ḥōqq*) is that which, like the Ten Commandments, has been permanently "carved in stone" and, like Truth, is perfect, being authored by God, and it can never be altered or changed. Expounding on the biblical passage, "The [two] Tablets are the work of God, and the writing is the writing of God, engraved (*ḥarūṭ*) upon the Tablets,"[15] *Pirkēi Avōt*, playing with words, suggests, "Do not read *ḥarūṭ* (engraved), but *ḥerūt* (freedom), for no man is free but he who is engaged in the study of Torah."[16] This is why Jewish sages suggested that "Torah scholars [who study the scriptural text] increase peace in the world."[17] Unless we, Jews and Muslims, continuously engage in a critical study of the Law and occupy ourselves in the reinterpretation of our scriptures, we would remain rigid, fixated, and intolerant toward others. If we do, however, go back to our sacred texts and revisit our teachings, a free space may be opened up to revise old prejudices and embrace other peoples' truths.

An Illustrating Parable

Much of the interreligious strife and the resulting potential calamity to humanity is the influence of truth in our life, as we can see from the following Midrash.[18] Expounding on the verse, "Loving-kindness and truth met together, righteousness and peace kissed each other,"[19] this Midrashic parable tells, the moment God was about to create the first Adam, the ministering angels broke up into factions. Some of them said, "Let him be created," while others said, "Let him not be created." The argument centered around four heavenly factions:

1. The Angel of Loving-Kindness (*ḥēsed*) said, "Let him be created, for he will do acts of loving-kindness."
2. The Angel of Truth (*'emēt*) said, "Let him not be created, for he will be drenched in lies."
3. The Angel of Righteousness (*tzēdeq*) said, "Let him be created, for he will do righteous deeds."
4. The Angel of Peace (*shalōm*) said, "Let him not be created, for he will be all discord and quarrelsomeness."

What did God do? He took Truth and cast it to the ground, as it is written (in Daniel 8:12): "Truth will be cast to the earth." The ministering angels immediately approached God, asking, "Why do you shame the leader of your court? Let Truth rise from the earth, they requested. Thus it is written (in Psalms 85:12), 'Truth will arise from the earth.'"

What did God gain by casting Truth to the ground, if Peace remains? After all, Peace also said "Let him not be created." Because, when you cast Truth, Peace stays. The source of any conflict is that every one fights for his own truth. When you set truth aside, there is nothing to quarrel about. As we are told, "Wherever the law of truth reigns there is no peace, and wherever peace reigns there is no need for judgment of truth."[20] Truth is crucial to peace, at least the kind of peace we all aspire to. Peace without truth may be a peace of lies. We hope, however, that truth and peace would support each other, as it is written, "Truth and peace love each other."[21] But, when we are unable to get rid of divisive and hostile "truths," we can still live in peace and harmony hoping that we will ultimately discover the authentic truth. This leads directly to the next question.

Why didn't God cast Peace to the ground? Because nothing can exist if there is no peace. The word "*shalōm*," peace, is etymologically rooted in the Hebrew word "*shalēm*," which means "complete" or "whole." So, when we maintain peace, we eventually arrive at truth. The rabbinic sages even suggested that one may deviate from the truth in the interests of peace.[22] Peace was so important for them that a special Chapter on Peace (*Perēk ha-Shalōm*) was dedicated to peace, in the Talmud (see Appendix 3). This text lists several cases from the Bible, where a "good" lie was told "in order to make peace" like between Abraham and Sarah and Joseph and his brothers.[23] The Talmudic sages held the opinion that a "true" truth is a state of peace, whether between spouses, brothers, or anybody else in the world. Violating the truth for the sake of peace, love, and brotherhood is marginal. In other words, an absolute, uncompromising commitment to tell the truth sometimes might unnecessarily jeopardize the most desirable state of human affairs, which is peace. We are even told, "So great is peace that, even if [the People of] Israel were to worship idols yet manage to maintain peace among themselves at the same time, the Blessed Holy One says, 'I cannot wield power over them, because peace prevails among them.'"[24] This is why it is better to throw away truth.

And what about Loving-kindness and Righteousness? Truth is without effect if not accompanied by these two virtues. The angels, who supported the creation of Adam, recognized that these two virtues are essential for the survival of God's creation. Judaism and Islam may differ in their conception of Truth and in their understanding of what Peace means, but for sure they are in agreement about the precedence that should be given to both loving-kindness and righteousness over all other ethical values.

Shimon the Righteous says in *Pirkēi Avōt* that "the world is based upon three principles: on the Torah, on the worship [of God], and on acts of loving-kindness."[25] A Hebrew derivative of loving-kindness is mercy or compassion and one of God's Names is "The Merciful" (*Ha-Raḥamān*) or "Merciful Father" (*Av Ha-Raḥamān*). The Talmud states that "anyone who is not compassionate to mankind cannot truly be of the descendent of Abraham, our father,"[26] and that "one who is kind to humankind, the Heavens are kind to him, and those who are not kind to humankind, the Heavens are not kind to him."[27] As to righteousness, it is written in the Bible, "Blessed are they who observe justice and do righteousness at all times,"[28] and "The righteous man is the foundation of the world."[29]

Likewise in Islam, as we have seen (see Chapter 2), "The Merciful" (*Al-Raḥmān*) is one of the most popular of the Ninety-Nine Beautiful Names of God. It forms the traditional prelude to every verse in the Qur'ān—"*Bismillāh ar-Raḥmān ar-Raḥīm*" (In the Name of God, the Merciful, the Compassionate). The Qur'ān, like the Jewish tradition, teaches to be kind and compassionate to others as He is to you. It says, "Be kind as God has been kind to you,"[30] and also, "The Merciful is kind to those who are kind to others."[31] As to righteousness, the Qur'ān states, "Those who have faith and do righteous deeds, they are the best of creatures."[32] And Prophet Muhammad stated in his farewell sermon, "The noblest among you in the eyes of God is the one with the most righteous conduct."[33]

Monotheism Redefined

The narrow definition of monotheism—the belief in a single, universal, all-encompassing deity—has many ramifications. Some of these are destructive to interreligious relations, as each religious group incorporates other absolutist elements into their "mono": the belief in a single Truth, the belief in a single image for the human being, and the belief that a single religion is needed for humanity. Some of them, however, are constructive, which we need to reinforce, such as the universalistic idea of the brotherhood of humankind under the Fatherhood of God. The complementary relationship between the brotherhood of mankind and the Fatherhood of God is a central doctrine in the Jewish religion. Malachi, the famed Hebrew prophet of universalism, affirms this monotheistic concept by asking the following questions: "Have we not all one Father? Has not the One God created us? So why do we deal treacherously every man against his brother?"[34]

It is time we expand the definition of monotheism and spread the idea of so-called ethical monotheism, one that professes a single God from which emanate ethical imperatives for human conduct, one that considers the ritual precepts governing the relationship between man and his God and the ethical precepts governing the relationship between man and his fellow as equally important; one that finds the unity of God and the diversity of human expressions as complementary and noncontradictory; one that regards the divine love of God and the earthly love of man as one and the same. In both Judaism and Islam, love of fellow human beings is an essential and integral part of love of God and faith in Him.

This idea was presented in an open letter, titled "A Common Word between Us and You," sent in September 2007 by 138 Muslim scholars, clerics, and intellectuals who had unanimously come together for the first time since the early days of Islam to declare the common ground between Christianity and Islam. Sponsored by the The Royal Aāl al-Bayt Institute for Islamic Thought in Jordan, this historical epistle, which was addressed to the leaders of all the world's churches, speaks of the love of God and the love of man as the most fundamental common ground between Islam and Christianity and the best basis for future dialogue and understanding between them.[35] Never before had Muslims delivered this kind of definitive consensus statement on Christianity. Rather than engage in polemic, the signatories of this letter have adopted the traditional and mainstream Islamic position of respecting the Christian scripture. While this reconciliation letter was timely and commendable, one cannot help but be troubled by the position taken by the initiators and signatories to ignore Judaism, the parent of Christianity and Islam, and the Hebrew Bible, the originator of the Two Commandments of Love. This epistle appears to reduce Judaism to a footnote. To broaden the dialogue to include Judaism and acknowledge its contribution to, and kinship relation with, the religious groups it gave birth to, would be seen as a decent, worthy approach. Such a move would be true to their message of peace among all People of the Book and be consistent with the words of the Qur'ān, "We make no distinction between anyone of them," that is, all revelations.[36] For sure, such an unprecedented dialogue would receive joyous accolades all over the world.

One such effort took place in January 2002, when more than a dozen senior Jewish and Muslim and Christian leaders from Israel/Palestine met in Alexandria, Egypt, and concluded an unprecedented joint declaration pledging themselves to work together for a just and lasting peace. The agreement, which was thereafter known as the First Declaration of Alexandria of the Religious Leaders of the Holy Land (see Appendix 4), pledges the spiritual leaders to use their religious and moral authority to work for an end to violence and the resumption of the peace process. It also envisages the establishment of a permanent committee of leaders from the three religions in Israel/Palestine to pursue the implementation of the declaration.[37] Such an event was a good start and should continue on a global level to include religious leaders from all over the world, as were the following interfaith and international gatherings: The Cordoba Initiative founded in 2002,[38] the Alliance of Civilizations established in 2005 under the United Nations,[39] and the Council of 100 Leaders also established in 2005 under the World Economic Forum.[40]

We live in an age of competing truths, where "truth-bearers" compete with the others over whom God loves best and are willing, in the name of God, to kill for it. This is a total misunderstanding of God, Whose love is infinite and boundless. We should all concern ourselves with how best to love God and His creation and follow what the Qur'ān asks of humankind, "Compete with one another in doing what is good,"[41] and "enjoin that which is good (*ma'arūf*) and forbid that which is evil (*munkar*)."[42]

We live in an abundant universe, where man is the only vehicle for God's love, grace, and goodness to be expressed. With this role comes responsibility—to express those divine qualities on the planet and show up as God's true servant on earth. On the sixth day of creation, after creating man in His image and likeness, "God saw all that He had made, and behold, it was very good."[43] This is an empowering reminder that we are charged with the awesome responsibility of perfecting God's Creation. After seven days, on the eighth day, we began where God left off, and assumed our role as God's fellow architects in the building of a better world, or at least maintaining it as God left it off—"very good."

Unfortunately, however, the state of the world is not what God had in mind. We have been a witness to a world turned upside down, where the violence of the few has instilled a sense of chaos and fear. At the basis of this violence is the growing religious polarization in the world. We find the three Great Religions still theologically dividing the world into two universal blocs—the faithful and the unfaithful—maintaining a state of conflictive, even belligerent, relations between them. Judaism makes a distinction between the People of Israel and the "gentile nations," or *goyyīm*. This distinction is imprinted in the Jewish collective consciousness as polar opposites. Christians have historically divided the world by religion and civilization to Christendom and all the rest of the nations and communities, known as infidels, and aspired to Christianize them and subordinate the whole world to one religion. Islam has divided the civilized world into two blocs, *Dār al-Islām* ("House of Islam") and *Dār al-Ḥarb* ("House of War"). The first one corresponded to the region under Islamic rule, and the second consisted of all the states and communities outside the Muslim dominated region. In theory, *Dār al-Islām* was always in a state of war (Arabic: *jihād*) with *Dār al-Ḥarb*. Although a common practice in the late medieval age, this Islamic international law that was concocted by Muslim classical jurists to contend with the problems of their time is still prescribed today by a few Islamist groups, such as Ḥamās and Ḥizballah, in their fight against the Jewish state of Israel and for the revival of the medieval Islamic caliphate. From their perspective, the renewal of the ancient conflict between Islam and the "Crusaders and Jews" justifies a war against Israel, an "illegitimate entity" on the frontline between the two civilization blocs. We should be reminded, however, that the contemporary generation of mainstream Muslim scholars discards the practically and Islamically unwarranted framework of this classical division of the world.[44] The division of humanity into warring blocs may have had a rationale in medieval times, but in today's era of globalization, where nations strive to be part of the developed world, such a belligerent framework of international relations has to be tossed away into the wastebasket of history.

This pervasive tendency to define the world in absolute terms, to color it in black and white, and divide it using rigid formulations of good and evil, may be attractive to promoters of fundamentalism and global confrontations, but it ultimately yields tragedy and devastation to humanity as a whole. It is time we divide the world according to ethical categories instead, namely: those who do good and those who do evil; those who partner in Creation and those who destroy the world of God; those who create, sanctify, and preserve life and those who destroy, desecrate, and ruin life; those who liken the moral nature of the human being to that of their Creator and emulate His benevolent attributes in their own life and those who misinterpret and misrepresent their scripture to advance their narrow, particularistic doctrine and, in the name of God, foment hostilities and divisions in the world; those who create boundaries and walls of separation and those who create bridges of peace and understanding; those who use faith and religion to promote the teachings of love and those who spread hatred.

One Truth and Many Truths

There is one universal rule, and one only, that is consistent with the idea of ethical monotheism, that can stand by itself in this warring world, in the face of the contending religious groups and apart from their creed. It is the Golden Rule—*Do to others, as you would have others do to you.* Both Judaism and Islam prescribe this ethic of reciprocity. In keeping with the central and admirable biblical commandment that is a preamble to the Jewish Morning Prayer—"You shall love your fellow as yourself"[45]—the great Jewish master and one of the foremost sages of the Talmudic period, Rabbi Akiba (ca. 50—ca. 135 CE) drew the conclusion that this biblical commandment is "a great principle of the Torah."[46] Another sage, Ben Azai, said, "The verse, 'When God created man He created him in His image' (Genesis 5:1) is an even greater principle."[47] In other words, love of a fellow human being, which is not motivated and nourished by the realization that man was created in God's image, is doomed to failure. When we realize that man is fashioned in the image of God and he carries His spark, interpersonal relationships will be more significant and the life of the other will be treated as sacred.

The Jewish preeminent teacher and scholar, Rabbi Hillel the Elder, went further by making the famous statement, "What is hateful to you do not do to your fellow: this is the whole Law, and the rest is interpretation."[48] Similarly, a famous *ḥadīth* states, "None of you has faith [in God] until he wishes for his brother what he wishes for himself."[49] The Golden Rule does not offer solutions, but a way to approach relationships. It does not prescribe a certain kind of treatment of others, but only the spirit in which we should treat them. It can be a starting point for a constructive dialogue between Islam and Judaism.

The renowned playwright George Bernard Shaw (1856–1950) once said that "the golden rule is that there are no golden rules." In making this statement, he may have gone too far to the extreme; but there is an element of truth in it. When we do away with those divisive "truths" asserted in the name of God that are particular to each of our religions, and adopt all-embracing universalistic ideas instead, we will be able to overcome the divisiveness existing between Islam and Judaism and will be well on the way to peace and reconciliation between them. When we accept the notion that the Truth, the "whole truth," belongs to neither Islam nor Judaism, and that each holds but a part of God's "whole truth," Muslims and Jews will realize that they are intimately connected to each other. The difference in letter composition between the Hebrew words for The Truth אמת (*'emēt*) and a truth אמיתה (*'amitāh*) is יה (Yod-Hay) that signifies the

Name of God; meaning that a truth is also God's living truth, even if it is not His "whole truth."

When people accept their religion as the best faith for them, but at the same time recognize that there are other religions that adhere to other systems of belief and morality, and when they develop a degree of doubt that their religion is the one and only true way to reach God, there might be fewer people willing to defend their "truth" by oppressing, discriminating against, killing, or committing genocide against followers of other faiths such as has happened throughout history.

Martin Buber (1878–1965), a famous Jewish philosopher and thinker, who is best known for his dialogic principle, *I and Thou*, said, "Truth is the Seal of the Blessed Holy One, and we are the wax with which it seeks to be stamped."[50] We are God's manifestation on earth. We are His living truth. As human beings we each have our own separate truths. We are asked to mirror His positive attributes, to "walk the talk" of Truth by spreading His goodness everywhere, as Buber beautifully explains:

> Resting above your head is the Truth, and One Truth for all. But it does not enter into your world, unless you implement it, *everyone [implementing] his own truth*. When you live with yourselves consistently and faithfully, then it takes place, then you find it as your own truth, the human truth. What our sages say—Truth is the Seal of the Blessed Holy One—makes this point more remarkable. If it is His Seal, then where is the [human] multicolored wax in which He stamps his Seal? To be good means to be quick and ready like the wax. "Conscience" is the living knowledge, one that knows when there is harmony between the Seal and us, and when there is not. When man pulls himself away from the [divine] stamping hand, it disappears; the light vanishes from our world. Yet, this is not a teaching that can be fulfilled with talks [only]. It wants to be learned in life itself [...] It is impossible to start out truth, but everyone doing it by himself (emphasis added).[51]

There is no better way to present the argument—that there is One Truth and many truths and that both Islam and Judaism are *true* religions—than with the words of the great Sufi master, Hafiz. Imagine he dedicated this prophetic poem to Islam and Judaism—"two birds on a limb":

> Both of our mouths can fit upon this flute I carry.
> My music will sound so much sweeter that way
> With your breath and my breath
> Poking each other in the ribs and kissing.
> I saw two birds on a limb this morning
> Laughing with the sun.
> They reminded me of how we will one day exist.
> My dear, keep thinking about God,

Keep thinking about the Beloved
And soon our nest will be the whole firmament.
Forget about all your desires for Truth,
We have gone far beyond that,
For now it is just pure need.
Both our hearts are meant to sing.
Both our souls are destined to touch and kiss
Upon this holy flute God carries.[52]

When this flute will be heard, Hafiz continues in another poem, the world will enjoy the "holy dance" of peace:

No
Conflict
When the flute is playing
For then I see every movement emanates
From God's
Holy
Dance.[53]

Final Thoughts

Nowadays, when a growing number of "truth-bearers," who set themselves as the arbiters of absolute truth, dominate global politics and attempt to create a new world order of divisions and hostilities, is the time to remind ourselves what Aristotle wrote in the fourth century BCE, "The least initial deviation from the truth is multiplied later a thousandfold."[54] We are unfortunately all paying a heavy price for keeping silent in the face of those marginal, but vocal and militant, "truth-bearers" and their misguided followers, who have successfully expanded over centuries the deviation from the universal Truth that "God is One." *So are we.*

People need to understand that true religion is not about possessing the Truth. No religion does. It is rather the recognition of many particular spiritual journeys to the Divine. They need to know that the higher the truth, the fewer boundaries it knows. When they embrace the divine notion that peace is when the plurality of truths finds a higher Oneness, peace will be created. The multitude of human beings as living truths is the condition that causes the plentitude of the One Truth. At the surface, we look as if we are individual islands in the ocean of humanity. But, if you are willing to dive deep into the very bottom, you will find that all the islands are connected to each other at the seabed. So are religions—they are all universally connected at the deeper level to one foundation of perennial wisdom.

The only question is, "Will we acknowledge that?" When we all do, when we would no longer be separated and severed from each other, as peoples and faiths, we could truly then say, "God is One." When we ourselves become an embodiment of this higher truth, the planet becomes what God wanted it to be, the Garden of Eden. God assigned us as its gardeners to enjoy its fruits and participate in all its abundance as long as we fulfill the divinely prescribed responsibility "to cultivate it and protect it."[55]

On the other hand, as long as we treat each other the way Cain did when he killed his younger brother Abel, the planet will always be saturated with blood. The reason Cain's offering was not accepted by God, a response that triggered the blood feud, was his failure to realize that the physical world we inhabit is not meant to be a world of singularity reflecting God's absolute oneness, but a world of plurality. Unity does not mean uniformity. Our strength is in our diversity. This is a powerful message to all contemporary religions that each, in its competition for God's favor, builds its own altars, believing that its offering is the one to be accepted by God. And their militant followers are willing, in the name of God and His Truth, sometimes to kill for it.

Our challenge is to create a context large enough to contain all of our truths, including the ones that you and I take issue with. When you have such a broad context, a communication free of right-wrong dualism, conversation is possible. Positions are expressed as positions and welcomed as a contribution, which in turn leads to peace and reconciliation. When you do not have such a context, positions offered as the truth are conceived as judgment or confrontation, which in turn leads to conflict and war.

In the prevailing context of the Arab-Israeli conflict, unholy differences that might be tolerable under normal circumstances and easily resolved by negotiations are turned into absolute stands that can only collide. The dispute often invokes the sanctions of religion to convert ordinary differences into total hostilities, and make those who differ into devil or Satan figures. No antagonism is so strong and no enmity is so great, as that aimed against those who are depicted as the enemies of God and the violators of His Truth.

The Jewish sages always were aware of the complexity of God's Truth embodied in the Torah and the difficulty of human beings living by the heavenly code on earth. Therefore, while aspiring to live ideally by the Torah of Truth (*torāt 'emēt*), they argued, human beings should practically follow the dictum, "[human] conduct comes before Torah" (*dērekh 'ēretz qodēmet la-torāh*).[56] In other words, one cannot truly serve God without serving man first; one cannot live by God's Ultimate Truth without "inter-living" with human truths, which is the foundation of peace. The Psalmist wrote, "Truth will arise from the earth,"[57] for a reason—to express God's will that truth emerges from humanity below, not from the heaven above. Meaning, the Torah becomes the Torah of Truth when human beings practice it.

Inspired by the concept of the singularity of Truth and the plurality of truths, I wrote the following poem simply entitled "Truth":

No such thing as truth.
        There is Truth
        and many truths.
When your truth
        merges with mine
        like a river joining the vast sea,
        they become one whole,
        the "whole truth," a universal truth;
Not just yours or mine, but ours,
all blend together and blossom
like a petalled rose emerging from one stem
offering its sweet fragrance and infinite beauty
to humanity.

Epilogue

A Poetic Conclusion

Over the years, as I was walking down the path of life, I came to recognize that I have three principal commitments in my relationship with the world: first, as a human being, I am committed to cultivating interpersonal relationships that are in line with the Golden Rule of reciprocity, "You shall love your fellow as yourself"; second, as a religious man, I am committed to promoting interreligious understanding and harmony, particularly between Jews and Muslims; and third, as a man of nationality, I am committed to forwarding the peaceful resolution of the Middle East conflict, particularly between the Israelis and the Palestinians. As a context for this book, I chose the Gate of Mercy for two reasons—one is that it represents a symbolic site "where Islam and Judaism join together," a place of possibilities for their reconciliation; and two is that it represents my conviction of the centrality of mercy, compassion, and love as fundamental spiritual values shared by all religions.

In the book, I have tried to convince you that Islam and Judaism are two sister religions that are closely related to one another with roots intertwined in the land, in the language, and in the memories of shared history. Of all religions, they are by far the closest to each other in their fundamental religious tenets, practices and systems of law, and their social, cultural, and ethical traditions. The challenge before us is to overcome the doctrinal differences, which have been manipulated by religious zealots, and combat all divisive acts of exclusivism and extremism. We all need to embrace the spirit of religious tolerance and coexistence and emphasize the beauty of the colorful tapestry of our various religions.

I agree with the Psalmist's statement, "The heavens are God's and the earth He entrusted to mankind,"[1] with the responsibility to establish unity and harmony among all human beings here in Paradise on Earth, and to cocreate with God's help a new future for humanity. In a true religion, the horizontal relationship with other human beings and the vertical relationship with God are equally important and each is meaningless without the other. It is clearly expressed in the famous two-word *ḥadīth*, "Ad-dīn al-mu'āmalatu" (see p. 30), which literally means, your religion is what you do; your faith is judged by your treatment of others. You cannot claim to be a person of piety by simply going to a place of worship and praying to God in heaven. You cannot truly serve God without serving man, as we are told by the Midrash, "A [human] conduct comes before Torah." I grew up with the dictum, "Be a Jew inside your home, and a man outside [on the street]," where you are able to reach out to people of different faiths and convictions.

I could not find a better way to conclude the argument—that our plurality of religions and cultures is transcended by the singularity of our humanity and that *we* are one mirroring the One—than the following four poems I wrote under the title, "You and I Are the Same: A Quadrilogy on Oneness."

I. **Beyond Separateness**

you
and I
are the same
members of the
human commonwealth
of beings invisibly one with
the universe corporeally divided
into separate physical entities anxious
to open up to relationship eager to transcend the
illusion of plurality through metaphorical acts of
oneness in flesh and in spirit
we
share common bread and drink from the same cup
in the spirit of brotherhood
we
shake hands in greeting and hold each other in arms
in the spirit of friendship
we
caress our lips together and join in carnal union
in the spirit of love

II. A Flower of Being

you and I
are the same if
you believe the
Lord created us
all human beings
like colored flowers
of different traits to
decorate mother earth
with our beautiful faces

if you are willing to take a look
deep in your heart of compassion
remove the corolla from your head
and peel off the petals of your ego
leaving yourself truly naked
in your bud of innocence
you will find out
we're the same
you and I

III. In the Heart of Hearts

you
and I
are the same
beyond the walls of suspicion that separate us
beyond the barriers of hatred that set us apart
beyond the gulf of bloody conflict
beyond the hostility
there
in the heart of hearts
in the realm of human oneness
in the sphere of spiritual inter-connectedness
in the world of peace, compassion and empathy
you and I
are the
same

IV. A House of Worship

you and I
are the same
praying in the House of the Lord
with the foundation laid by Moses
with the walls erected by Jesus Christ
with the roof built by Prophet Muhammad
each sharing his own contribution to the Oneness of
God God
man man
and and
faith faith faith faith faith faith faith faith faith faith

בֵּית תְּפִלָּה

אַתָּה וַאֲנִי

אוֹתוֹ דָּבָר

בְּבֵיתוֹ שֶׁל אֱלֹקִים

עִם הַיְּסוֹד שֶׁהֵנִיחַ מֹשֶׁה

עִם הַקִּירוֹת שֶׁהֵקִים יֶשׁוּ

וְעִם הַגַּג שֶׁבָּנָה הַנָּבִיא מֻחָמַד

כָּל אֶחָד נָתַן אֶת תְּרוּמָתוֹ לְאַחְדוּת

הָאֵל הָאֵל

הָאָדָם הָאָדָם

וְ וְ

הָאֱמוּנָה הָאֱמוּנָה הָאֱמוּנָה הָאֱמוּנָה הָאֱמוּנָה

بيت العبادة

أنت وأنا

كلانا نفس الإنسان

نصلّي في بيت الرب

على الأساس الذي وضعه موسى

داخل الجدران التي أقامها يسوع المسيح

تحت سقف بناه النبي محمد

كل منهم يشارك مساهمته إلى وحدة

الله الله

الإنسان الإنسان

و و

الإيمان الإيمان الإيمان الإيمان الإيمان

The fourth and last poem, "A House of Worship," including its Hebrew and Arabic translations, is a perfect ending for the book and a great reminder to take to heart the words of Isaiah, considered the most universal of all prophets. His vision of peace is relevant today to all the three monotheistic religions, which compete for God's favors to the exclusion of others: "It shall come to pass in the days to come that the mountain of the Lord's house shall be established at the top of the mountains, and shall be exalted above the hills; and all nations shall flow unto it [. . . .] And He shall judge between the nations, and shall decide for many peoples; and they shall beat their swords into plowshares, and their spears into pruning hooks; nation shall not lift up sword against nation, neither shall they learn war any more."[2]

May this prophetic call inspire Jews and Muslims to embrace each other as brothers and sisters, who share God's Truth, and join together for a prayer of peace! May Jerusalem, the City of Peace, *Where Islam and Judaism Join Together*, become a place of their reconciliation and a beacon for Prophet Isaiah's vision of peace! May God's mercy fill their hearts with courage to transform their relations into His mirror of love and compassion!

Appendix 1: Parallels between Jewish and Islamic Systems of Law

	Jewish Law (Halakhāh)	**Islamic Law (Sharī'ah)**
Jurisprudence	Mishpāṭ	Fiqh
Written Law	Torah (Pentateuch) (Torāh she-bi-Khtāv)	Qur'ān (Kitāb)
Oral Law	Mishnah & Gemarah (Torah She-be-'Al-Peh)	Sunnah (Ḥadīth)
Analogy	Sevarāh	Qiyās
Consensus	Aḥarēi ha-Rōv	Ijmā'
Custom	Minhāg	'Urf or 'Ādah
Response	She'elōt u-'Teshuvōt	Fatāwa (sing. Fatwā)
Injunction	Taqanāh	
Decree	Gezeirāh	
Exegesis	Midrāsh	Tafsīr
Legist	Posēq	Faqīh
Religious Judge	Dayyān	Qāḍi
Religious Court	Beit Dīn	Maḥkamah

Source: Hava Lazarus-Yafeh, "Hitpatḥūt ha-Torāh she-be-'Al-Peh ve-ha-Halakhāh" [The Development of Oral Tradition and Law], in Yafeh, ed., *Perakīm be-Toldōt ha-'Aravīm ve-ha-Islām* [Studies in the History of the Arabs and Islam] (Tel Aviv: Reshafim Publishing House, 1967), 156–175; S. D. Goitein, *Jews and Arabs: Their Contacts Through the Ages* (New York: Schocken Books, 1974), 59–61; S. D. Goitein, "The Interplay of Jewish and Islamic Laws," in B. Jackson, ed., *Jewish Law in Legal History and the Modern World*, (Leiden: Brill, 1980), 61–77; David Steinberg, *Islam and Judaism: Influences, Contrasts and Parallels*, in http://www.houseofdavid.ca/.

Appendix 2: Seeking Unity in Diversity Article

THE HAMMOND TIMES

Monday, December 13, 1993

SEEKING UNITY IN DIVERSITY

'If we don't unite we will be broken.' – Jamal Aessa

Peace advocates: Jews, Muslims should celebrate common link

By ROBIN BIESEN
Times Correspondent

MICHIGAN CITY – After years of looking at each other's differences with animosity and distrust, it is time for Jews and Muslims to seek out the similarities that join them, Shai Har-El said Sunday.

Har-El, president of the Middle East Peace Network and a native of Israel, spoke to more than 100 Muslims during a service at the Islamic Center in Michigan City.

The international Middle East Peace Network is devoted to fostering peace between Arabs and Israelis.

With the historic, albeit tentative, peace agreement for Palestinians living in the Israeli-Occupied West Bank at hand, Har-El said it is a sign the two groups can live together after years of strife in the Holy Land.

While he is sometimes disheartened over the ongoing skirmishes and loss of life over which religious group will rule the Gaza Strip, Suheil S. Nammari, another member of the Middle East Peace Network, said that whenever he sees renewed tensions in the Middle East, he sees even more the need for the two groups to come together in peace.

"This didn't start overnight and it won't disappear overnight," said Nammari, a native of Palestine who lives in Lowell.

See PEACE, Page A-4

Times photo by Zbigniew Bzdak

Shai Har-El, president of the Middle East Peace Network, left, greets Sheyku Hisham of Kalamazoo, Mich., after Har-El spoke to Muslims from Northwest Indiana.

Peace

Continued from Page A-1

Har-El agreed and said the differences that have so long divided Jews and Muslims should be celebrated, not scorned.

"God did not create human beings as clones," he said. "He made human beings different so we can be enriched by our differences and grow."

Despite the theological differences between Muslims, Jews and Christians, Har-El said members of all three of the major world religions that trace their faith to Jerusalem should be reminded of their common link to Abraham and bound by their faith to one God.

"My God and your God is one," he said.

Quoting extensively from the Koran, the Islamic holy book, Har-El said it is incumbent upon all Muslims, as it is for all Jews and Christians, to work toward creating peace.

"One cannot love God without loving human beings," Har-El said.

Borrowing from the Muslim tradition of kneeling with the forehead down in prayer as an example of placing the heart above the head, Har-El said that if all people would communicate with their hearts, conflicts would be easily overcome.

"We need to speak to one another heart-to-heart," he said.

While the tensions in the Middle East have evolved from religious differences, Nammari and Har-El said the people fostering the conflict are not closest to the teachings of God.

"It is those who are farthest from God who look for the differences," Nammari said.

Mohammad Aessa, of Wakarusa, southeast of South Bend, said that warring over religious differences should be over.

"If we can go to war, then why can't we go to peace," Aessa said. "There is one God. We are one humanity. Why don't we act like it."

His son, Jamal Aessa, 16, said he was heartened by what Har-El said.

Still, he said he thinks it will be a long road to peace, a road made longer by western interference in the Middle East.

"I think the United States has been trying to help, but I think it has made things worse," Jamal Aessa said.

"I believe what he (Har-El) said was absolutely correct," he added. "We have to unite. If we don't unite we will be broken."

Still, he said he doesn't expect a real peace accord in the region during his lifetime.

Nammari was more hopeful.

"There is no going back," he said. "We've been going on that road for too long and we know it is the wrong way. The only way we can go now is forward. It's the only way."

Appendix 3: The Chapter on Peace: A Jewish Sacred Text

(*Pērek ha-Shalōm* in Tractate *Dērekh 'Ēretz Zuṭā*)

Rabbi Jehoshua ben Levi said: Great is peace, for peace is to the land what yeast is to the dough. If the Blessed Holy One had not given peace to the land, the sword and the beast would depopulate it, as it is written (in Leviticus 16:6): "And I will give peace in the land." And there is no land like Israel, as it is written (in Malachi 13:12): "And all nations shall call you happy, for you shall be a delightsome land." And it is also written (in Zechariah 1:11): "And behold all the land sits still and is at rest."

It is written (in Ecclesiastes 1:4): "One generation passes away, and another generation comes, but the earth endures for ever." One kingdom comes and another kingdom passes, but [the People of] Israel lives forever. [King] Solomon meant to say thus: Although one generation passes away and another one comes, one kingdom disappears and another one appears; and although evil decrees are enacted one after another against Israel, still they endure forever. [The Lord] does not abandon them, and they are never abandoned. They are never annihilated, neither do they decrease, as it is written (in Malachi 3:6): "For I the Lord have not changed: and you, sons of Jacob, have not ceased to be." As I have never changed and will never change, so you, sons of Jacob, have never ceased and will never cease to be. But [it is written] (in Deuteronomy 4:4): "You that did cleave unto the Lord your God are alive, every one of you, this day."

Rabban Shimon ben Gamliel said: The world rests upon three things: On justice, on truth, and on peace. Said Rabbi Mona: Those are one and the same thing. For if there is justice, there is truth, and there is peace. And these three are expressed in one and the same verse, for it is written (in Zechariah 8:16): "Execute the judgment of truth and peace in your gates."

Wherever there is justice, there is peace, and wherever there is peace, there is justice.

Rabbi Jehoshua said: Great is peace, for at the time [the People of] Israel arose and said (in Exodus 24:7): "All that the Lord has spoken will we do and obey," the Blessed Holy One was pleased to give them His Torah and blessed them with peace, as it is written (in Psalms 29:11): "The Lord will bless His people with peace."

Hezekiah said: Great is peace, for at every commandment in the Torah it is written: "If you see," "if you hit," "if he calls," "if you build." Meaning, *if* such a thing occurs to you, you must do the commandment. But concerning peace, what is written? (In Psalms 34:15): "Seek peace, and pursue it," which means, seek peace at the place where you are, and [if you do not find it,] seek it in other place. Hezekiah [also] said: Great is peace: In all the journeys of [the Children of] Israel it is written, "and they moved," "and they encamped," which means they moved in strife and encamped in strife; but when they came to Sinai, there was no more strife, and they all encamped in peace, as it is written (in Exodus 29:2): "And Israel encamped there." The Blessed Holy One said: "Because Israel hated discord and loved peace, and they all became one encampment, this is a favorable time that I should give them my Torah." Adoniah [the son of David], was killed because he was quarrelsome, and it is permitted to support the accusation of a quarrelsome man, as Nathan the Prophet did when he said to Bath-Sheba [accusing Adoniah] (in I Kings 1:14): "I myself will come in after you, and fulfill your words."

And Rabbi said: All manner of lying is prohibited, except when making peace between one and his fellow. Bar Kappara said: Great is Peace, as we found that the Torah spoke a lie in order to make peace between Abraham and Sarah, as it was said (in Genesis 18:12): "And Sarah laughed within herself, saying [...] and my lord is old," and at the end it is written "and I am old." Bar Kappara said: Great is Peace, as we found that the Prophets spoke a lie in order to make peace between Manoah and his wife, as it was first said (in Judges 13:3): "Behold now, you are barren," and then it was said "you shall conceive," and nothing was mentioned of "barren." Bar Kappara said: Great is Peace, as among the angels there is no animosity, no jealousy, no hatred, no commanding, no quarrelling, because the Blessed Holy One has made peace among them, as it is written (in Job 15:2): "Dominion and dread are with Him: he makes peace in his heavens." "Dominion" is [the angel] Michael and "Dread" is [the angel] Gabriel, one of whom is of fire and the other one of water, and still they do not oppose each other, [for the Blessed Holy One has made peace between them]. Not to mention human beings who carry all these qualities.

Rabbi Ishmael said: Great is peace, as we found that the Blessed Holy One gave up His Name [Peace] that was written with holiness, in order to make peace between man and his wife. Rabbi Jehoshua said: Great is peace, in that the covenant of the priests was made with peace, as it is written (in Numbers 25:12): "I give to him my covenant of peace." Rabbi Jehoshua said: Great is peace, as the name of the Blessed Holy One is [also] Peace (*Shalōm*), as it is written (in Judges 6:24): "And called it Adonāi-Shalōm." Rabbi Hiya Bar Abba said: From this we deduce that greeting one's fellow with Shalōm in a dirty place is forbidden. Why? [It is written] (in Judges 6:24) "Then Gideon built an altar there to the Lord, and called it Adonāi-Shalōm." Why an altar that does not eat, drink or smell, and is not built but for the purpose of absolving [the People of] Israel is called Shalōm? [To teach us that] whoever loves peace and pursues peace, offers [the greeting of] peace first and responds with [the greeting of] peace, all the more so forges peace between [the People of] Israel and their Father in Heaven.

Rabbi Jose the Galilean said: The name of the Messiah is also Shalōm, as it is written (in Isaiah 9:5): "My Everlasting Father is the Ruler of Peace." Said Rabbi Jehoshua: Great is peace, for Israel is also called Shalōm, as it is written (in Zechariah 8:12): "For [Israel] there shall be the seed of peace [the vine shall give her fruit]." Peace for whom? For [Israel,] the Seed of Peace. Rabbi Jose the Galilean said: Great is peace, as when the Messiah shall come to Israel, he will open with Shalōm, as it is written (in Isaiah 32:7): "How beautiful upon the mountains are the feet of the messenger of good tidings that announces peace." Rabbi Jose the Galilean [also] said: Great is peace, for even in time of war we begin in no other way than with [the call for] peace, as it is written (in Deuteronomy 20:10): "When you draw nigh to a city to make war against it, then summon it with [the call for] peace."

Rabbi Jehoshua said: Great is peace, for in the future the Blessed Holy One will uphold the righteous with peace, as it is written (in Isaiah 26:3]: "The mind that confides on You keeps [us in perfect] peace." [Again] Rabbi Jehoshua said: Great is peace, because it accompanies the living as well as the dead. Why for the living? As it is written (in Exodus 14:18): "And Jethro said to Moses, Go in peace"; why for the dead? As it is written (in Genesis 15:15): "And you shall come to your fathers in peace."

Rabban Shimon ben Gamliel said: Great is peace, for we found that the Tribes told lies in order to make peace between Joseph and his brothers; as is written (in Genesis 50:16) "And they sent a message to Joseph, saying 'your father did command [before he died].'" We cannot find [in the Torah] that he commanded them anything. Rabban Shimon ben Gamliel [also] said: Great is peace, for Aaron the Priest was praised only because he was a peaceable man. For it was he who loved peace, who pursued peace, who was first to offer [the greeting of] peace, and responded with [the greeting of] peace; as it is written (in Malachi 2:6): "He walked with Me in peace and uprightness." And what is written thereafter "And did turn many away from iniquity." This teaches us that whenever he saw two men hating each other, he went to one of them and said to him: Why do you hate that man? For he already came to my house, and prostrated himself before me and said: I have sinned against him. Go and reconcile with him! And Aaron left him and went to the second man and spoke to him as to the first. Thus it was his way to set peace and friendship between man and his fellow, and he "did turn many away from iniquity."

R. Jehoshua of Sichnin said in the name of Rabbi Levi: Great is peace, in that all benedictions and all prayers conclude with "peace." The Reciting of Shemā' is concluded with "peace"—"Spread the tabernacle of peace"; the Prestly Blessing = concludes with "peace"—"and give you peace;" and the [prayer of Eighteen] Benedictions conclude with "peace"—"He Who makes peace."

Said Rabbi Jehoshua ben Levi: The Blessed Holy One said to [the People of] Israel, You have caused me to destroy my House and to exile my children, now pray for peace [of Jerusalem] and I will forgive you; as it is written (in Psalms 122:6): "Pray for the peace of Jerusalem." And it is written (in Jeremiah 29:7): "And seek the peace of the city." And it is written (in Psalms 122:7): "May there be peace be within your walls." And it is said (in Psalms 122:8): "For the sake of my brethrens and friends [I ask that there be peace be within you]." Therefore he who loves peace, who pursues peace, who offers [the greeting of] peace first, and responds [the greeting of] peace, the Blessed Holy One will make him inherit the life of This World and the life of the World-to-Come, as it is written (in Psalms 37:11): "But the humble shall inherit the land, and delight themselves in the abundance of peace."

Source: Original Hebrew text is available at http://www.daat.ac.il/daat/toshba/zuta/11-2.htm.

Appendix 4: First Alexandria Declaration of the Religious Leaders of the Holy Land, January 21, 2002

In the name of God who is Almighty, Merciful and Compassionate, we, who have gathered as religious leaders from the Muslim, Christian, and Jewish communities, pray for true peace in Jerusalem and the Holy Land, and declare our commitment to ending the violence and bloodshed that denies the right to life and dignity.

According to our faith traditions, killing innocents in the name of God is a desecration of his Holy Name, and defames religion in the world. The violence in the Holy Land is an evil which must be opposed by all people of good faith. We seek to live together as neighbors, respecting the integrity of each other's historical and religious inheritance. We call upon all to oppose incitement, hatred, and the misrepresentation of the other.

1. The Holy Land is holy to all three of our faiths. Therefore, followers of the divine religions must respect its sanctity, and bloodshed must not be allowed to pollute it. The sanctity and integrity of the Holy Places must be preserved, and the freedom of religious worship must be ensured for all.
2. Palestinians and Israelis must respect the divinely ordained purposes of the Creator by whose grace they live in the same land that is called Holy.
3. We call on the political leaders of both parties to work for a just, secure, and durable solution in the spirit of the words of the Almighty and the Prophets.
4. As a first step now, we call for a religiously sanctioned cease-fire, respected and observed from all sides, and for the implementation of the Mitchell and Tenet recommendations, including the lifting of restrictions and return to negotiations.

5. We seek to help create an atmosphere where present and future generations will co-exist with mutual respect and trust in the other. We call on all to refrain from incitement and demonization, and to educate our future generations accordingly.
6. As religious leaders, we pledge ourselves to continue a joint quest for a just peace that leads to reconciliation in Jerusalem and the Holy Land, for the common good of all our peoples.
7. We announce the establishment of a permanent joint committee to carry out the recommendations of this declaration, and to engage with our respective political leadership accordingly.

Host & Chair: His Eminence Sheikh Mohammed Sayed Tantawi, Grand Mufti of the Al-Azhar, and His Grace the then-Archbishop of Canterbury, Dr. George Carey.

Signatories

- The Shephardi Chief, Rabbi Bakshi Doron
- The Deputy Foreign Minister of Israel, Rabbi Michael Melchior
- The Rabbi of Tekoa, Rabbi Menachem Fromen
- Rabbi David Rosen, President of the World Conference on Religion and Peace
- The Rabbi of Savyon, Rabbi David Brodman
- Rabbi Yitzak Ralbag, Rabbi of Maalot Dafna
- Chief Justice of the Sharia Courts, Sheikh Taisir Tamimi
- Minister of State for the Palestinian Authority, Sheikh Tal El Sider
- Mufti of the (Palestinian) Armed Forces, Sheikh Abdusalam Abu Schkedem
- The Mufti of Bethlehem, Sheikh Taweel
- Representative of the Greek Patriarch, Archbishop Aristarchos
- The Latin Patriarch, His Beatitude Michel Sabbah
- The Melkite Archbishop, Archbishop Boutros Mualem
- Representative of the Armenian Patriarch, Bishop Arist Shrivinian
- The Bishop of Jerusalem, The Right Reverend Riah Abu El Assal

Source: http://www.usip.org—the website of United States Institute of Peace.

Appendix 5: A Muslim's Commentary on Qur'ānic Support of Intolerance and Violence

Imam Jamal Rahman

Scriptural and Institutional Support for Violence

Sadly, today many Muslims live in environments of economic deprivation and political oppression. Their feelings of anger and powerlessness are exploited by politicians and clerics with an agenda. Crying "God is great!" some of them have unleashed terror at home and abroad, falsely invoking the name of God and quoting the Qur'ān for their own violent purposes. People who get their knowledge of Islam from the media reports on Al-Qaeda and other extreme terrorist groups may perhaps be forgiven for thinking the Qur'ān is a violent scripture filled with "sword verses" calling for non-Muslim blood, but the truth is quite otherwise. In a volume of more than six thousand verses, less than sixty verses mention fighting or warfare in any context. Such verses are offensive to our twenty-first-century sensibilities, but we simply have to acknowledge that they are there, and interpret them from a higher, more evolved consciousness.

Three Qur'anic verses that speak to intolerance and violence against nonbelievers are:

> But when the forbidden months are past, then fight them, beleaguer them, and lie in wait for them in every stratagem [of war]; but if they repent, and establish regular prayers and practice regular charity, then open the way for them; for God is Oft-forgiving, Most Merciful (9:5).
>
> I will instill terror into the hearts of the Unbelievers: Smite ye above their necks and smite all their fingertips off them (8:12).
>
> O Prophet! Strive hard against the Unbelievers and the Hypocrites and be firm against them. Their abode is Hell—an evil refuge indeed (9:73).

These and similar verses are quoted by fundamentalists to justify acts of terror and by non-Muslims to prove that the Qur'ān is calling for their blood. In the next section, we shall dig a little further into what the verses really meant at the time they were revealed and explore the ways we can heal the damage their misinterpretation has done to both Muslim and non-Muslim psyches.

Damage has also been done by early classical jurists, who divided the world into the Abode of Islam and the Abode of War and claimed that it was the religious duty of Muslims to "Islamicize" the world, using military force, if necessary. At the time, the religion of Islam was spreading exponentially throughout the Middle East and beyond, and some Muslim leaders relied on their jurists to support war as a means of imperialist expansion that had nothing to do with religion. In modern times, with the political and economic fortunes of Islam drastically reduced, many Islamic extremists take their inspiration from the influential Egyptian scholar Sayyid al Qutb, who stated in his extensive writings that Muslims are mandated to establish Allah's sovereignty on earth. Though he died more than forty years ago (in 1055), his writings still inspire Islamic extremists who call for jihad against the world of nonbelievers.

Commentary on Violence

First, let us consider the "sword verse" of the Qur'ān (9:5), which has been so tragically misrepresented by Islamic extremists and misunderstood by fearful Westerners. First, the verse is seriously limited and defined by its historical context. This seventh-century revelation came at a time when the Islamic community in Arabia was a tiny embryonic group in Medina under constant attack by the Quraish tribe and their allies in Mecca, who were overwhelmingly superior in arms and numbers. Second, the verse is even more seriously qualified by its textual context. The sword verse also appears in chapter 2, where it is hedged by two Qur'anic commandments. The verse immediately preceding the sword verse in chapter 2 says, "Fight in the cause of God those who fight you, but do not transgress limits; for God loveth not transgressors" (2:190), while the verses immediately following it say, "But if they cease, God is Oft-forgiving, most Merciful. . . . let there be no hostility. . . . and know that God is with those who restrain themselves" (2:192–194). Thus the verses that surround the sword verse soften its sharp edges and establish a clear context: The verse refers to defensive fighting, and if the attacker is inclined to peace, the Muslim must cease fighting.

A general principle of Qur'anic interpretation is that if a verse does not seem to support the overall message of the Qur'ān or reflect God's divine attributes, we have to dig deeper to reach a more enlightened understanding. So in addition to establishing the contextual limits on this particular revelation—allowing one to kill only in self-defense—it is critical to emphasize that this verse is not about divine permission to kill nonbelievers simply because of their nonbelief or to gain power or control. Such an interpretation would place the verse in direct conflict with the spirit and content of the universal verses in the Qur'ān. In an abundance of verses celebrating pluralism and diversity, the Qur'ān explains that God could easily have made all of humanity "one single people," but instead created us in beautiful diversity so that we might "vie, then, with one another other in doing good works!" (5:48) and "come to know one another" (49:13). The Holy Book asks rhetorically, "Wilt thou then compel humankind against their will, to believe?" and emphasizes that no matter how much one disapproves of the other's religion, the Muslim is commanded to live and let live: "To you be your Way, and to me mine" (109:6). The Qur'ān clearly states that entrance to heaven depends not on religious affiliation but on doing "righteous deeds" (4:124 and 5:69). Except when in mortal danger at the hands of an enemy, Muslims are commanded to repel evil with something better, so that an enemy becomes a bosom friend (41:34).

Making Peace with the Sword Verse

Now, how can we make peace with the sword verse? Even if we know that it refers only to self-defense, it is extremely uncomfortable and confusing to read words like, "kill the unbeliever," as a divine revelation. Why would the All-Merciful and All-Powerful God, who has infused every human with divine breath and holds every human heart between divine fingers, instruct anyone to kill? Why would the "Light of the Heavens and Earth" advise a Muslim engaged in battle against his attackers to "smite at their necks" (47:4)? Some of my co-religionists may call me naïve, but when presented with such a puzzlement, I take refuge in Rumi's utterance, "Sell your cleverness and buy bewilderment." What else can one do with a verse like this?

In a continuing attempt to advance my understanding of this difficult verse, I have discussed it with both scholars and students. Some of the scholars, Hindus who are fully conversant with the Qur'ān, believe the revelation in question is about God's exhortation to humanity to be courageous and take action in the face of attack by others. Indeed, this line of thought is consistent with another revelation in the Qur'ān: "For if God had not enabled people to defend themselves against one another, monasteries and churches and synagogues and mosques—in which God's name is abundantly extolled—would surely have been destroyed" (22:40).

Reinforcing the need for courage when under attack, the scholars cite an epic conversation in the Bhagavad-Gita between Krishna, a Divine Being, and the mortal Prince Arjuna on the eve of engaging in the battle of Kurukshetra. Viewing the multitude of soldiers on the opposing side, the prince laments to Krishna about spilling the blood of "cousins." Krishna berates the prince for using false piety to cover up his fear and lack of courage. Without action, Krishna says, the cosmos would fall out of order.

My students, high school Muslims, suggested that the verse should be interpreted metaphorically. After all, they argued, the Qur'ān clearly states that some verses are literal and some are metaphorical (3:7), but it doesn't say which ones are which! To these young, creative minds, the sword verse is about slaying the idols of arrogance and ignorance within ourselves.

Finally, the thirteenth-century sage Rumi claims that any interpretation depends on our level of consciousness and our intention on what we hope to learn. "A bee and wasp drink from the same flower," says Rumi. "One produces nectar and the other, a sting." When I'm troubled by the way the sword verse could be interpreted, I remember that the way of Islam is to produce nectar.

Understanding Jihad

Now, about that terrifying word jihad: Thanks to misinformation in the media and misrepresentation by Islamic extremists, many Westerners associate the word jihad with "holy war" and suicide bombing. To set the record straight, jihad literally means "effort" and refers primarily to the spiritual effort to evolve into the fullness of one's being, to improve relationships with family and neighbors, and to work for justice. The more militant concept of jihad that so threatens the Western mind refers only to self-defense when under attack. The idea of jihad as "holy war" simply does not exist in the Qur'ān, even though this is the prevailing notion not only in the media but also, unfortunately, among some Islamic militants.

What is often overlooked is that for a thousand years after Islam's inception in the seventh century, there was a tradition of vigorous and lively debate among scholars and jurists on contentious issues, including war. The classical jurists' notion of dividing the world into the Abode of Islam and the Abode of War has been hotly contested and refuted by other Islamic jurists. In the fourteenth century, the conservative jurist Ibn Tamiyya argued definitively that such a concept violated the basic Qur'anic principle forbidding "compulsion in religion" (2:256). Even in the twentieth century, when ideological debate among peers and scholars was comparatively lame, the inflammatory views of Sayyid al Qutb were opposed by many of his colleagues and upon his death he was declared a heretic by the scholars of Al-Azhar University, one of the premier universities in the Muslim world.

In recent times, however, the classical doctrine of jihad as holy war has seen a resurgence among militants who chafe against the Muslim experience of colonialism, wars, and occupation. What underlies the resurgence of militancy is not religion but politics. An exhaustive six-year Gallup poll in thirty-five Muslim countries concluded that 7 percent of Muslims are "radicals," and that Islamic militancy is based not on Islamic principles but on political radicalization. In every suicide bombing attack from 1980 to 2004, the primary motive was to overthrow foreign occupation, not to further religious views. Robert Pape, a leading expert on suicide terrorism from the University of Chicago, reports that the vast majority of Islamic suicide bombers come from middle-class backgrounds with a significant level of education. He asserts that the "taproot of suicide terrorism is nationalism." According to Islamic sages, if we focus on religion as the primary cause, we are searching in the branches for what really appears in the roots.

As is so often the case, the remedy for misunderstanding and fear lies in the same texts and traditions that give rise to the problem in the first place. Muhammad proclaimed that the ink of the scholar is more holy than the blood of the martyr, and the word *ilm* (knowledge) is the second-most-repeated word in the Qur'ān. It is the sacred task of Muslims and non-Muslims alike to humbly and mindfully examine the scriptural sources of religious violence and allow for a knowledge of the heart to understand and interpret the sacred texts.

The historic "Arab Spring" began in early 2011, when nonviolent, grassroots movements in Tunisia and Egypt astonishingly overthrew autocratic and repressive regimes in a short span of time. This stunning turn of events is reminiscent of how the Prophet Muhammad finally achieved victory in the face of overwhelming odds.

Source: An excerpt from *Religion Gone Astray: What We Found at the Heart of Interfaith* by Pastor Don Mackenzie, Rabbi Ted Falcon, and Imam Jamal Rahman (Woodstock, VT: SkyLight Paths, 2011), "Violence in Islam" by Jamal Rahman, pp. 68–74.

Notes

Acknowledgments

1. The dissertation was published as Shai Har-El, *Struggle for Domination in the Middle East: The Ottoman-Mamluk War, 1485–1491* (Leiden: E. J. Brill, 1995).
2. Talmud Bavlī, Nedarīm 50a.

Introduction: Jerusalem's Gate of Mercy as a Context

1. Genesis 28:17.
2. *The Midrash on Psalms*, trans. William G. Braude, vol. 2 (New Haven, CT: Yale University Press, 1959), 105.
3. Albert Hourani, *A History of the Arab Peoples* (Cambridge, MA: Harvard University Press, 1991), 28.
4. Qur'ān 17:1.
5. For a recent historical and archeological study of the Old City of Jerusalem and its ancient gates, see the illustrated work by Meir Ben-Dov, *In the Shadow of the Temple: The Discovery of Ancient Jerusalem* (New York: Harper & Row, 1985), a translation of a work originally published in Hebrew under the title *Ḥafīrōt Har Ha-Bāyyit* [Excavations of the Temple Mount] (Jerusalem: Keter Publishing House, 1982). See also his book of archeology and architecture of the Old City, *Adām Va-'Ēven Bi-Yerushalāyim* [Man and Stone in Jerusalem] (Tel Aviv: Modan Publishing House, 1989), and his illustrated history of Jerusalem updated and expanded to the year 2000, *Yerushalāyim Bi-R'ī Ha-Dorōt* [Jerusalem in the Mirror of Generations] (Jerusalem: Carta, 2000).
6. Qur'ān 57:13.
7. Meir Ben-Dov, *In the Shadow of the Temple*, 286.
8. Qur'ān 3:103.
9. In his speech at St. Louis, March 22, 1964. See "Memorable Quotes and quotations from Martin Luther King Jr.," in http://www.memorable-quotes.com.
10. See, for example, Jacob Neusner, *Jews and Christians: The Myth of Common Tradition* (Eugene, OR: Wipf & Stock, 2003).

11. Bernard Lewis, *The Jews of Islam* (Princeton, NJ: Princeton University Press, 1984), 22–33. Cf. Mark R. Cohen, *Under the Crescent and Cross: The Jews of the Middle Ages* (Princeton, NJ: Princeton University Press, 1995), 66–67, 88.
12. Talmud Bavlī, 'Eruvīn 13b.
13. Qur'ān 10:37. Cf. 5:48.
14. Qur'ān 41:34.
15. See, for example, William Muir, *The Life of Muhammad from Original Sources*, ed. T. H. Weir (Edinburgh: John Grant, 1923); Charles Torrey, *The Jewish Foundation of Islam* (New York: Jewish Institute of Religion Press, 1933); W. S. Clair Tisdall, *The Original Sources of the Qur'an* (London: Society for the Promotion of Christian Knowledge, 1991); Abraham Katsh, *Judaism and the Koran* (New York: A. S. Barnes, 1962); Abraham Geiger, "Was hat Mohammed aus dem Judenthume aufgenommen," trans. F. M. Young (1896), *Judaism and Islam* (New York: Ktav, 1970); Arent Jan Wensinck, *Muhammad and the Jews of Medina*, trans. and ed. Wolfgang Behn (Freiburg: K. Schwartz, 1975); Bat-Sheva Garsiel, *Miqrā', Midrāsh and Qur'ān: 'Iyyūn Intertextuāly be-Ḥomrēi Sippūr Meshutafīm* [Bible, Midrash and Qur'ān: An Intertextual Study of Common Narrative Materials] (Tel Aviv: Hakibbutz Hameuchad, 2006).
16. See this claim in Qur'ān 3:78, 7:162. The term used in Islam for changing, twisting, falsifying, distorting, or altering portions of the Bible is called *taḥrīf*. For a study of Islamic polemical claims, see Hava Lazarus-Yafeh, "Muslim Arguments against the Bible," in Hava Lazarus-Yafeh, ed., *Intertwined Worlds: Medieval Islam and Bible Criticism* (Princeton, NJ: Princeton University Press, 1992), 19–49, and Appendix 143–160; Moshe Perlstein, "The Medieval Polemics between Islam and Judaism," in S. D. Goitein, ed., *Religion in Religious Age* (Cambridge: AJS, 1974), 103–138.
17. On the controversial search for the historical Abraham, see Israel Finkelstein and Neal Asher Silberman, *The Bible Unearthed: Archeology's New Vision of Ancient Israel and the Origin of its Sacred Texts* (New York: Touchstone, 2002), Hebrew edition, 49–53; Thomas L. Thompson, *The Historicity of the Patriarchal Narratives* (Berlin: de Gruyter, 1974) (reissued in Harrisburg: Trinity Intl', 2002); John Van Seters, *Abraham in History and Tradition* (New Haven, CT: Yale University Press, 1975).
18. Quoted from the Jewish Sabbath Morning Prayer.
19. Qur'ān 21:107.
20. Quoted from the Jewish Daily Morning Prayer.

Prologue: Our Father Avrahām/'Ibrāhīm

1. See the organization's web site www.MEPNetwork.org.
2. Qur'ān 49:13.
3. Samuel Huntington, *The Clash of Civilizations and the Remaking of World Order* (New York: Simon & Schuster, 1996). Cf. response by Jonathan Sacks, *The Dignity of Difference: How to Avoid the Clash of Civilizations* (London and New York: Continuum, 2002).

4. On the Spanish Golden Age, see Vivian B. Mann, Thomas E. Glick, and Jerrilynn Denise Dodds, eds. *Convivencia: Jews, Muslims, and Christians in Medieval Spain* (New York: George Braziller, in conjunction with The Jewish Museum, 1992); and Alan C. Brownfeld, "A Look at Spain's Age Encourages Efforts Toward Future Muslim-Jewish Understanding," published by *The American Council for Judaism* in http://www.acjna.org/acjna/articles_detail.aspx?id=413.
5. The Dalai Lama, *Toward a True Kinship of Faiths: How the World's Religions Can Come Together* (New York: Doubleday, 2010).
6. Philip Jenkins, "The Next Christianity," *Atlantic Monthly* (October 2002): 56.
7. See, for example, Marc Gopin, *Holy War, Holy Peace: How Religion Can Bring Peace to the Middle East* (New York: Oxford University Press, 2002); Marc Gopin, *Between Eden and Armageddon: The Future of World Religions, Violence and Peacemaking* (New York: Oxford University Press, 2000); R. Scott Appleby, *The Ambivalence of the Sacred: Religion, Violence and Reconciliation* (Lanham, MD: Rowman & Littlefield, 1999); Mohammed Abu-Nimer, *Nonviolence and Peace Building in Islam: Theory and Practice* (Gainesville, FL: University Press of Florida, 2003); Nathan C. Funk, *Peace and Conflict Resolution in Islam: Precept and Peace* (Lanham, MD: University Press of America, 2001); Nathan C. Funk and Abdul Aziz Said, eds., *Islam and Peacemaking in the Middle East* (Boulder, CO: Lynne Rienner, 2008).
8. See a recent study by Thomas F. Farr, "Diplomacy in an Age of Faith," *Foreign Affairs* (March/April 2008): 110–124. See also Douglas Johnson, *Faith-Based Diplomacy: Trumping Realpolitik* (New York: Oxford University Press, 2008); Douglas Johnson and Cynthia Sampson, eds., *Religion: The Missing Dimension of Statecraft* (New York: Oxford University, 1995).
9. David Smock, "Faith-Based NGOs and International Building," *United States Institute of Peace Publications*, Special Reports No. 76 (October 2001), 1. For more on the subject, see David Smock, ed., *Interfaith Dialogue and Peacebuilding* (Washington DC: United States Institute of Peace, 2002); and David Smock, "Religion in World Affairs: Its Role in Conflict and Peace," *United States Institute of Peace Publications*, Special Reports No. 201 (February 2008).
10. Khaled Abou El Fadl, "The Place of Tolerance in Islam: On Reading the Qur'an and Misreading It," *Boston Review* (December 2001/January 2002), quoted from http://www.bostonreview.net.
11. For a study on the difficulties scholars face in initiating a critical evaluation of their own traditions and opening up to revising old prejudices, see Mohammed Arkoun, "New Perspectives for a Jewish-Christian-Muslim Dialogue," in Leonard Swidler, ed., *Muslims in Dialogue: The Evolution of a Dialogue*, (Lewiston, NY: The Edwin Mellen Press, 1992), 224–229.
12. Talmud Bavlī, Berakhōt 64a, Yevamōt 122b, Nazīr 66b, Keritōt 28b, Tamīd 32b.
13. Talmud Bavlī, Berakhōt 64a.
14. Psalms 34:15.
15. Avōt d'Rabbi Nathan, version 1, 12:33–34.
16. Psalms 122:6.
17. Talmud Yerushālmi, Ḥagigāh 2:6.

18. Published in http://www.mepnetwork.org/an-open-letter-to-my-muslim-friends/.
19. *The Wisdom of Gibran: Aphorisms and Maxims,* ed. Joseph Sheban (New York: Philosophical Library, 1966), 17.

1 The Gate of Unity: We Are Bound Together—an Appeal to Muslims

1. Qur'ān 20:25–28.
2. It is part of the '*Alēinu* Prayer that concludes every Jewish prayer.
3. Qur'ān 42:15.
4. See morning and afternoon *Shmonēh 'Esrēh* prayers in the Jewish prayerbook.
5. Psalms 95:2–3.
6. Musnad Ahmad ibn Hanbal, *Ḥadīth* # 19774; Sahih al-Bukhari, *Aḥadīth* # 1623, 1626, 6361.
7. Malaachi 2:10.
8. Qur'ān 4:1.
9. Qur'ān 32:7–9.
10. Al-Rabghūzī, *The Stories of the Prophets: Qiṣaṣ al-Anbiyā', an Eastern Turkish Version*, vol. 2, translation (Leiden: E. J. Brill, 1995), 16–17. Cf. Al-Imam Imaduddin Abul-Fida Ismail Ibn Kathir, *Stories of the Prophets*, trans. Muhammad Mustapha Geme'ah, Al-Azhar (Riadh: Darussalam, 1999), 5–6, at httm://www.islamguiden.com/arkiv/stories_of_the_prophets.pdf.
11. Pirkēi d'Rabbi Eliezer in *Pirke De Rabbi Eliezer: The Chapters of Rabbi Eliezer the Great,* trans. and annotated Gerald Friedlander (New York: Sepher-Hermon, 1981), 76–77.
12. Qur'ān 30:22.
13. Mishnah, Sanhedrīn 4:5.
14. Qur'ān 20:30.
15. Qur'ān 49:13.
16. See, for example, Suhail H. Hashmi, "The Qur'an and Tolerance: An Interpretive Essay on Verse 5:48," *Journal of Human Rights* 2 (1) (March 2003): 81–104.
17. Qur'ān 10:19.
18. Qur'ān 11:118–119.
19. Qur'ān 5:48.
20. Qur'ān 2:177.
21. Qur'ān 2:148.
22. See Hashmi, "The Qur'an and Tolerance," 79–80.
23. Qur'ān 49:13.
24. The Sabians, referred to in the Qur'ān, are adherents of beliefs of a community, which was based in the Harran region of southeastern Anatolia and northern Syria.
25. Qur'ān 2:62.
26. Qur'ān 8:2–3.
27. Qur'ān 49:10.

28. Psalms 118:19–20.
29. Midrāsh Rabbāh, Exodus 19:4.
30. Qur'ān 21:105. Cf. Psalms 25:13, 37:11, 29.
31. Qur'ān 42:15.
32. Qur'ān 2:136, 3:84.
33. Qur'ān 42:13.
34. Qur'ān 3:7, 13:39, 43:4, 85:21–22.
35. Qur'ān 24:35.
36. See poems published in the Epilogue.
37. Qur'ān 4:152.
38. Qur'ān 2:256.
39. Qur'ān 109:1–6.
40. Qur'ān 5:2.
41. Qur'ān 2:256.
42. Qur'ān 3:64.
43. Qur'ān 16:125.
44. Qur'ān 29:46.
45. Qur'ān 28:77.
46. Qur'ān 12:92.
47. Qur'ān 60:7.
48. Abd al-Rahman Nasir Sa'di, *Taysīr al-Latīf al-Mannān fī Khulāsat Tafsīr al-Qur'ān* (Cairo: Maktabah al-Islamiyyah, 2000), 55.
49. *The Gift: Poems by Hafiz, The Greater Sufi Master*, trans. Daniel Ladinsky (New York: Penguin Compass, 1999), 325.
50. Qur'ān 33:4.
51. *Bringing Heaven Down to Earth: Meditations and Everyday Wisdom from the Teachings of the Rebbe, Menachem Schneerson*, ed. Tzvi Freeman (Holbrook, MA: Adams Media Corporation, 1999), 119.
52. http://www.twf.org/Sayings/Sayings3.html.
53. Tanḥumā, Netzavīm a.
54. Qur'ān 77:25.
55. Deuteronomy 14:1.
56. Edmond Bordeaux Szekely, *The Essene Gospel of Peace, Book 2: The Unknown Books of the Essenes* (Nelson, British Columbia: International Biogenic Society, 1981). Quoted in Gabriel Cousens, *Sevenfold Peace* (Tiburon, CA: H. J. Kramer, 1990), 85.
57. Qur'ān 3:68.
58. Genesis 13:8.
59. Psalms 133:1.
60. Abraham Isaac Ha-Cohen Kook, *Orōt* [Lights] (Jerusalem: Mosad Ha-Rav Kook, 1993), 152.
61. Qur'ān 2:125.
62. Qur'ān 114.
63. Psalms 1:1–6.
64. Psalms 25:13.
65. Proverbs 17:5.

66. Qur'ān 4:114.
67. Qur'ān 10:81.

2 The Gate of Discourse: Holy Tongue—A Cultural Commonality

1. See, for example, *The Bahir*, trans. and ed.. Aryeh Kaplan (York Beach, ME: Samuel Weiser, 1990), 75–76.
2. Genesis 11:1.
3. Genesis 10:5, 20, 31; Talmud Yerushālmi, Megillāh 1:9; Torah Temimāh's commentary on Genesis 11:1.
4. Qur'ān 30:22.
5. Midrāsh Rabbāh, Exodus 5:9.
6. Sifre, Deuteronomy, Parashāt ve-Zot ha-Berakhāh.
7. On the Semitic family, see Patrick R. Bennett, *Comparative Semitic Linguistics: A Manual* (Winona Lake, IN: Eisenbrauns 1998).
8. Shimon Federbush, *Ha-Lashōn Ha-'Ivrīt Be-Yisraēl Uva-'Amīm* [The Hebrew Language in Israel and the Nations] (Jerusalem: Mosad Ha-Rav Kook, 1967), 12–15.
9. Joel 2:13; Jonas 4:2; Psalms 111:4, 112:4, 145:8; Nehemiah 9:17,31; 2 Chronicles 30:9.
10. Psalms 86:15, 103:8.
11. Based on Exodus 34:6.
12. Samson Raphael Hirsch, Commentary on Genesis 43:14.
13. Psalms 103:13.
14. For a comprehensive review of God's Names, see "Names of God," http://JewishEncyclopedia.com, taken from *The Jewish Encyclopedia*, 160–165; "Names of God in Judaism," http://en.wikipedia.org/wiki/Names_of_God_in_Judaism; "Names of God in the Hebrew Bible," in *The Oxford Companion to the Bible*, eds. Bruce M. Meltzer and Michael D. Coogan (New York: Oxford University Press, 1993), 548–49; Judah Halevi, *The Kuzari* (New York: Schocken Books, 1978), 83–88; Israel Knohl, *Me-'Āyin Bānu: Ha-Tzōfen Ha-Genēti shel Ha-Tanākh* [Where Have We Come From: The Bible's Genetic Code] (Tel Aviv: Dvir, 2008), 69–76.
15. Rabbi Moshe ben Maimon, *Mishnēh Torāh*, Sēfer Ha-Madā' [Book of Knowledge], Hilkhōt Yesodēi Ha-Torāh [Fundamentals of the Torah] (Jerusalem: Mosad Ha-Rav Kook, 1972), 30–31.
16. See, for example, Psalms 150:6: "*Qol ha-neshamāh tehallēl Yah halellū-Yah*" (Let every soulful being praise the Lord, praise the Lord).
17. Exodus 3:14.
18. See an illuminating discussion on this topic in Midrāsh Rabbāh, Exodus 3:6.
19. Aryeh Kaplan, *Meditation and Kabbalah* (York Beach, ME: Samuel Weiser, 1982), 125–136.
20. Genesis 12:8.

21. Genesis 14:22.
22. Genesis 15:2.
23. Genesis 17:1.
24. Genesis 17:8.
25. Genesis 21:33.
26. Mishnah, Pirkēi Avōt 4:22.
27. See Sheikh Al-Islam Ahmad Ibn Taimiyah, *Principles of Islam* [Al-'Aqīdah Al-Wasitīyah], trans. Asaad Nimer Busool (Chicago: IQRA', 1992), 9–25.
28. On the Name "Allah," see Abul Kalam Azad, *The Tarjumān al-Qur'ān*, ed. Syed Abdul Latif, vol. 1, (Hyderabad: Dr. Syed Abdul Latif's Trust for Quranic & Other Cultural Studies, 1981), 14–16.
29. Saḥīḥ Muslim, vol. 4, no. 1410.
30. Qur'ān 7:180.
31. Qur'ān 17:110.
32. Qur'ān 59:22–24.
33. Qiṣaṣ al-Anbiyā', vol. 2, 21 (cf. vol. 1, 17).
34. Deuteronomy 28:9.
35. Genesis 1:26–27.
36. See analysis in Rabbi Joseph Ber Soloveitchik, *'Ish ha-Halakhāh: Galūy ve-Nistār* [The Halakhic Man: Revealed and Hidden] (Jerusalem: Jewish Agency, 1979), 180–86.
37. Mishnēh Torāh, Sēfer Ha-Madā' [Book of Knowledge], Hilkhōt De'ōt [Laws of Ethical Ideas], 1:6.
38. Sifrei, Deuteronomy 49.
39. Talmud Bavlī, Soṭāh 14a.
40. Talmud Bavlī, Shabbāt 133b; Mekhilta de'Rabbi Ishmael 18:II 3.
41. Talmud Bavlī, Beitzāh 32b.
42. Mishnēh Torāh, Sēfer Qinyān [Book of Acquisition], Hilkhōt 'Avadīm [Laws of Slaves], 9:8.
43. Shmuel David Luzzatto, *'Al Ha-Ḥemlāh ve-Ha-Hashgaḥāh* [On Compassion and Providence] (Tel Aviv: Miskal—Yediot Aharonot, 2008), 40, 47, 95–96, 100.
44. Qur'ān 21:107.
45. Qur'ān 90:17.
46. Qur'ān 7:151.
47. Qur'ān 12:64, 12:92, 21:83.
48. Amos 5:15.
49. Psalms 34:13–15.
50. Qur'ān 28:77.
51. Qur'ān 10:26.
52. Qur'ān 18:88.
53. Qur'ān 3:134.
54. Qur'ān 7:56.
55. Qur'ān 17:53.
56. Qur'ān 41:33.
57. Qur'ān 61:2–3.

58. Talmud Bavlī, Ḥagigāh 14b.
59. Mishnah, Pirkēi Avōt 1:17.
60. This Jewish prayer ends every *Shmonēh 'Esrēh*, the standing silent meditation.
61. Avōt d'Rabbi Nathan, version 2, 24:4.

3 The Gate of Practice: Rituals and Rites—Closer than Apart

1. Qur'ān 22:78.
2. Qur'ān 2:286.
3. On the position of Maimonides and his treatment of Islam in his writings, see G. F. Hourani, "Maimonides and Islam," in W. M. Brinner and S. D. Ricks, eds., *Studies in Islamic and Judaic Traditions* (Atlanta: Scholars Press, 1986), 153–165; D. Novak, "The Treatment of Islam and Muslims in the Legal Writings of Maimonides" in *ibid.*, 233–250; Yoseph Kapach, "Islām ve-ha-Yāḥas la-Muslemīm be-Mishnēh Torāh" [Islam and the Treatment of Muslims in Mishnēh Torāh], *Maḥanāyim* 1 (1991–92); Dov Maimon, "Sovlanūt lamrōt 'l-ha-Haskamāh be-Mitzrāyim ha-Yemēi Benāyimit: Rabbi Abraham ben-ha-Rambam ve-ha-Mistikanīm ha-Muslemīm" [Tolerance despite Lack of Agreement in Medieval Egypt: Rabbi Abraham, son of Maimonides, and the Muslim Mystics], in Shlomo Fischer and Adam B. Seligman, eds., *'Ol ha-Sovlanūt: Nasorōt Datiyyōt ve-Etgār ha-Pluralism* [The Burden of Tolerance: Religious Traditions and the Challenge of Pluralism] (Jerusalem: Van Leer Jerusalem Institute / Hakibbutz Hameuchad Publishing House, 2007), 289–292; [Gerald] Jacob Blidstein, "Ma'amād ha-Islām ba-Halakhāh ha-Maimōnit" [The Status of Islam in the Halakhah of Maimonides], in Menachem Mautner, Avi Sagy, and Ronen Shamir, eds., *Rav-Tarbutiyyūt be-Medināh Demoqrāṭit ve-Yehudīt* [Multiculturalism in a Democratic and Jewish State] (Tel Aviv: Ramot, Tel Aviv University, 1997–1998), 465–476.
4. Mishnēh Torāh, Sēfer Shofṭīm [Book of Judges], Hilkhōt Melakhīm [Laws of the Kings], 11:7–8
5. M. Bar-Joseph, ed. Rabeinu Moshe Ben Maimon: *Igrotāv ve-Toldōt Ḥayāv* [Maimonides: His Epistles and Biography] (Tel Aviv: Mordechai Institute for Publishing Judaica, 1970), 144.
6. On Rabbi Abraham ben Maimon and the Sufi influence, see Dov Maimon, "Sovlanūt lamrōt 'l-ha-Haskamāh," 292–296; S. D. Goitein, "Abraham Maimonides and his Pietist Circle," in A. Altmann, ed., *Jewish Medieval and Renaissance Studies* (Cambridge, MA: Harvard University, 1967), 145–164.
7. See Paul B. Fenton "Judaism and Sufism," in Seyyed Hossein Nasr and Oliver Leaman, eds., *History of Islamic Philosophy*, vol. 1 (London: Routledge, 1996), 755–768; Paul B. Fenton, "Judaeo-Arabic Mystical Writings of the XIIIth–XIVth Centuries," in Norman Golb, *Judaeo-Arabic Studies: Proceedings of the Founding Conference of the Society for Judaeo-Arabic Studies*, Studies in Muslim-Jewish Relations, vol. 3 (Amsterdam: Harwood Academic Publishers, 1997),

89–102. Diana Lobel, *A Sufi-Jewish Dialogue: Philosophy and Mysticism in Bahya ibn Paquda's Duties of the Heart* (Philadelphia: University of Pennsylvania Press, 2006).

8. On Jewish life under Islam, see Bernard Lewis, *The Jews of Islam* (Princeton, NJ: Princeton University Press, 1984); Bat Ye'or, *The Dhimmi: Jews and Christians under Islam*, trans. David Maisel, Paul Fenton, and David Littman (Rutherford, NJ: Fairleigh Dickinson University Press, 1985); Mark R. Cohen, *Under Crescent and Cross: The Jews in the Middle Ages* (Princeton, NJ: Princeton University Press, 1995).
9. On the Cairo Genizāh and its research as it is related to Jewish-Muslim relations in Medieval Cairo, see the masterful five-volume work of S. D. Goitein, *A Mediterranean Society: The Jewish Communities of the Arab World as Portrayed in the Documents of the Cairo Genizāh* (Los Angeles and London: University of California Press, 1969–1993); Yoseph (Paul) Fenton, "Yaḥasīm bein Yehudīm le-Muslemīm le-'Or Mismakhēi ha-Genizāh" [Relations between Jews and Muslims based on the Genizāh Documents], *Te'udāh* 15 (1998–1999): 351–364.
10. Qur'ān 15:87.
11. Psalms 51:17.
12. See, for example, Psalms 146, 147, 148, 149, 150, 155.
13. Maimonides used this prefatory phrase in the *Commentary on the Mishnah*, the *Sefēr ha-Mitzvōt*, and the *Essay on Resurrection*, a postscript that was possibly eliminated from other printed editions. See analysis in Marvin Fox, *Interpreting Maimonides* (Chicago: The University of Chicago Press, 1990), 262–264.
14. Genesis 21:33.
15. See, for example, Talmud Bavlī, Yomā 87b, Berakhōt 60b.
16. Proverbs 20:8.
17. See, for example, Talmud Bavlī, 'Avodāh Zarāh 18a.
18. 1 Samuel 7:3.
19. Psalms 27:11, 107:7.
20. Proverbs 3:6.
21. Qiṣaṣ al-Anbiyā', vol. 2, 3.
22. Rabbi Ovadia Yosef, *Yebī'a 'Ōmer*, vol. 7, Yorēh De'āh, 12.
23. Maimonides: His Letters and Biography, 173.
24. Tur in *Shulḥān 'Arūkh*, Yorēh De'āh, 124.
25. Yitzchak Elchanan Spektor, *'Ain Yitzḥāq*, Part A (Vilna, 1889), Siman 11b.
26. David Novak, *Jewish-Christian Dialogue: A Jewish Justification* (New York: Oxford University Press, 1989), 53–56. On Rabbi Ha-Meiri's views on non-Jews, see Jacob Katz, "Sovlanūt Datīt be-Mishnatō shel Rabbi Menachem Ha-Meiri" [Religious Tolerance in the Study of Rabbi Menachem Ha-Meiri], *Zion* 18 (1953): 15–30; Gerald J. Blidstein, "Maimonides and Meiri on the Legitimacy of Non-Judaic Religion," in Leo Landman, ed., *Scholars and Scholarship: The Interaction between Judaism and Other Cultures* (New York: Yeshiva University Press, 1990).
27. Menachem Ha-Meiri, *Beit ha-Beḥirāh* [The Chosen House], ed. Y. Dickman (Jerusalem, 1965), 226.

28. *The Life of Muhammad: A Translation of Ibn Ishaq's Sirat Rasul Allah*, trans. Alfred Guillaume, vol. 1 (New York: Oxford University Press, 1990), 619.
29. Qur'ān 2:125.
30. Qur'ān 5:97.
31. Qur'ān 22:77.
32. Genesis 17:3.
33. Numbers 16:20–22.
34. Job 1:20.
35. Talmud Bavlī, Tamīd 6:1–3, 7:1–3, Yomā 1:8, 6:2.
36. Talmud Bavlī, Berakhōt 34 a. Cf. Eliezer Levy, *Yesodōt ha-Tefillāh* [The Basics of Prayer] (Tel Aviv: Avraham Tziyoni, 1963), 109.
37. Maimonides, *Mishnēh Torāh*, Sefer Ahavāh [Book of Love (of God)], Hilkhōt Tefillāh [Laws of Prayer], 5:14.
38. Mishnah, Pirkēi Avōt, 5:5.
39. Talmud Bavlī, Berakhōt 31a.
40. Psalms 99:5.
41. Isaiah 66:1.
42. Leviticus 26:1; Talmud Bavlī, Megillāh 22b. Cf. Maimonides, *Mishnēh Torāh*, Sēfer Ha-Madā' [Book of Knowledge (of God)], Hilkhōt 'Avodāh Zarāh ve- Ḥuqqōt ha-Goyyīm [Laws of Idolatry and Heathenism], 6:6–7.
43. Adin Even-Yisrael Steinsaltz, *Ha-Siddūr ve-ha-Tefillāh* [the Prayerbook and the Prayer], vol. 2 (Tel Aviv: Yediot Ahronot, 2001), 80; cf. Rabbi Hayim Halevy Donin, *To Pray as a Jew: A Guide to the Prayerbook and the Synagogue Service* (New York: Basic Books, 1980), 41.
44. Exodus 30:19.
45. Psalms 26:6.
46. Psalms 24:3–4.
47. Shulḥān 'Arūkh, 'Oraḥ Ḥayyīm, 4, 18, 158–165.
48. On Mikvāh, see Aryeh Kaplan, *Waters of Eden: The Mystery of the Mikvah* (New York: NCSY / Orthodox Union, 1982).
49. On the Islamic ḥammām, see http://www.cyberbohemia.com/Pages/Islam-hammam.
50. Leviticus 12:3.
51. Genesis 17:7–8.
52. Genesis 17:9–12.
53. Muhammed Salih Al-Munajjid, Question #9412: Circumcision: how it is done and the rulings on it, http://www.islam-qa.com.
54. Ibid., Question #7073: The health and religious benefits of circumcision, http://www.islam-qa.com.
55. Muhammad Lutfi al-Sabbagh, *Islamic Ruling on Male and Female Circumcision* (Alexandria: World Health Organization, 1966), 16.
56. Ḥadīth #377 in *Ṣaḥīḥ Muslim* [Arabic only].
57. Ḥadīth #4368 in *Ṣaḥīḥ Muslim* [Arabic only].
58. Genesis 17:23–27.
59. Leviticus 11:3; Deuteronomy 14:6.
60. Qur'ān 5:1.

61. Leviticus 11:9; Deuteronomy 14:9.
62. Qur'ān 5:96.
63. Deuteronomy 12:21–24.
64. Qur'ān 6:118.
65. Qur'ān 6:121.
66. Deuteronomy 14:21.
67. Qur'ān 5:3, 16:115.
68. Leviticus 7:26–27, 17:10–14.
69. Qur'ān 5:3, 16:115.
70. Leviticus 11:7.
71. Qur'ān 16:115, 5:3.
72. Qur'ān 5:5.
73. Qur'ān 52:19.
74. Leviticus 11:4.
75. Qur'ān 3:93.
76. Qur'ān 4:86.
77. Qur'ān 24:61. Cf. 24:27.
78. Mishnah, Pirkēi Avōt 4:15.
79. Pērek ha-Shalōm [Chapter on Peace], in Tractate Dērekh 'Ēretz Zuṭā, quoted from http://www.daat.ac.il/daat/toshba/zuta/11-2.htm.
80. Talmud Bavlī, Berakhōt 17a.
81. Mishnah, Shevi'īt 4:3, 5:9; Giṭṭīn 5:9.
82. *The Essential Rumi*, trans. Coleman Barks (New York: HarperCollins, 1996), 165–168.
83. Qur'ān 2:177.
84. Qur'ān 5:48.
85. Psalms 51:12.
86. Psalms 24:3–5.
87. Qur'ān 26:89.
88. Yitzhaq Yehudah (Ignac) Goldziher, *Hartza'ōt 'al Ha-Islām* [Lectures on Islam, a translation of *Vorlesungen über den Islam*] (Jerusalem: Mosad Biyalik, 1951), 125.

4 THE GATE OF LEGACY: THE RELIGION OF ABRAHAM—A COMMON GROUND

1. Genesis 23:2.
2. The land acquisition is fully recorded in Genesis 23:1–20.
3. Based on Talmud Bavlī, Soṭāh 34a.
4. Midrāsh Rabbāh, Numbers 2:12.
5. Isaiah 51:1–2.
6. Qur'ān 19:41.
7. Qur'ān 4:125.
8. Qur'ān 16:120, 123.

9. Qur'ān 16:120.
10. Qur'ān 2:135.
11. Qur'ān 2:130.
12. Qur'ān 2:13.
13. Qur'ān 3:68.
14. Qur'ān 16:123.
15. Qur'ān 16:121.
16. Qur'ān 6:161.
17. Qur'ān 1:6. These commandments are repeated in detail in Qur'ān 17:22–37.
18. Qur'ān 6:151–153.
19. Qur'ān 4:68–69.
20. *The Tarjuman al-Qur'ān*, vol. 1, xviii.
21. Genesis 22:12.
22. Genesis 20:7.
23. Talmud Bavlī, Minḥōt 53:72.
24. Genesis 17:1.
25. Midrāsh Rabbāh, Song of Songs 3:5.
26. Nehyemiah 9:7–8.
27. Luzzatto, 116.
28. Genesis 17:1.
29. Genesis 18:19.
30. Jeremiah 9:22, 22:15–16.
31. Nehama Leibowitz, *Studies in Bereshīt (Genesis)* (Jerusalem: The Jewish Agency Publisher, 1976), 169–170.
32. Deuteronomy 6:18, 12:25, 13:19, 21:25.
33. Judges 4:1.
34. Samuel I 12:23.
35. Jeremiah 31:8.
36. Yehezkel Kaufmann, *The Religion of Israel* (New York: Schocken Books, 1972), 221–23.
37. Raphael Patai, *The Seed of Abraham: Jews and Arabs in Contact and Conflict* (New York: Charles Scribner's Sons, 1986), 17.
38. Mishnah, Pirkēi Avōt 2:1.
39. Mishnēh Torāh, Sēfer HaMadā', Hilkhōt De'ōt, 1:4, 7.
40. Luzzatto, 162, 168.
41. Rabbi Naftali Tzvi Yehudah Berlin, "Petiḥāh Le-Sēfer Bereshīt [Introduction to the Book of Genesis]," in *Ha'amēq Davār* (Jerusalem: Yeshivat Volozhin, 1999). Cf. Gil S. Perl, "No Two Minds Think Alike: Tolerance and Pluralism in the Work of Neziv," *The Torāh U-Maddā' Journal*, vol. 12 (2004), 74–98.
42. Genesis 26:2–5.
43. *Pentateuch and Rashi's Commentary*, vol. 1—Genesis, trans. Abraham ben Isaiah and Benjamin Sharfman (Brooklyn, NY: S. S. & R., 1948), 248–249.
44. *Ramban (Nacmanides) Commentary on the Torah, Genesis*, trans. Charles B. Chavel (New York: Shilo Publishing House, 1971), 329.
45. Sēfer ha-Yovlīm 20:1–5. Based on Book of Jubilees in R. H. Charles, ed., *The Apocrypha and Pseudepigrapha of the Old Testament* (Oxford: Clarendon Press,

1913), http://wesley.nnu.edu/biblical_studies/noncanon/ot/pseudo/jubilee.htm.

46. Ibid.
47. Mahmoud M. Ayoub, "Abraham and His Children: A Muslim Perspective," *Dinika* 3(1) (January 2004), 19–34.
48. Maimonides: His Epistles and Biography, 170.
49. Abraham ben David Halevi, *Sēfer Ha-'Emunāh Ha-Rammāh* [The Book of the Sublime Faith] (Jerusalem, 1967), 104.
50. A hymn (*piyyūṭ*) chanted during the *Minḥāh* prayer of Yom Kippur, the Jewish Day of Atonement.
51. Qiṣaṣ al-Al-Anbiyā', 93.
52. Genesis 18:1–8.
53. Mishnah, Pirkēi Avōt 1:5.
54. Talmud Bavlī, Shabbāt 127a.
55. Quoted from the text in http://www.newadvent.org.
56. Genesis 13:1–12.
57. Genesis 21:22–34.
58. Genesis 26:12–33.
59. Leviticus 19:16.
60. Genesis 14:1–24.
61. Qur'ān 11:75.
62. Deuteronomy 16:20.
63. Genesis 18:25.
64. Genesis 18:19.
65. Genesis 18:26–33.
66. See Genesis 9:3–6. For comprehensive studies on the Seven Noahide Laws, see "Ben Noah" in *Encyclopedia Talmudīt*, vol. 3, 348–362; David Novak, *The Image of the Non-Jew in Judaism: An Historical and Constructive Study of the Noahide Laws* (New York and Toronto: E. Mellen Press 1983), and his work, *Jewish-Christian Dialogue*, 26–41; Yirmiyahu Bindman, *The Seven Colors of the Rainbow* (Colorado Springs, CO: Scheuller House, 2000); Michael Dallen, *The Rainbow Covenant: Torah and the Universal Law* (Springdale, AR: Lightcatcher Books, 2003).
67. See an excellent analysis by Irshaad Hussain in his article "Basic Commandments and the Straight Path," *Islam from the Inside Out,* http://islamfrominside.com/Pages/Tafsir/Tafsir(6–151%20to% 20153).html.
68. For the Seven Noahide Laws as a foundation for Jewish-Christian Dialogue, see Novak, *The Image of the Non-Jew in Judaism,* 114–156.
69. Talmud Bavlī, Sanhedrīn 105a.
70. Qur'ān 6:161.
71. Qur'ān 10:35.
72. Qur'ān 3:64.
73. Genesis 17:5.
74. See, for example, Talmud Bavlī, Beitzāh 32b, Baba Qāma 97, Baba Bātra 15, 91; Midrāsh Rabbāh, Genesis 41:8; Talmud Yerushālmi, Berakhōt 9:5.
75. Tosefta, Berakhōt, 1.

76. Maimonides, *Pirūsh Ha-Mishnāh*, Bikkurīm, 81.
77. Romans 4:9–17; Galatians 3:9.
78. Romans 4:12.
79. Qur'ān 3:67.
80. Qur'ān 22:78.
81. Qur'ān 3:68.
82. Qur'ān 16:120.
83. Qur'ān 25:67.
84. Talmud Bavlī, Beitzāh 32b.
85. This is a literary translation from a article in Hebrew on October 17, 2007, http://www.Haaretz.co.il

5 The Gate of Ancestry: Abraham and Ishmael—a Scriptural Reconstruction

1. See "Epistle to Yemen," in Maimonides: His Epistels and Biography [in Hebrew], 60.
2. For a detailed biographical list, see Yechiel ben Shlomo Halperin, *Sēfer Sēder ha-Dorōt* [The Book of the Order of the Generations] (New York), 245–253.
3. On Rabbi Ishmael ben Elisha, see Nissan Mindel's article in http://www.chabad.org/library/article_cdo/aid/112326/jewish/Rabbi-Ishmael-Ben-Elisha.htm. The famous 13-principle list is included as part of the preliminary prayers and readings of the Jewish Prayerbook. See details in Nissan Mindel, *My Prayer* (Brooklyn, NY: Merkos L'Iyonei Chinuch, 1972), 97–109.
4. Genesis 16:12.
5. Zohar, Parashāt Va-Yerā', 463, in *Sēfer ha-Zōhar*, vol. 4 (Jerusalem: Press of Yeshivat Kol Yehuda, 1988), 137–138.
6. Pirkēi d'Rabbi Eliezer, 218.
7. Sēfer ha-Yashār 21:6–20.
8. Pirkēi d'Rabbi Eliezer, 218–219. Cf. Sēfer ha-Yashār, 21:22–45, and Qiṣaṣ al-Anbiyā', 120.
9. Sēfer ha-Yashār 22:1–3.
10. Ibid., 22:40–45. Cf. Talmud Bavlī, Sanhedrīn 89b.
11. Talmud Bavlī, Sanhedrīn 89b. Cf. Pentateuch and Rashi's Commentary (on Genesis 22:1–2), vol.1, 199–200.
12. Sēfer ha-Yashār 23:20–28; Pirkēi d'Rabbi Eliezer, 224–225.
13. Midrāsh Rabbāh, Genesis 61:1, 4. Cf. Louis Ginzberg, *The Legends of the Jews* [Philadelphia: Jewish Publication Society, 1909], ch. 5.
14. Zohar, Parashāt Ḥayēi Sarāh, 257. Cf. Midrāsh Rabbāh, Genesis 61:4; and Pentateuch and Rashi's Commentary (on Genesis 25:1), 233–234.
15. Sēfer ha-Yovlīm 20:1–5.
16. Ibid., 22:1–9.
17. Ibid., 23:1–8.
18. Ramban (Nacmanides) Commentary on the Torah, Genesis, 213.
19. RaDak on Genesis, 16:6.

20. See, for example, Midrāsh Rabbāh, Genesis 45:4–5, 53:11; Midrāsh Rabbāh, Exodus 1:1.
21. Pentateuch and Rashi's Commentary (on Genesis 21:9), 190.
22. Tosefta, Soṭāh, 5:7, 6:3.
23. Ramban (Nacmanides) Commentary on the Torah, Genesis 269–271.
24. Deuteronomy 21:10–23. See an excellent commentary in Ben-Zion Firer, *Panīm Ḥadashōt ba-Torāh* [New Faces in the Torah], vol. 5, Deuteronomy (Jerusalem: Feldheim Publishers, 1975), 118–124.
25. Ibid., 21:10–14.
26. Ibid., 21:15–17. Cf. Maimonides, *Mishnēh Torāh*, Sēfer Mishpaṭīm [Book of Civil Code], Hilkhōt Neḥalōt [Laws of Inheritance], 2:1–9, 3:1.
27. Ibid., 21:18–23.
28. Genesis 13:17.
29. Genesis 12:6–9.
30. Menasheh Harel, *Masa'ōt ve-Ma'arakhōt bi-Ymēi Qēdem* [Journeys and Campaigns in the Ancient Days] (Tel Aviv: Israel's Ministry of Defense, 1984), 11–21.
31. Genesis 12:10.
32. Pirkei De Rabbi Eliezer, 217–217; Yalqut Shimoni on Genesis, ch. 21.
33. Pirkei De Rabbi Eliezer, 218–219; Yalqut Shimoni on Genesis, ch. 21; Qiṣaṣ al-Anbiyā', vol.2, 120–121.
34. Pirkei De Rabbi Eliezer, 219.
35. See analysis by Reuven Firestone, *Journeys in Holy Lands: The Evolution of the Abraham-Ishmael Legends in Islamic Exegesis* (Albany: State University of New York Press, 1990).
36. Qur'ān 2:125, 127.
37. Qiṣaṣ al-Anbiyā', vol. 2, 129–132.
38. Qur'ān 3:97.
39. Genesis, 25:9.
40. Pentateuch and Rashi's Commentary (on Genesis 25:9), 236.
41. Midrāsh Rabbāh, Genesis 62:3.
42. Pentateuch and Rashi's Commentary (on Genesis 25:17), 237–238.
43. Talmud Bavlī, Baba Bātra, 1:16b.
44. Genesis, 25:12.
45. Genesis, 25:19.
46. Genesis 25:13–16.
47. Chronicles I, 1:27–28.
48. Talmud Bavlī, Berakhōt 13a.
49. Genesis 17:5.

6 The Gate of Morality: The Sacrifice of Isaac/Ishmael—Some Forgotten Lessons

1. For the entire speech, see https://www.jewishvirtuallibrary.org/jsource/Peace/sadat_speech.

2. Genesis 22:1.
3. Mishnah, Pirkēi Avōt 5:3.
4. Rabbi Moshe ben Maimon [Rambam], *Pirūsh le-Masēkhet Avōt* [Commentary to the Tractate of Avot] (Jerusalem: Mosad Ha-Rav Kook, 1969), 173–174.
5. Pirkēi d'Rabbi Eliezer, 187–230. Cf. other versions in Avōt d'Rabbi Nathan 33:2; and Sēfer ha-Yovlīm 17:17.
6. See Genesis 22:1–19.
7. Pentateuch and Rashi's Commentary (on Genesis 22:2), 200.
8. Qur'ān 2:124.
9. Qur'ān 102–109.
10. Qiṣaṣ al-Anbiyā', vol. 2, 121–123.
11. Abu Ja'far Muhammad ibn Jarir Al-Tabari, *The History of al-Tabari*, vol. 2: *Prophets and Patriarchs*, trans. William M. Brinner (Albany, NY: SUNY Press, 1987), 82–89. Cf. Sam Shamoun, "Abraham and the Child of Sacrifice—Isaac or Ishmael," in http://www.answering-islam.org/Shamoun/sacrifice.htm.
12. See a study by Amer Yunis, "The Sacrifice of Abraham in Islam," in Frederic Manns, ed., *The Sacrifice of Isaac in the Three Monotheistic Religions*, Proceedings of a Symposium on the Interpretation of the Scriptures held in Jerusalem. March 16–17, 1995 (Jerusalem: Franciscan Printing Press, 1995).
13. Qiṣaṣ al-Anbiyā', vol. 2, 123–129.
14. Zev Vilnay, *Legends of Palestine* (Whitefish, MT: Kessinger Publishing, 2003), 24–25. This is a reprint of a Hebrew volume published by the same author under the title *Aggadōt 'Ēretz Yisraēl* (London, 1929).
15. Psalms 121:1–2.
16. Exodus 3:5.
17. Qiṣaṣ al-Anbiyā', vol. 2, 121–122.
18. Qur'ān 17:1.
19. See a full analysis by Uriel Simon, "'Ḥavayāh Mekhonēnet Aḥāt" [A Single Transformational Experience], in http://acheret.co.il/?cmd=articles.181&act=read&id=1060.
20. For a good discussion on religious myths, see Neil Gillman, *Sacred Fragments: Recovering Theology for the Modern Jew* (New York: The Jewish Publication Society, 1990), 26–30, 84–88, 234–236.
21. Joseph Campbell, *The Power of Myth* with Bill Moyers, ed. Betty Sue Flowers (New York: Doubleday, 1988), xvii.
22. Qur'ān 3:154.
23. Ramban (Nacmanides) Commentary on the Torah, Genesis, 275.
24. Midrāsh Rabbāh, Genesis 51:1.
25. Psalms 23.
26. See references to Job in the Qur'ān 6:84, 21:83–84, 38:41–44. This Islamic tradition is fully covered in Qiṣaṣ al-Anbiyā', vol. 2, 280–299.
27. Pentateuch and Rashi's Commentary (on Genesis 22:2), 200.
28. Qur'ān 3:156. Cf. 15:23.
29. Mishnah, Pirkēi Avōt 5:22.
30. Genesis 22:12.
31. Deuteronomy 6:26.

32. Micah 6:7.
33. Genesis 9:6.
34. Mishnah, Sanhedrīn 4:5.
35. Qur'ān 5:32.
36. Qur'ān 6:151.
37. Qur'ān 4:29–30.
38. Qur'ān 2:190.
39. Exodus 23:2.
40. Isaiah 56:7.
41. I Samuel 15: 22.
42. Hosea 6:6.
43. Proverbs 21:3.
44. Genesis 22:12.
45. Qiṣaṣ al-Anbiyā', vol. 2, 125.
46. Qur'ān 37:102.
47. Qur'ān 37:103.
48. Jewish morning prayer.
49. For a full analysis of the distinction between love of God and fear of God, see Louis Jacobs, *A Jewish Theology* (West Orange, NJ: Behrman House, 1973), chs. 11, 12.
50. Job 1:1.
51. Deuteronomy 6:5.
52. Leviticus 19:18.
53. Pirkēi d'Rabbi Eliezer, 233–234
54. Qur'ān 5:91.
55. Qur'ān 2:256.
56. Deuteronomy 12:31. Cf. Jeremiah 7:31; Ezekiel 16:20–21, 23:37, 39; Isaiah 57; 7:31; II Kings 15:3, 21:6, 23:10; II Chronicles 33:6; Psalms 106:37–38.
57. Proverbs 34:14.

7 The Gate of Peace: Rights to the Holy Land—a Theological Reexamination

1. For a balanced synopsis of the complex history of the Arab-Israeli conflict, see the web site of the Council on Foreign Relations http://www.cfr.org/crisisguide_mideast.
2. The entire text can be found at http://www.jewishvirtuallibrary.org/jsource/History/Dec_of_Indep.html.
3. Genesis 13:15, 13:17.
4. Midrāsh Tanḥumā, Lekh Lekhā, 9.
5. Ramban (Nacmanides) Commentary on the Torah, Genesis, 169.
6. *Sha'arēi 'Ēretz Yisraēl* (Jerusalem: Heikhal Menachem, 2002), 35–36, 103.
7. Ḥōshen Mishpāṭ 190.
8. Midrāsh Rabbāh, Genesis 79:7.

9. Genesis 23:16.
10. Genesis 33:19.
11. I Chronicles 21:25.
12. For a halakhic study of the sanctification of the Land of Israel, see Shlomo Yosef Zevin, *Le-'Or Ha-Halakhāh* [In Light of the Halakhah] (Jerusalem: Qol Mevaser, 2004), 91–111.
13. Genesis 12:1–2.
14. Genesis 12:7.
15. Genesis 15:18–21.
16. Genesis 17:7–8.
17. Genesis 26:3.
18. Genesis 35:12. Cf., Genesis 28:4, 28:13.
19. Genesis 48:4.
20. Genesis 50:24.
21. Exodus 6:5–8.
22. Exodus 20:12.
23. Numbers 34:1–2.
24. Numbers 34:3–12.
25. For a study of the Land of Canaan and its borders, see Yehoshafat Nevo, "Gevulōt 'Ēretz Yisraēl Lefī Ha-Torāh [The Borders of the Land of Israel According to the Torah], in *Shema'atin* 137–138 (1999) published in *http://www.daat.ac.il.*; Yehoshua M. Grinitz, *Motza'ēi Dorōt: Meḥkarīm be-Qadmoniyūt ha-Mikrā' ve-Rehsīt Toldōt Yisraēl ve-Sifrutō* [Origins of the Generations: Studies in Early Biblical Ethnology and History] (Tel Aviv: HaKibbutz HaMeuchad, 1969), 130–70.
26. Zohar, Parashāt Va-Yerā', 591, in *Sēfer ha-Zōhar*, vol. 4, 144.
27. Zohar, Parashāt Va-'Erā', 202–3, in *Sēfer ha-Zōhar*, vol. 7, 189.
28. S. D. Goiten, *Jews and Arabs: Their Contacts through the Ages* (New York: Schocken Books, 1967), 5, 21–22.
29. Psalms 83:2–13.
30. Talmud Bavlī, Sanhedrīn, 11:91a. Cf. Midrāsh Rabbāh, Genesis 51:6.
31. Genesis 25:57.
32. Ginzberg, *The Legends of the Jews*, vol.1, ch. 5.
33. Genesis 21:20.
34. Genesis 23:16–18.
35. 1 Samuel 15:7.
36. See, for example, Grinitz, *Motza'ēi Dorōt*, 35–50; Cornelis Houtman, *Exodus 1: Historical Commentary on the Old Testament* (Kampen: Kok Publishing House, 1993), 127.
37. Stated by Jacob in Genesis 49:29, 49:31.
38. See analysis in Yehudah Elitzur, "'Ēretz Yisraēl be-Maḥshēvet ha-Miqrā' " [The Land of Israel in Biblical Thought], in *Hagūt be-Miqrā' B* (Jerusalem, 1973), published in http://www.daat.ac.il.
39. Genesis 17:7–8.
40. Paul Johnson, *A History of the Jews* (New York: Harper & Row, 1987), 18–19.
41. Deuteronomy 10:14–15.

42. Nehemiah 9:6–8.
43. Deuteronomy 25:23.
44. Psalms 104:24.
45. Exodus 19:5.
46. Mishnah, Pirkēi Avōt 6:10.
47. *Midrash on Psalms*, trans. William G. Braude, vol. 1(New Haven, CT: Yale University Press, 1959), 337–338.
48. Talmud Bavlī, Berakhōt 5a.
49. Nehama Leibovitz, *Studies in Shemot*, trans. Aryeh Newman (Jerusalem: World Zionist Association, 1976), 1–4.
50. *Pentateuch and Rashi's Commentary* (on Genesis 1:1), vol.1, 1.
51. Nachmanides argues with Rashi and suggests instead that at the roots of God's arbitrary gifting of the Land to the People of Israel is a moral consideration—the corruption and evildoing of the nations that had inhabited it. Nachmanides, Commentary on Genesis, 17–20. See a thorough discussion by 'Uzi Kalchaim, "Ha-Zekhūt ha-Musarīt bi-Yrushāt ha-'Āretz bi-Kitvēi ha-Rambān" [The Moral Right of Inheriting the Land in the Writings of the Nachmanides], *Niv Ha-Midrashiyāh* (Winter 1968), published in http://www.daat.ac.il.
52. Psalms 105:1–15.
53. Genesis 12:10.
54. Genesis 26:1–3.
55. Exodus 6:4–5; cf. 3:7–8, 16–17.
56. Qur'ān 3:26.
57. Qur'ān 7:128.
58. Qur'ān 5:21.
59. Qiṣaṣ al-Anbiyā', vol. 2, 140.
60. Qur'ān 38:45–48.
61. Qur'ān 44:30–33.
62. Qur'ān 45:16.
63. Qur'ān 2:47.
64. Qur'ān 2:63.
65. Qur'ān 5:20–21.
66. Qur'ān 10:93.
67. Qur'ān 30:5–7.
68. Qur'ān 17:5–8.
69. II Maccabees 5:19–20.
70. Isaiah 40:1–2.
71. Jeremiah 29:10, 29:14.
72. Amos 9:11, 9:14–15.
73. Zechariah 8:7–8.
74. Isaiah 51:2–3.
75. Qur'ān 2:136, 3:84, 42:13.
76. Qur'ān 6:84, 16:44, 38:17–26.
77. Psalms 136:21–23.
78. Psalms 105:8–14.
79. Psalms 102:14–17.

80. Psalms 137:1–6.
81. See Yaakov Zisberg, "Vittūr 'al Ḥalaqīm me-'Ēretz Yisraēl" [Relinquishment of Parts of the Land of Israel], *Ha-Ma'ayān* (Sept.–Oct. 1995), published in http://www.daat.ac.il.
82. Talmud Bavlī, Soṭāh 34a.
83. Early discussion of confederative solutions for the Israeli-Palestinian conflict can be found in the *Jerusalem Center for Public Affairs*' papers published in the late 1980s and early 1990s by Daniel J. Elazar under the titles: "What About Confederation?," "Self-Rule and Shared Rule," "Two Peoples—One Land: Federal Solutions for Israel, the Palestinians, and Jordan," and "Federal/Confederal Solutions to the Israeli-Palestinian-Jordanian Conflict: Concepts and Feasibility" and reprinted in http://www.jcpa.org. See also Jerome M. Segal, "A Binational Confederation," *Boston Review* (December 2001/January 2002), reprinted in http://www.bostonreview.net; and Yitzhak Hayutman, "The Abraham Federation: A Proposal for a Radical Solution to the Arab-Israeli Conflict," a 1993 reprint of a 1975 proposal (unpublished).
84. Rav Ovadia Yosef. "Ceding Territory of the Land of Israel in Order to Save Lives," *Crossroads: Halacha and the Modern World*, vol. 3 (Alon Shvut, Israel: Machon Zomet, 1990), an English translation of the article in Hebrew published in *Teḥumīm* 10 (Alon Shvut, Israel: Machon Zomet, 1989).
85. This folktale is recorded and discussed in Eliezer Segal, *Holidays, History, and Halakhah* (Northvale, NJ: Jason Aronson, 2001). Among Jews, this fable is often cited as a Talmudic legend taken from the Midrash, yet there is no mention of it in either the Talmud or the Midrash. According to the research of the late Professor Alexander Scheiber of Budapest, the first time "The Tale of Two Brothers" appeared in print was in 1851 written by a French historian, who claimed to have heard it from an Arab peasant. Some Jewish scholars believe the story is indeed of Talmudic origin, though for some reason it was not recorded, and that Arabs had preserved it over the centuries. It's equally plausible the story was originally Arabic. See Alexander Scheiber, *Essays in Jewish Folklore and Comparative Literature* (Budapest: Akademiai Kiado, 1955).
86. Genesis 4:1–16.
87. Qiṣaṣ al-Anbiyā', vol. 2, 41–42.
88. Ibid.
89. Qur'ān 4:114.
90. Qur'ān 9:61.
91. Qur'ān 7:56.
92. Ibid.
93. Qur'ān 42:40.
94. Mishnah, Pe'āh 81:41.
95. Hosea 2:20.
96. Proverbs 29:18.
97. More on the subject of vision of peace, read Shai Har-El's essays at http://www.mepnetwork.org/where-there-is-a-vision-the-people-flourish/ and http://www.worldpolicy.org/blog/2012/04/03/peace- process-actual-peace.

98. For Shai Har-El essays on ways to create a paradigm shift in the Middle East peace process in general and the Israeli-Palestinian relations in particular, please visit his blog at http://www.mepnetwork.org/mepn-blog/.

8 The Gate of Humanness: The Problem of Truth—the Truth of the Problem

1. Psalms 15:2, 19:10, 25:10, 31:6, 85:11, 86:15, 117:2, 119:43, 142.
2. Mishnah, Pirkēi Avōt 1:18.
3. Talmud Bavlī, Shabbāt 55a.
4. Midrāsh Rabbāh, Genesis 81:2.
5. Deuteronomy 7:6.
6. On the doctrine of Israel as God's chosen people, see Louis Jacobs, *A Jewish Theology* (West Orange, NJ: Behrman House, 1973), ch. 19.
7. Cf. Shmuel David Luzzatto, *'Al Ha-Ḥemlah ve-Ha-Hashgaḥah*, 101, 105, 169–170, 174–175.
8. Qur'ān 6:62, 22:6, 23:16, 31:20.
9. Qur'ān 32:3, 35:31.
10. Qur'ān 17:9.
11. Qur'ān 41:42.
12. Qur'ān 2:256.
13. Qur'an 3:110.
14. Qur'ān 9:33, 48:28, 61:9. Cf. 3:85.
15. Exodus 32:16.
16. Mishnah, Pirkēi Avōt 6:2.
17. Talmud Bavlī, Berachōt 64a.
18. Midrāsh Rabbāh, Genesis 8:4–5.
19. Psalms 85:10.
20. Tosefta, Sanhedrīn 1:3.
21. Zechariah 8:19.
22. Talmud Bavlī, Yevamōt 65b.
23. Dērekh 'Ēretz Zuṭā, Pērek Ha-Shalōm [Chapter on Peace], published in http://www.daat.ac.il/daat/toshba/zuta/11–2.htm. For the text, see Appendix 3.
24. Midrāsh Rabbāh, Genesis 38:6.
25. Mishnah, Pirkēi Avōt 1:2.
26. Talmud Bavlī, Beitzāh 32b.
27. Talmud Bavlī, Shabbāt 151b.
28. Psalms 106:3.
29. Proverbs 10:25.
30. Qur'ān 28:77.
31. Qur'ān 12:92.
32. Qur'ān 99:7–8.
33. Qur'ān 49:134.

34. Malachi 2:10.
35. See the official websites of A Common Ground, http://www.acommonword.com, and of *The Royal Aāl al-Bayt Institute for Islamic Thought*, http://www.aalalbayt.org.
36. Qur'ān 2:136, 3:84.
37. On the Alexandria Process and Declaration, see the website of the United States Institute of Peace http://www.usip.org/programs/projects/alexandria-process. For the text, see Appendix 4.
38. See details in http://www.cordobainitiative.org.
39. See details in web site http://www.unaoc.org.
40. See details in http://www.weforum.org.
41. Qur'ān 5:48.
42. Qur'ān 9:71.
43. Genesis 1:31.
44. See e.g. Mohammad Omar Farooq, "Does the Qur'an or Muhammad promote violence?" *IslamiCity.com,* April 20, 2007, http://www.islamicity.com/articles/Articles.asp?ref=IC0704-3268.
45. Leviticus 19:18.
46. Talmud Yerushālmi, Nedarīm 24:7; Midrāsh Rabbāh, Genesis 24:7.
47. Talmud Yerushālmi, Nedarīm 9:4.
48. Talmud Bavlī, Shabbāt 31a.
49. An-Nawawi's Forty Hadith 13 (http://archive.is/V40F2). Cf. "None of you has faith until you love for your brother what you love for yourself," in *Saḥīḥ Al-Bukhārī, Kitāb al-'Imān, Ḥadīth* no.13; and, "None of you has faith until you love for your neighbour what you love for yourself," in *Saḥīḥ Muslim, Kitāb al-'Imān, 67–1, Ḥadīth* no. 45.
50. Mordecai Martin Buber, "Ha-'Emēt ve-ha-Teshu'āh" [Truth and Salvation (1947)], in *'Am ve-'Olām* [People and World], vol. 2 (Jerusalem: Jewish Agency Publisher, 1961), 342.
51. Ibid, "Ha-Mashbēr ve-ha-'Emēt" [The Crisis and the Truth (September 1945)], 80–81.
52. *The Gift: Poems by Hafiz, The greater Sufi Master*, trans. Daniel Ladinsky (New York: Penguin Compass, 1999), 138.
53. Ibid. 91.
54. Aristotle, *On the Heavens*, trans. J. L. Stocks (eBooks@Adelaide, 2004), book 1, ch. 5.
55. Genesis 2:15–16.
56. Midrāsh Rabbāh, Leviticus 9:3.
57. Psalms 85:12

EPILOGUE: A POETIC CONCLUSION

1. Psalms 115:16.
2. Isaiah 2:2–4.

Glossary

Islamic Terms

Arabic is the universal language of Islam even though Muslims speak many different languages. Islamic terms, therefore are generally Arabic or Arabic-derived. Arabic is the largest member of the Semitic language family. It is spoken by more than 280 million people as a first language and by 250 million more as a second language.

Ādhān. A call to prayer; therefore the one who performs the call is called Mu'adhdhin.

'Adl. Justice; in Islamic theology, it refers to God's divine justice.

Ahl al-Kitāb. Lit., "People of the Book"; Islamic reference to Jews and Christians, who each had their own book of revelation, the Torah and the Gospels respectively, prior to the advent of Prophet Muhammad.

'Ākhirah. The Hereafter, Afterlife; as opposed to *Dunyā*, the world we live in.

Akhlāq. The practice of virtue; morals.

Allah. The most common Arabic name for God used by all Muslims.

'Aqīdah. The Islamic creed, or the six articles of faith, which consist of the belief in God, Angels, Messengers and Prophets, Scriptures, the Day of Judgment, and Destiny.

Arkān. Lit., "Pillars"; the primary practices observed by Muslims: *shahādah, salāh, zakāt, ḥajj, ṣaum*; known as the Five Pillars of Islam.

'Asmā' Allah al-Ḥusnā. Lit., "The Beautiful Names of God"; refers to God's 99 Names.

'Āyah. A sign, or more specifically, a verse in the Qur'ān.

Barakah. Spiritual wisdom and blessing transmitted from a master to his pupil.

Bid'ah. Lit., "innovation"; an action that is considered a deviation and a serious sin.

Bismillāh. Muslims' common blessing; the invocation that precedes the sūrahs of the Qur'ān: *Bismillāh al-Raḥmān al-Raḥīm*.

Dhimmī. Lit., "protected person." It refers primarily to Jews and Christians living in an Islamic state, whose right to practice their religion is tolerated under Islamic law.

Farḍ. A religious obligatory duty.

Fātiḥah. The short, opening *sūrah* of the Qur'ān.

Fatwā. Decree, legal opinion of a religious scholar, not covered by the *Fiqh* books.

Fī Sabīl Allah. Lit., "in the path of God" or "for the cause of God"; a common Islamic expression for performing acts such as charity or jihad.

Fiqh. The jurisprudence built around the Islamic Law, the *Sharī'ah*.

Ḥadīth. Sayings and actions of Prophet Muhammad, attributed to one of his early followers, which help interpret the Qur'ān and govern Islamic life.

Ḥajj. The annual pilgrimage to Mecca, required, if possible, for every Muslim once in their lifetime.

Ḥalāl. Permissible and lawful, particularly in reference to Islamic dietary laws. Opposite of Ḥarām.

Ḥanīf. Pre-Islamic monotheist.

Hijrah. Lit., "migration." The migration of Muhammad and his followers from Mecca to Medina in 622 CE, the first year of the Islamic calendar.

'Ibādah. Act of worship to God.

'Īd al-Aḍḥā. "Feast of the Sacrifice" that commemorates the attempted sacrifice of 'Isma'īl (Ishmael).

'Īd al-Fiṭr. "Festival of Fitr (Breaking the Fast)" that marks the end of the fast of Ramaḍān.

'Ikhlās. Genuine in religious beliefs.

'Imām. Lit., "leader"; specifically a man who *leads* a community or *leads* the prayer.

'Imān. Personal faith.

'Injīl. Islamic denotation of the Gospels revealed to Prophet 'Īsā (Jesus).

Jāhiliyyah. Lit., "ignorance"; the time of before Islam was realized when polytheistic religions existed.

Jamā'ah. Congregation gathering to pray with others behind an *'imām*.

Jannah. Paradise, Heaven, the Garden of Eden.

Jihād. Struggle, fighting against the enemies of Islam, thus commonly called "holy war"; any earnest striving "in the path of God," whether physical or spiritual; thus Mujāhid is a fighter for Islam.

Ka'bah. The holiest shrine in Islam located in Mecca; the point toward which Muslims pray and the focal point of the *ḥajj*.

Kufr. Disbelief in God and denial of His Truth.

Khitān. Male circumcision.

Khuṭbah. The sermon at the Friday (*Jumu'ah*) prayer.

Madhhab. Traditional school of religious jurisprudence, school of thought; there are four schools: al-Ḥanafī, al-Mālikī, al-Shāfi'ī, and al-Ḥanbalī.

Masjid. Mosque; a place of worship; also called *jāmi'*.

Makkah. Mecca in Arabic; Islam's holiest city, located in Saudi Arabia.

Mi'rāj. The Ascension of Prophet Muhammad from Jerusalem to the Seven Heavens during the Night Journey.

Muftī. Jurist; Islamic scholar who is an interpreter or expounder of Islamic Law (*Sharī'ah*), and capable of issuing a legal ruling or "*fatwā*."

Mu'min. Believer; one who belongs to the community of the "faithful."

Muslim. A follower of the religion of Islam; one who submits his will to God.

Qadar. Predestination, divine decree.

Qāḍī. Judge of Islamic Law.

Qiblah. The direction to the holy city of Mecca that Muslims face during prayer.

Qiṣaṣ al-Anbiyā'. "Stories of the Prophets"; stories of the lives of Prophet Muhammad and many biblical prophets starting with Adam; based primarily on the popular text of Al-Imām Ibn Khathīr.

Qur'ān. The holy book of Islam; a compilation of "recitations" of the Word of God as revealed to Prophet Muhammad.

Ramaḍān. The ninth month of the Islamic calendar during which fasting is obligatory for all Muslims.

Rasūlullāh. "Messenger of God"; the name of Prophet Muhammad.

As-Salāmu 'Alaykum. Lit., "Peace be upon you"; the Islamic greeting. In addition, there is "wa-Raḥmatullāhi wa-Barakātuhu," which means "and the Mercy of God and His Blessing." The full response to this greeting is "wa-'Alaykum us-Salām wa-Raḥmatullāhi wa-Barakātuhu"–"may the Peace, the Mercy of God and His Blessing be upon you."

Ṣadaqah. Freewill offering to the needy.

Ṣalāh. Prayer; Muslims are obligated to pray five times a day.

Ṣawm. Fasting from dawn to sunset throughout the month of Ramaḍān.

Sīrah. The life or biography of the Prophet Muhammad.

Ṣirāṭ al-Mustaqīm. The Straight Path.

Shahādah. The profession of faith: "There is no God but God and Muhammad is his Messenger."

Shahīd. Martyr; usually refers to a person killed while fighting "*fi sabīl Allah*" (in the path of God).

Shayṭān. Satan, the devil; also known as Iblis.

Shī'ah. "The faction of Ali"; the largest dissident sect of Islam; the state religion of Iran.

Shirk. Accepting partners with God; regarded as the worst sin in Islam. The one who does it is called a Mushrik.

Sharī'ah. The sacred law of Islam; the legal code governing the life of a Muslim, founded on the *Qur'ān* and *Sunnah* and codified by various *Fiqh* interpretations.

Ṣūfī. One who practices Sufism, the mystical school in Islam.

Suḥūf. Islamic denotation of the Books revealed to the Prophet 'Ibrāhīm (Abraham).

Sujūd. The Muslim practice of kneeling down in praying.

Sunnah. The "path" of Prophet Muhammad, that is, the words and actions of the Prophet; thus called *Sunnat al-Nabī*; best example that Muslims are to follow.

Sunnī. The largest denomination of Islam. The word derives from the word Sunnah.

Sūrah. A "chapter" of the Qur'ān; There are 114 "chapters."

Tafsīr. An interpretation, a commentary, usually referring to the commentary of the Qur'ān.

Takbīr. The call to prayer, which begins with *Allāhu Akbar*, meaning "God is Greatest."

Taqwā. The virtue of piety obtained by fearing the punishment of God.

Tawbah. "Turning" to God; repentance.

Tawḥīd. The Oneness of God; The centermost doctrine of Islam.

Tawrāt. The Torah as revealed to Prophet Mūsā (Moses).

'Ulamā' Muslim scholars who function as religious leaders in Islam.

Ummah. Denotation for the global community of Muslims.

'Umrah. The lesser pilgrimage performed in Mecca, which unlike *ḥajj* can be performed throughout the year.

Waḥy. Revelation of God to His prophets for all humankind.

Waqf. An endowment of money or property for a charitable cause.

Wuḍū'. Ablution for ritual purification from minor impurities before prayer.

Yawm ad-Dīn. Day of Judgment.

Zabūr. Denotation for the Book of Psalms revealed to Prophet Dāwūd (King David).

Zakāt. Obligatory almsgiving for the poor.

Jewish Terms

Hebrew, a Semitic language like Arabic, is the universal language of Judaism; therefore its religious terms are generally either in Hebrew or are Hebrew-derived. The core of the Tanakh (the Hebrew Bible) is written in Classical Hebrew, which has been used for prayer or Torah study in Jewish communities around the world for over two millennia. Hebrew in its modern form is spoken by more than seven million people in Israel.

Adonāi. One of the most common Jewish Names for God, used especially during prayer.

Aggadāh. Nonlegal material in the Talmud and Midrash, including stories and legends.

Alef-Bet. The Hebrew alphabet.

'Alēinu. Closing prayer of every synagogue service, proclaiming God's sovereignty.

'Aliyāh. Lit., "going up." It means to be called up to recite the blessing before the Torah reading.

'Amidāh. Lit., "standing"; Another name for the Eighteen Benedictions, a silent standing prayer in every synagogue service.

Aramaic. Semitic language closely related to Hebrew. Was once the common language of the Jewish world.

Arōn Qōdesh. "The Ark." The cabinet in the synagogue that holds the Torah scrolls, usually located at the front of the sanctuary.

'Asēret ha-Shevaṭīm. Lit., "The Twelve Tribes." They were descended from and named after the sons and grandsons of the Jewish forefather Jacob. Together they make up the People of Israel.

Ashkenazi. A term used to designate the Jews who lived, and to some extent still live, primarily in eastern and northern Europe; to be distinguished from Sephardic Jews. It also refers to the religious practices performed by the Ashkenazi community.

Bar (Bat) Mitzvāh. Lit., "Son (or Daughter) of the Commandment"; the term refers to a boy or a girl who has reached the age of 13 or 12 respectively and is thereafter obligated to observe the divine commandments. Term is also used for the ceremony marking this occasion.

Beit Knēset. Lit., "House of Assembly"; the synagogue. The central institution of Jewish communal prayer and study since ancient times.

Beit Midrāsh. Lit., "House of Study"; a place designated for the study of sacred texts, usually a part of the synagogue.

Ben. "Son," "Son of" in Hebrew; Aramaic "bar"; Arabic "ibn"; Used in traditional Hebrew names, such as Rabbi Moses ben Maimon is Moses, the son of Maimon.

Beit Dīn. Lit., "House of Justice"; a rabbinal court convened to resolve business disputes, grant divorces, decide about conversion, and so on.

Brīt. "Covenant"; the special agreement between God and the Jewish people.

Brīt Milāh. Lit., "Covenant of Circumcision"; the physical sign of the Covenant; colloquial name for the ritual of circumcision performed on the eighth day of a boy's life; commonly known as *brīt.*

Ḥuppāh. "Canopy" under which the Jewish marriage ceremony takes place, representing the marriage chamber or the couple's new home.

'Ēser ha-Dibrōt. "The Ten Commandments"; the most famous part of the Covenant between God and the People of Israel made at Mount Sinai.

Galūt. Lit., "exile"; It refers to the exile of the Jewish people from the Land of Israel. Also refers to the Diaspora, the Jewish dispersion outside Israel. Strictly speaking, "*galūt*" refers to the condition of exile, while "*golāh*" refers to the geographic situation and communities of the Diaspora, but the terms are used interchangeably.

Gemarā. Recorded commentaries, discussions and debates contributed by rabbinical scholars in the Land of Israel and Babylon. The Gemara and the Mishnah constitute the Talmud.

Geṭ. Divorce decree granted by a Beit Dīn.

Goy. Lit., "nation"; refers to a "gentile," or a non-Jew.

Hafṭarāh. Portion of the Prophets read in synagogue services.

Halakhāh. Lit., "the walk"; refers to the Jewish Law, consisting of the 613 mitzvōt of the Torah plus rabbinic law and custom.

Ḥanukkāh. Lit., "dedication"; also spelled Chanukah. An eight-day holiday beginning on 25 Kislēv (mid-December) that commemorates the revolt of the Maccabees in 164 BCE and the miraculous oil that burned for eight days.

Hashēm. Lit., "The Name [of God]." Used especially by Orthodox Jews to avoid pronouncing the Name.

Hekhshēr. "Seal of Approval" on kosher foods.

Kashēr. "Permissible" to eat, fit to make a food, or fit for ritual. Known in its Anglicized form *Kosher*.

Kashrūt. Jewish dietary laws.

Ketubbāh. A marriage contract, written in Aramaic, in which the husband sets out and agrees to his responsibilities toward his wife.

Kippāh. Head covering; also known in Yiddish as "*yarmulke*."

Kol Nidrē. Lit., "All Vows"; a hymn sung during Yom Kippūr releasing Jews of all religious vows made in the previous year.

Lashōn Qōdesh. "The Holy Tongue"—Hebrew.

L'Ḥayim. "To Life"—A Jewish toast.

Maḥzōr. A special prayer book for the High Holidays of Rosh Hashanāh and Yom Kippūr.

Mashgīaḥ. Lit., "supervisor"; A trained inspector appointed to guard against any violation of the Jewish dietary laws in food processing plants, meat markets, restaurants, and to certify the foods as kosher.

Mashīaḥ. Lit., "annoited one"; the Messiah; a saving figure, who is expected to come at the End of Days and to rule over Israel. He will carry out God's will and will restore Israel's fortunes, and make the People of Israel great again.

Matzāh. "Unleavened Bread"; unleaved (non-yeast) bread used during Passover or in Hebrew Pēsach.

Mazāl Tov. Lit., "good luck"; usually said at the end of a wedding or upon hearing good news.

Menorāh. "Candelabrum"; a seven-branch candlestick. Part of the furnishings of the tabernacle in the wilderness and the Temple in Jerusalem. In 1948 it became the official symbol of the State of Israel. Often used to refer to the *ḥanukkiyyah* lit during Ḥanukkāh.

Mezuzāh. "Doorpost"; a small parchment of Torah verses placed on the right doorpost of Jewish homes in obedience to the biblical passage (Deuteronomy 6:4).

Midrāsh. From the Hebrew verb "derash"; interpretations of the Bible, especially retellings and expansions of biblical stories.

Mikvāh. Lit., "a [water] gathering place"; a body of natural water used for ritual cleansing.

Minhāg. Lit., "custom"; a custom that evolved for worthy religious reasons and has continued long enough to become a binding religious practice.

Minyān. Lit., "counting"; quota of ten adult Jews required for certain prayers and observances.

Mishnāh. Lit., "repetition"; rabbinic six-volume commentary on the Torah and part of the Talmud codified c.200 CE by Yehudah Ha-Nasi in order to record and preserve the canon of religious legislation, laws, and customs.

Mishnēh Torāh. Lit., "repetition of Torah"; the code of law written by Maimonides, one of the most respected compilations of Jewish law ever written.

Mitzvōt. "Commandments" (singular *mitzvāh*); 613 religious actions sanctioned in the Torah.

Mohēl. A trained religious person who performs the ritual of circumcision.

Ha-'Olām Ha-Bā'. The "World-to-Come"—The Jewish afterlife, as opposed to This World or *Ha-'Olām Ha-Zēh*.

Qaddīsh. A prayer proclaiming the greatness of God. Used as the mourners' prayer, but also used during service.

Qedushāh. Lit., "holiness"; also a noun referring to a portion of the communal repetition of the Amīdah prayer.

Pareve. "Neutral" in Yiddish. Kosher foods that contain no meat or dairy.

Pēsach. Passover; a spring religious festival usually occurring in April that commemorates Exodus from Egypt.

Purīm. Festive holiday in the early spring, celebrating the story of Esther and Mordecai.

Rav. Rabbi; a spiritual leader, a teacher; one that is certified with a "*semikhāh*" (ordination).

Rosh ha-Shanāh. "New Year"; a joyous holiday celebrated in the fall, usually in September, which begins the new Jewish year.

Sefirāt ha-'Ōmer. "Counting of the 'Ōmer"; the ritual counting of 49 days between *Pēsach* (Passover) and *Shavu'ōt* (Festival of Weeks).

Sephardic. A term used to designate the Jews, whose ancestors lived in Spain (in Hebrew "Sepharād") until the exile of 1492. Many of these Jews immigrated to the Arab or Muslim countries. Thus, today Sephardic Jews are usually thought of as Jews from Arab countries.

Se'udāt Mitzvāh. A festive meal following the fulfillment of a *mitzvāh* such as circumcision.

Shabbāt. The seventh day of the week recalling the completion of the six days of Creation. It is a biblically ordained day of rest, starting at sundown Friday evening and lasting to sundown on Saturday. In the synagogue, this is a special day for worship.

Shalōm. "Peace"; the greeting of hello or goodbye; the state of peace.

Shavu'ōt. "Festival of the Weeks"; commemorates the giving of the Torah on Mount Sinai.

Shekhināh. "Indwelling Presence"; the Holy Spirit. In Kabbalistic thought, the feminine aspect of God.

Shemā'. The confession of faith. It is essentially taken from Deuteronomy 6:4, "Hear O Israel, the Lord our God, the Lord is One." This prayer is said several times a day as part of the fixed prayers and it also is contained within a *mezuzāh*.

Shulḥān 'Arūkh. Lit., "organized table"; it is a medieval codification of *halakhāh* written by Joseph Caro in the late 1500s. This easily used book guides Jews in daily practice and answers questions that might come up in everyday Jewish life.

Siddūr. Lit., "order"; the prayer book used in Jewish liturgy.

Simḥāh. Lit., "rejoicing"; any Jewish celebration.

Sukkōt. "Feast of Tabernacles"; an eight-day autumn festival commemorating the Exodus and celebrating the harvest. During the festival, Jews eat inside a booth (*sukkāh*).

Ṭallīt. A prayer shawl worn by men in the synagogue on Shabbat and holidays, and while reciting morning prayers (*Shaḥarīt*).

Talmud. Lit., "teaching"; the Oral Torah, made up of the Mishnah and the Gemara.

Tanākh. The Hebrew term for the Bible; an acronym for "Torah" (the Pentateuch, i.e., the first five books of Moses), "Nevi'īm" (the Prophets, i.e., Joshua through Kings and the "Writing Prophets" such as Isaiah, Jeremiah), and "Ketuvīm" (the Writings, i.e., everything else, including the Psalms, Proverbs, Esther, and so on).

Taryāg Mitzvōt. "613 commandments" given in the Torah and enumerated by Maimonides.

Tefillāh. A central act of worship taking place in a congregational setting in a synagogue, or individually at home (so called *tefillāt yaḥīd*, or solo prayer). This includes three daily prayers: in the morning (*shaḥarīt*), afternoon (*minḥāh*), and after sunset (*ma'arīv*), as well as an additional prayer (*musāf*) in Shabbāt.

Tefillīn. Phylacteries, a pair of black leather boxes containing scrolls of parchment inscribed with verses from Torah. Jewish men wear them on their heads and their upper arms during weekday morning prayers.

Ṭreifāh. Food that is not kosher and may not be eaten. Also pronounced and spelled in Yiddish *treyf.*

Teshuvāh. Lit., "returning" to God; repentance; self-evaluation. Thus, *ḥozēr bi-teshuvāh* is one who left the secular way of life and became an observant Jew.

Tiqqūn 'Olām. Reparation, perfecting and healing of the world.

Torah. Lit., "teaching"; the first five books of the Bible, known as the Five Books of Moses or the Pentateuch. Also refers to the dual Torah, both the Written (the Five Books or Ḥumāsh) and the Oral (Talmud, i.e., Mishnah and Gemara).

Yahrzeit. Anniversary of a loved one's death in Yiddish.

Yerushalayim. Jerusalem in Hebrew. The holiest city in Judaism, King David's capital and the site of King Solomon's Temple and the Second Temple. Since ancient times, Jews all over the world have faced this holy city during prayer, and have prayed daily for a return to it.

Yiddish. A dialect of German written in Hebrew characters and spoken by Jews living in Germany, or whose ancestors had lived there before migrating elsewhere in Eastern Europe, during the late medieval period and the modern period. Today it remains the language of the ultraorthodox groups.

Yizkōr. A memorial prayer for the deceased recited at the end of each festival.

Yom Kippūr. The Day of Atonement; a day of fasting falling after *Rosh Ha-Shannāh*. The two together are called *Yamīm Nora'īm*, or the Days of Awe.

Yom Ṭōv. Lit., "good day"; one of the three festivals (*Sukkōt, Pēsach*, and *Shavu'ōt*), when Jews performed their pilgrimage, or *'Aliyāh la-Rēgel,* to Jerusalem.

Zohar. The most important text of Kabbalah, Jewish mysticism.

Selected Readings

The books listed below represent a small sampling of literature that informs the interested nonspecialist about Islam and Judaism, particularly about their relationship and the ways to forge better understanding between them.

Scriptures in Translation

Arabic Translation of the Bible

Van Dyke translation. http://www.arabicbible.com/arabic-bible/pdf/van-dyke-arabic.htm.
Arabic Bible. http://www.biblica.com/bibles/arabic/.
Easy-to-Read Version. http:/www.biblegateway.com/versions/?action=getVersionInfo&vid=171.

Hebrew Translation of the Qur'ān

Ben-Shemesh, Aaron. הקֻראַן [The Qur'ān].Translated into Hebrew. Tel Aviv: Karni Publishers, 1978.
Rivlin, Yosef Yoel. אַלקֻראַן [The Qur'ān]. Translated into Hebrew. 2 vols. Tel Aviv: Dvir Publishers, 1987.
Uri Rubin, Uri, הקוראן [The Qur'ān]. Translated into Hebrew. Tel Aviv: Tel Aviv University Press, 2005.

Jews and Muslims in Dialogue

Al-Faruqi, Ismail Raji, ed. *Trialogue of the Abrahamic Faiths*. Romford, UK: Amana Books, 1995.
Bretton-Granatoor, Gary M. and Andrea L. Weiss, eds. *Shalom/Salaam: A Resource for Jewish-Muslim Dialogue*. New York: UAHC Press, 1993.

Chittister, Joan, Saadi Chishti Shakur, and Arthur Waskow. *Tent of Abraham: Stories of Hope and Peace for Jews, Christians and Muslims*. Boston: Beacon Press, 2007.
Halevi, Yossi K. *At the Entrance to the Garden of Eden: A Jew's Search for God with Christians and Muslims in the Holy Land.* New York: HarperCollins, 2002.
Mackenzie, Don, Ted Falcon, and Jamal Rahman. *Religion Gone Astray: What We Found at the Heart of Interfaith*. Woodstock, VT: SkyLight Paths, 2011.
Shafiq, Muhammad and Mohammed Abu-Nimer, eds. *Interfaith Dialogue: A Guide for Muslims*. Herndon, VA: International Institute of Islamic Thought (IIIT), 2007.
Smock, David, ed. *Interfaith Dialogue and Peacebuilding*. Washington, DC: United States Institute of Peace, 2002.
Swidler, Leonard, ed. *Muslims in Dialogue: The Evolution of a Dialogue*. Lewiston, NY: The Edwin Mellen Press, 1992.
Swidler, Leonard, Khalid Duran, and Reuven Firestone. *Trialogue: Jews, Christians, and Muslims in Dialogue*. New London, CT: Twenty-Third, 2007.

Abraham as a Unifying Force

Feiler, Bruce. *Abraham: A Journey to the Heart of Three Faiths*. New York: William Morrow, 2002.
Firestone, Reuven. *Journeys in Holy Lands: The Evolution of the Abraham-Ishmael Legends in Islamic Exegesis*. Albany: State University of New York Press, 1990.
Klinghoffer, David. *Discovery of God: Abraham and the Birth of Monotheism*. New York: Doubleday, 2003.
Kritzeck, James. *Sons of Abraham*. Baltimore: Helicon Press, 1965.
Patai, Raphael, *The Seed of Abraham: Jews and Arabs in Contact and Conflict*. New York: Charles Scribner's Sons, 1987.
Wyschogrod, Michael. *Abraham's Promise: Judaism and Jewish-Christian Relations*. Grand Rapids, MI: William B. Eerdmans Publishing, 2004.

Introducing Islam

Ahmed, S. Akbar. *Discovering Islam: Making Sense of Muslim History and Society*. New York: Routledge, 2002.
Duran, Khalid and Abdelwahab Hechiche, eds. *Children of Abraham: An Introduction to Islam for Jews*. Jersey City, NJ: Ktav Publishing House, 2001.
Eaton, Charles Le Gai. *Islam and the Destiny of Man*. New York: SUNY Press, 1985.
Firestone, Reuven. *An Introduction of Islam for Jews*. Philadelphia: Jewish Publication Society, 2008.
Hitti, Phillip K. *Islam: A Way of Life*. Chicago: Henry Regency, 1970.
Hodgson, Marshall G. C. *The Venture of Islam: Conscience and History in a World Civilization*. 3 vols. Chicago: The University of Chicago Press, 1974.

Hourani, Albert. *A History of the Arab Peoples*. Cambridge, MA: Harvard University Press, 1991.
Rahman, Fazlur. *Islam*. New York: Anchor Books, 1968.
Von Grunebaum, Gustave E. *Medieval Islam: A Study in Cultural Orientation*. Chicago: University of Chicago Press, 1956.
Von Grunebaum, Gustave E. *Modern Islam: The Search for Cultural Identity*. New York: Random House, 1962.

Introducing Judaism

Baron, Salo Wittmayer. *A Social and Religious History of the Jews*. 18 vols. New York: Columbia University Press, 1952.
De Lang, Nicholas. *An Introduction to Judaism*. New York: Cambridge Unuversity Press, 2000.
Firestone, Reuven. *Children of Abraham: An Introduction to Judaism for Muslims*. Jersey City, NJ: Ktav Publishing House, 2001.
Fishman, Sylvia Barack. *The Way into the Varieties of Jewishness*. Woodstock, VT: Jewish Lights Publishing, 2008.
Hartman, David. *A Heart of Many Rooms: Celebrating the Many Voices within Judaism* Woodstock, VT: Jewish Lights Publishing, 1999.
Kalir, Joseph. *Introduction to Judaism*. Washington, DC: University Press of America, 1980.
Neusner, Jacob. *The Way of Torah: An Introduction to Judaism*. Belmont, CA: Wadsworth, 1988.
Olitzky, Kerry M, Ronald H. Isaac, and Dorcas Gelabert. *The Complete How To Handbook For Jewish Living*. New York: Ktav Publishing House, 2004.
Steinberg, Milton. *Basic Judaism*. New York: Harcourt Brace Jovanovich,1947.
Telushkin, Joseph. *Jewish Literacy: The Most Important Things to Know About the Jewish Religion, Its People, and Its History*. New York: William Morrow, revised edition, 2008.

Comparing Judaism and Islam

Harry, Benjamin H., John L. Hayes, and Fred Astren, eds. *Judaism and Islam: Boundaries, Communication and Interaction*. Leiden: Brill, 2000.
Neusner, Jacob and Tamara Sonn. *Comparing Religions through Law: Judaism and Islam*. London and New York: Routledge, 1999.
Neusner, Jacob, Tamara Sonn, and Jonathan E. Brockopp, eds. *Judaism and Islam in Practice. A Sourcebook*. London and New York: Routledge, 1999.
Neusner, Jacob, Bruce Chilton, and William Graham. *Three Faiths, One God: The Formative Faith and Practice of Judaism, Christianity and Islam*. Boston: Brill Academic Publishers, 2002.

Peters, F. E. *The Children of Abraham: Judaism, Christianity, Islam: A New Edition.* Princeton, NJ: Princeton University Press, 2006.

Historical Encounters between Jews and Muslims

Brinner, W. and S. Ricks, eds. *Studies in Islamic and Judaic Traditions.* Atlanta: Scholars Press, 1986.

Bunzl, John, ed. *Islam, Judaism and the Political Role of Religions in the Middle East.* Gainsville: University Press of Florida, 2004.

Geiger, Abraham. *Judaism and Islam.* A New Edition. New York: Ktav Publishing House, 1970.

Goitein, S. D. *Jews and Arabs: Their Contacts Through the Generations.* New York: Schocken Books, 1967.

Hary, Benjamin H., John L. Hayes, and Fred Astren, eds. *Judaism and Islam: Boundaries, Communication and Interaction: Essays in Honor of William M. Brinner.* Leiden: Brill, 2000.

Lazarus-Yafeh, Hava. *Intertwined Worlds: Medieval Islam and Bible Criticism.* Princeton, NJ: Princeton University Press,1992.

Lewis, Bernard. *The Jews of Islam.* Princeton, NJ: Princeton University Press, 1984.

Lewis, Bernard. *Cultures in Conflict: Christians, Muslims, and Jews in the Age of Discovery.* New York: Oxford University Press, 1995.

Meddeb, Abdelwahab and Benjamin Stora, eds. *A History of Jewish-Muslim Relations: From the Origins to the Present Day.* Princeton, NJ: Princeton University Press, 2013.

Mann, Vivian B., Thomas F. Glick, and Jerrilynn Dodds. eds. *Convivencia: Jews, Muslims, and Christians in Medieval Spain.* New York: George Braziller, 1992.

Menacol, Maria Rosa. *Ornament of The World: How Muslims, Jews, and Christians Created a Culture of Tolerance in Medieval Spain.* Boston: Little, Brown, 2002.

Nettler, Ronald L. ed. *Medieval and Modern Perspectives on Muslim-Jewish Relations.*, vol. 2. Newark, NJ: Harwood Academic Publishers (Taylor & Francis Group), 1995.

Nettler, Ronald L. and Suha Taji-Farouki. eds. *Muslim-Jewish Encounters: Intellectual Traditions and Modern Politics.* Studies in Muslim-Jewish Relations, vol. 4. Newark, NJ: Harwood Academic Publishers (Taylor & Francis Group), 1998.

Peters, F. E. The *Monotheists: Jews, Christians, and Muslims in Conflict and Competition.* Princeton, NJ: Princeton Unversity Press, 2003.

Selengut, Charles, ed. *Jewish-Muslim Encounters: History, Philosophy, and Culture.* St. Paul, MN: Paragon House, 2001.

Index

The source of the words listed in this index is indicated in parentheses, using the following abbreviations: A – Arabic; H – Hebrew.

The manufacturer's authorised representative in the EU is Springer Nature Customer Service Centre GmbH, Europaplatz 3, 69115 Heidelberg, Germany. If you have any concerns regarding our products, please contact ProductSafety@springernature.com

Printed and bound by CPI Group (UK) Ltd, Croydon, CR0 4YY
23/04/2026
02095633-0002